LONDON 1
WE
SIL

No. ...  2063

This book to be RETURNED on or before the latest date stamped below unless a renewal has been obtained by personal call, post or telephone, quoting the above number and the date due for return.

-2. JAN. 1975			
25. JAN. 1975			
15 FEB 1975			
11. OCT. 1975			
-1. NOV. 1975			
14. FEB. 1976			
24. APR. 1976			
10. JAN. 1977			
25. APR. 1977			
18. AM '977			
21. OCT. 1977			
12-11-1977			

In the case of infectious illness, do not return books to the Library, but inform the Librarian.

Cloth Cap and After

Cloth Cap and After

by Innis Macbeath

London. George Allen & Unwin Ltd
Ruskin House   Museum Street

First published in 1973

This book is copyright under the Berne Convention.
All rights are reserved. Apart from any fair dealing for
the purpose of private study, research, criticism or
review, as permitted under the Copyright Act, 1956, no
part of this publication may be reproduced, stored in a
retrieval system, or transmitted, in any form or by
any means, electronic, electrical, chemical, mechanical,
optical, photocopying, recording or otherwise, without
the prior permission of the copyright owner. Enquiries
should be addressed to the publishers.

© George Allen & Unwin Ltd 1973

ISBN 0 04 331060 5 hardback
   0 04 331061 3 paperback

Printed in Great Britain
in 10 point Times Roman by
Clarke, Doble & Brendon Ltd
Plymouth

For Isobel, Elizabeth and Keith

'We often think that when we have completed our study of one we know all about two, because "two" is "one and one". We forget that we have still to make a study of "and".'

Sir Arthur Eddington

Contents

Introduction	page	13
1 Where Things Stand		19
2 Growth or Pseudo-Growth		39
3 Commissars and Fixers		66
4 Prejudices and Politics		85
5 High Hats and White Collars		113
6 Birds of a Feather		142
7 Tough at the Top		166
8 Quirks of Character		186
9 Day after Tomorrow		204
Index		227

Abbreviations

ACTSS   Association of Clerical, Technical and Supervisory Staffs (white-collar section of TGWU)
AEU   Amalgamated Engineering Union (now engineering section of AUEW)
AFL   American Federation of Labour.
APEX   Association of Professional, Executive, Clerical and Computer Staff (formerly CAWU)
ASCW   Association of Scientific Workers (now merged in ASTMS)
ASLEF   Associated Society of Locomotive Engineers and Firemen
ASSET   Association of Supervisory Staffs, Executives and Technicians (now merged in ASTMS)
ASTMS   Association of Scientific, Technical and Managerial Staffs
ASW   Amalgamated Society of Woodworkers (now merged in UCATT)
AUBTW   Amalgamated Union of Building Trade Workers (now merged in UCATT)
AUEW   Amalgamated Union of Engineering Workers
CAWU   Clerical and Administrative Workers' Union (now APEX)
CEU   Constructional Engineering Union (now construction section of AUEW)
CIO   Congress of Industrial Organisations
CIR   Commission on Industrial Relations
COHSE   Confederation of Health Service Employees
CWS   Co-operative Wholesale Society
CWU   Chemical Workers' Union (now merged in TGWU)
DATA   Draughtsmen's and Allied Technicians' Association (now TASS, the technical and supervisory section of AUEW)
DGB   Deutsche Gewerkschaftsbund (the West German central trade union organisation)

EETU/PTU	Electrical, Electronic and Telecommunications Union/Plumbing Trades Union
ETU	Electrical Trades Union (now EETU section of EETU/PTU)
FTAT	Furniture, Timber and Allied Trades Union
GGWU	Glass and General Workers' Union (attempted NUGMW splinter union)
GKN	Guest Keen and Nettlefold, Ltd
GMWU	General and Municipal Workers' Union (variant style for NUGMW)
HDV	Union of Heating, Domestic and Ventilating Engineers (now merged with SMW)
ICF	International Federation of Chemical and General Workers' Unions
IMF	International Metal Workers' Federation
IPCS	Institution of Professional Civil Servants
IRIS	Industrial Research and Information Services
ISTC	Iron and Steel Trades Confederation
ITT	International Telephone and Telegraph Corporation
JIB	Joint Industrial Board (for electrical contracting industry)
LTS	London Typographical Society (now merged in NGA)
MATSA	Managerial, Administrative, Technical and Supervisory Association (white collar section of NUGMW)
NACODS	National Association of Colliery Overmen, Deputies and Shotfirers
NALGO	National and Local Government Officers' Association (formerly National Association of Local Government Officers)
NASD	National Amalgamated Stevedores' and Dockers' Union
NATSOPA	National Society of Operative Printers, Graphical and Media Personnel (temporarily merged in SOGAT and originally National Association of Operative Printers and Assistants)
NBPI	National Board for Prices and Incomes
NEDC	National Economic Development Council
NGA	National Graphical Association
NUBE	National Union of Bank Employees
NUFTO	National Union of Furniture Trade Operatives (now merged in FTAT)
NUGMW	National Union of General and Municipal Workers

NUJ	National Union of Journalists
NUM	National Union of Mineworkers
NUPBPW	National Union of Printing, Bookbinding and Paper Workers (now SOGAT)
NUPE	National Union of Public Employees
NUR	National Union of Railwaymen
NUT	National Union of Teachers
NUVB	National Union of Vehicle Builders (now merged in TGWU)
POEU	Post Office Engineering Union
PTU	Plumbing Trades Union (now merged in EETU/PTU)
SLADE	Society of Lithographic Artists, Designers, Engravers and Process Workers
SLL	Socialist Labour League
SMW	National Union of Sheet Metal Workers, Coppersmiths, Heating and Domestic Engineers
SOGAT	Society of Graphical and Allied Trades
STA	Scottish Typographical Association
TASS	Technical and Supervisory Section of the AUEW (formerly DATA)
TGWU	Transport and Genral Workers' Union
TSSA	Transport Salaried Staffs' Association
TUC	Trades Union Congress
UAW	United Auto Workers
UCATT	Union of Construction, Allied Trades and Technicians
UCS	Upper Clyde Shipbuilders, Ltd
UKAPE	United Kingdom Association of Professional Engineers
UPW	Union of Post Office Workers
USDAW	Union of Shop, Distributive and Allied Workers
WPWU	Wall Paper Workers' Union

Introduction

We have had trade unions in Britain for a very long time now – longer than any man can remember. In many parts of the world this is not true, and in almost none is it true in the sense that it is true in Britain. Not only has the British union movement compelled recognition for more than a century, but until very recently Governments have left its development to take its own course, apart from a few not very important provisions about political contributions and political strikes, and others to end obscurities and arguments about the exact state of the law. There has always been a framework of law, of course; it was a paradox in 1970 that people said on the one hand that we must have a framework of law, and on the other that a particular kind of legislation would succeed because British trade unions had never defied a court order.

This book is based on study and practice of trade unionism for some twenty years. It tries to explain why we have trade unions at all, what manner of institution they are, and what sort of pressures they face. It is almost entirely about British trade unions, but the basic considerations are common in all countries. Their expression is different. Borrowings from the experience of one country have taken fresh forms in others. Obviously no country can exactly repeat the experience of another. For this reason (among many others) we do not need to be unduly pessimistic in Britain. If we look at our particular situation, we may find our particular solutions. No one else is likely to produce them for us.

Unfamiliar institutions are difficult to understand. We all know that. But familiar institutions can be difficult to understand as well, and this book attempts to provide a key to understanding institutions which we hear about every day; two out of five British workers are members of them, yet a great deal of the daily talk we hear about them is simply daft. Consequently I have begun by asking very simple and obvious questions. I have tried to illustrate my answers by homely detail from my experience. I have tried not to take sides in any current controversy, although of course my prejudices must be obvious.

The basic considerations derive simply from the common behaviour of groups of people in responding to outside events, outside people, things which are beyond their control as individuals. Once groups become well enough set in their ways, they develop collective habits of their own. If they survive and maintain their membership they become institutions and may themselves have a great effect on outsiders. Outsiders affect the individual judgment of individuals who take part in the group's discussions, but they do not take part in the discussions. Outsiders may also control, persuade or wheedle representatives of the group, individual members of the group, or even the group itself if it is small enough. They may destroy the group, especially if it is only a little one, but if this happens often, little groups will band together to form bigger ones that will survive.

If we do not remember this, we shall not go very far to understand the development of trade unions. We may apply the wrong words to describe their position: for example, it is very common to talk about the 'power', 'authority' or 'responsibility' of unions, or even about the 'monopoly' they enjoy. If we use these words as we use them of great companies or captains of industry we are merely confusing ourselves. Trade unions are not commercial institutions, although they have commercial interests and commercial effects. Some of them are particularly sensitive to commercial changes: Roy Grantham, general secretary of APEX, which organises clerical and technical workers in private industry, points out that its membership started to fall in the autumn of 1970, when recession was beginning to bite, and to rise again in the spring of 1972 as the economy recovered.

Besides, trade unions are not in origin structures of authority. They exist at all in reaction against unacceptable authority. They keep watch on employers' behaviour, bargain about terms, resist if necessary. Unappeased, they have an impressive power of interdiction. It can take the form either of a strike, which is a blank refusal to work as usual until something has been put right, or of collective low performance. (There is some evidence from other countries more strictly regulated than Britain that where workers are prevented from striking and have their performance dictated by machines, as on standard production lines, they will leave the industry in droves. In Germany and Sweden, only about half the workers in such industries are Germans and Swedes respectively.) Yet the direct contact of union officials is bound to be less than the direct contact of employers' officials with their members; it was to meet the authority of managers within the work group that shop stewards developed.

Work groups left to themselves, or any other groups for that matter, acquire leaders of their own whether there is a greater organisation like a union or not. They are not commercial leaders. In fact, consciously or unconsciously they give something up in return for leadership. What sort of leadership they provide depends on the circumstances in which they come to the centre of things. No one can take it for granted.

Unions in general have very little money or property in proportion to their membership, although some have much more than others. Unions do not normally attract servants with much capacity or taste for building up a fortune. Over the years, they have not been particularly successful at getting a bigger share of the country's wealth for their members. In Britain at least, there is still a tendency for the labour movement to assess a man as much by what he gives up, or goes without, as by his material success. So long as he is not just careless or lazy, a man who does not try to squeeze the last penny out of life earns respect because he is good-natured, or because he prefers to get on well with the next man. Yet because a general wage increase is normally the only way in which an individual can improve or maintain his standard of living in modern Britain, men like this often find themselves leading a struggle for more money for every one of their group, including themselves if they are lay officials like shop stewards.

Trade unions in other countries have had different achievements, different strengths and weaknesses. Without exception, they have developed under more formal constraints than British unions, sometimes because their political leaders could see British experience before their own people became active. Similar problems have had different expression in other countries. Members of trade unions, and the unions themselves, are part of society and come under the same general influences. They are also obliged to respond to employers' initiatives, not because they are necessarily run by a bunch of quaintly backward-looking men but because it is the employers and their managers who control the material and financial resources of society. Trade unions have developed from the collective action of workers who have only human resources – their own talents – and want a say in how they are rewarded and generally treated at work which is greater than the say most of them can get individually.

From this simple origin, the refusal to be kicked about without protest, have grown the great elaboration and various complexities and aims of trade unionism. For many years it was a movement of 'manual' workers. 'White-collar' workers were separated from them, and to some extent still are, by a range of social differences which made organisation difficult without an employer's consent. Since employers, by and large, did not object in public service, union membership there is eight out of ten. In private employment it is one out of ten. Commercial changes like mergers and takeovers that make authority remote, and computers and other mechanical devices that put clerks and checkers out of business, are setting the scene for trade union expansion among white-collar workers, but in spite of some notable successes it is still very slow.

For a great many people, carefully educated for the proper exercise of responsibility, trade unions are a bit of a mystery. If we have lawful authority already, what business have these anomalous institutions to get in its way? Who governs the country, the lawfully elected administration or the 'feudal barons' of the TUC? There is no answer to such questions because they are just oratory. The first principle of leadership is not to give orders that will not be obeyed. The effectiveness of all governments is limited by institutions and pressure groups that call a halt to policies at a certain point. Organised labour happens to be a particularly open and public pressure group in this respect, although not uniquely so.

Since 1970 we have seen it in action against the Industrial Relations Act and against an incomes policy contrived without consultation. The first campaign culminated in the threat of a national strike if five dockworkers were not released from prison, and they were released. The second culminated in the mining and railway strikes, which were absolutely solid, painful, damaging and to some people, in many respects, shocking. To anyone familiar with the British and other labour movements, this sequence of events was predictable, as was the fact that most unions would refuse to join the new register. One could also have predicted that the third London airport would not be built at Cublington, because that part of Hertfordshire has lobbying resources, and that when Greater London expanded to its present frontiers certain parts of East Surrey would remain outside them.

That does not necessarily mean that the policies resisted by the TUC were morally wrong. They were just impracticable. If one were to try to grow tea in the West Highlands of Scotland because the average annual rainfall is about the same as it is in Assam, one would expect a certain amount of criticism for not taking into account the temperature, the nature of the soil, and other determining factors. In the same spirit, we should not attempt to bend the mature institutions of British industrial society to alien or outdated patterns, in the hope that our economy will become more productive as a result.

Maturity, again, does not necessarily mean goodness. There is always room for improvement, but it will not come unless we match our plans to the realities of our present situation. This book describes some of them. I hope that it may help to make them comprehensible to some of the thousands of people who have found them as complicated and unexpected as I have done, but have had less opportunity to make comparisons and to savour different aspects of these matters in several different cultures.

For the past sixteen years I have been a Scotsman born in Ireland working for an English newspaper. For five of them I lived in the United States, and for three of these I travelled extensively in the Caribbean and Latin America. For the past three years I have combined the job of labour commentator with continuous activity as a lay trade union official at plant level. This has not left much time to develop tidy theories, and if there are some inconsistencies in my analysis I hope that they will be forgiven. At least I hope that I may avoid the suggestion that the book has been written in an ivory tower. If some of the matter seems unfamiliar, or seems to fly in the face of common sense, I can only plead that common sense is not much of a guide unless you are certain about what people have in common.

Chapter 1
Where Things Stand

*If you wait for the boss to raise your pay,
You'll still be waiting on Judgment Day:
 You'll all be buried.*
Pete Seeger, 'Talking Union'

What is Success?
When is a trade union successful? Perhaps the best answer is, 'When it is convincing'. Trade unions do not exist to get things done, but to set terms on which they are done. In order to play their part in setting terms, they must persuade members and potential members that they should support the union, and persuade employers that they should negotiate with the union. It is the employers who dispose of the money, materials and organisation which their particular business requires. The unions exist to see that employers do not deal cavalierly with the human resources which are all that union members have.

It follows that commercial success in the ordinary sense is not a priority with unions. They are not commercial organisations. For them success consists in providing certain satisfactions to their members. In the most general terms, these satisfactions are security and self-respect; the industrial system and the brute theories of the nineteenth century withheld these luxuries from working men in relation to their employment; perhaps it would be more apposite to call the satisfactions *maintaining employment* and some *collective substitute* for self-respect.

It follows that the first requirement for trade union success is simply survival. Beyond that success has something to do with the nature of membership. In fact, there are only two universal criteria for the performance of a union – *quality* and *size* of membership. Groups like the Institution of Professional Civil Servants or the British Air Line Pilots Association assess their position by the proportion of potential members who are fully paid up. Their proportions of more than nine out of ten give them great stability in representing and serving a clearly defined membership with a typically steady career pattern. In relation to the employers of professional civil servants and air line pilots they are extremely convincing. At the other end of the scale unions recruiting actively on a wide front – both the Transport and General Workers Union (TGWU) and the National Union of General and Municipal Workers (NUGMW) organise in something like a hundred industries and occupations – emphasise numbers on the books. So long as the numbers are buoyant, it is irrelevant whether they stand for much the same people for very long. When you examine unskilled occupations where workers often move from job to job, you find the union, like the company, is a comparatively stable institution in what is often a most unstable situation for most of the people in it. Many workers habitually leave the union when they leave a particular job, and join it (or another one) when they get another job in an 'organised' place of work.

Types of Trade Unions
Between these extremes many categories of trade union grow and flourish, decline and wilt in Britain. Sometimes they merge, sometimes they split (although the tendency has been much more to merge since 1960). Small unions slip under the wings of big ones because they no longer have the resources to be convincing enough. Unions which are much of a size band together because they are unconvincing separately; the most important recent example has been the building workers who have come together in the Union of Construction and Allied Trades and Technicians (UCATT) to halt declining overall membership, depletion of funds, and ineffectiveness in negotiation. In 1972 they took part in a stubborn strike with one principal objective: to raise national basic rates of pay closer to the national average earnings, on the reasonable assumption that a union cannot be convincing if its negotiators never set a rate within striking distance of what its members get for themselves. Unions also merge to provide better common services with what resources they have, although there has probably never been a merger in which this was an overriding consideration. They also respond to some extent to the behaviour of commercial mergers, even to the extent of going 'conglomerate'. There has always

been a hankering for 'one big union' in the background of working class aspiration, just as there is a theoretical socialism. But of course, we must remember that the divisions between unions may emphasise difference as much as the alliances among them express common interest. Trade unions in this country reached the level of institutions, with a continuing vigour of their own apart from other social influences on their members, well over half a century ago: many of them a century ago. The results have shown themselves in a great variety of forms, and there are now accepted labels for some of them:

A *craft union* – the oldest kind – is one which requires entry by apprenticeship and purports to maintain standards by joint control of apprenticeship and resisting 'dilution' by making this training a requirement for certain jobs.

A *general union* – the largest kind – takes in recruits without worrying about their level of skill, their occupation, the industry they work in or the status of the employers.

An *industrial union* is one which confines its recruiting to one industry (which is not necessarily easy to define, even if it is something apparently as straightforward as railway work); some sections of large unions are organised on an industrial basis within an overall structure.

A *sectoral union* is one which caters for one sector of employment only, usually the public service in general or the civil service in particular.

A *manual union* is one which recruits what are normally called manual workers, although the description has always been fatuous because anyone is employed because he has the brain to do what is required of him, and the term becomes increasingly outdated with the mechanisation of laborious jobs.

A *white collar union* includes workers who are removed by one or more degrees from direct production or direct service – clerks, supervisors, technicians, scientists, managers and others.

A *closed union* confines itself to a particular class or category of worker; an *open union* casts its net wider. Sometimes unions consciously convert themselves to catch what seems an appropriate kind of recruit, as NALGO (the National Association of Local Government Officers) did in becoming the National and Local Government Officers' Association. The National Health Service and the proliferation of other public bodies after the war opened up new territory.

What Brought About Trade Unions

Yet all these categories are abstractions, like 'economic man'. There is constant overlapping. Some of the big unions contain something of almost all these arbitrary qualities: they are probably best described as 'conglomerates', like their counterparts in commerce. There is no point in trying to analyse the trade union movement without reference to employers in any event. Perhaps the behaviour of workers and trade unions is an odd mirror of that of employers and professions, but it is a response to the initiatives of people who set the tone of society: usually a defensive response, to prevent the consequences of unsuccessful risk-taking falling less on the risk-taker than on his employees.

As we go on, we shall see the great variety of ways in which workers and workers' leaders have tried to do this. As long ago as the eighteenth-century printers' 'chapels' (the old word still survives today) tried to placate their employers by enforcing self-discipline. So rooted in respectability was the Society of Boilermakers a century later that one long-serving general secretary expended almost as much ink on denouncing the demon drink as on criticising shipbuilding employers. Trade unionism has always been associated with anxiety about all the influences that can demoralise workers, although the movement has not normally commanded complete agreement about what these influences are.

It is less than a century since a worker's breach of his contract of employment ceased to be a crime, and there was a discreditable period during which 'combinations' of workers were unlawful conspiracies. In this harsh ground the ancestors of today's trade unions took root and grew, eventually achieved recognition and established separate and continuous identities. The interaction of millions of individuals and the development of attitudes and habits have produced a much more complicated and ambiguous state of affairs than the original defensive simplicity. The unions have also matured in a strangely compounded climate of condescension, resistance, tolerance and denunciation from people who regard themselves as the 'natural' leaders of society. There have always been more than enough people to advise trade unions and their members about the right course of action, for one reason or another; there have been plenty who claim that with the development of society, trade unions have either outlived their usefulness or should change their character.

There is, however, an irreducible scepticism among trade union members. The most spectacular accomplishments by entrepreneurs and Conservative Governments may mean that Labour Governments are few and far between, but they do not mean that trade unions simply wither away. The extraordinary reversal of form when a Labour Government appointed a Royal Commission on Trade Unions in 1965 – all its predecessors had been appointed by Conservative Governments – was followed by an attempt to change the character of British trade unions by legislation. The Trades Union Congress beat off the Labour attempt and the Conservative attempt is now on the statute book. More than thirty unions are suspended from the TUC for registering under the Industrial Relations Act, but the Government that brought it in has been negotiating with the TUC for a tripartite incomes policy – another paradox in the world of labour relations, where orderly assumptions must constantly be tested in the light of what is actually going on.

Trade unions do not operate independently of society as a whole. They respond to the ordinary leadership of society and contribute to it. The process is far more various and complicated than any single commentator could describe, but over the piece one can see trade unions plucking ideas out of the air, responding to their leaders' initiatives and to the initiatives of employers, even just being fashionable and taking what seem to be appropriate decisions based on their collective perceptions, habits and circumstances. All human organisations and individuals behave like this. One of the problems in industrial relations is that an unusually large proportion of people seem to expect others to behave differently – in conformity with 'economic laws' and other abstractions.

Measures of Management
It is much easier to state a management's responsibility systematically than it is to state a union's. Managers are accountable to owners or shareholders, technically in purely financial terms; to their workers as a whole, with their various duties and rights and collective indispensability; to the customers, through the quality of the product, fair dealing and buying and selling on agreed terms; to the public interest, if only as expressed by statute; and to the institution itself, the business that they run. In general, these responsibilities are indivisible. A manager behaves as if one or other had priority at any given time,

because he cannot work on two problems simultaneously. Like every other sane person a sane manager does not have a system of priorities, one before the other, on every day of the week but a serial of different accountabilities which he keeps so far as possible in harmony, like an engineer lubricating a motor rather than a general looking for a fight; military analogy emphasises power and obscures function. Neglect of one responsibility eventually endangers them all, but in the end, the manager may respectably fall back on a framework of law. If the institution breaks up like Rolls-Royce (whose managers apparently assumed that no government would dare not to support such an institution), all creditors, including the employees and shareholders, are given residual pickings according to their degree of security in the contractual hierarchy. A business institution breaks up when it has run out of money and nobody will lend it any more.

The odd thing is that the exact allocation of ownership is possible only when the enterprise is dead. Accounting for a living enterprise is bound to be only an approximation, because accounting at regular intervals by the calendar requires assumptions about both the past and the future. Most manufacturing, for example, involves first working on raw materials which will in the end contribute to the added value of the final product; but if the company were to stop operations at that point, the accountant winding it up might get only scrap value for, say, 50 lb of metal rings which had been produced from 100 lb of metal by milling, boring and polishing. An accountant making up the books for the year would log the 50 lb of metal as worth more than the 100 lb because of the work that had gone into changing it and its prospective value in the next stage of manufacture.

The polarisation of one form of industrial discussion into distinctions between 'private ownership' and 'social ownership', or 'nationalisation' and 'free enterprise' has had the unfortunate effect of confusing real judgment of what goes on – and has had this effect for several generations. As a matter of observation, all ownership is social ownership because ownership itself is a social concept. There may be a conflict between our society's methods of control of very large organisations ('bureaucracy') and enterprise and initiative, but this seems to be a function of size and regulation rather than of who takes the dividends. When an institution gets big enough it will impose the collective will of its leadership where it can, whether it is the Transport and General Workers Union or Imperial Chemical Industries. Managers, with control of resources and an accepted line of authority, plan as widely and over as long a period as company size allows.

Unions for Protection
Trade unions are different. They dispose of very little of their members' money, too little, as a rule, to provide the service that their members ought to expect. Individual decisions by trade union leaders in the nature of things have less direct effect on the lives of individual members than the decisions of managers. Their decisions may also be less persuasive; they must certainly be less persuasive in terms of sanctions against individuals unless the management have made a deal to delegate discipline to the union, a very rare situation in Britain although not in some other countries. This is not surprising, since the whole point of a trade union in Britain, at all events, is to give its members protection against sanctions from their employers. A trade union leader is accountable to the union's members and to the institution itself. Some trade unions also have a lively sense of the quality of their members' product and in certain situations, like that of a small local authority, constantly exhort employers to use modern methods of work study and productivity planning to provide not only jobs but decently paid jobs. But the context is different. A trade union has no shareholders, only members linked to each other (at least until the passing of the Industrial Relations Act) by the same casual assumption of mutual obligation to every other member that exists in a club. It does not have to make a profit and until the passing of the Act did not need to meet auditors' standards of solvency. The Act changes these particulars for registered unions, but they are only marginally important. It changes something else as well: to narrow down and concentrate individual arrangements with employers to the status of contract binding on the union. They have always been binding on the individual member as implied terms of individual contract, but there is not much profit in suing a contract-breaking employee unless he is very eminent. Some unions have been accustomed to operate in a single, homogeneous occupation with either a sole employer or very similar ones, but none has to do so. Officers of general unions or unions with members in many different separately

owned establishments negotiate, and even compete, with an eye to the next negotiation, although like managers they can successfully concentrate on only one at a time. Whether this will change into a sequence of static, contractual settlements, each with its term, remains to be seen.

At the same time, trade unions have a representative function. Shop stewards' standing in a given situation may be greater than paid officials', and their interest is always more direct and often better informed. Many shop stewards – I have done it myself – use the paid official as a bogyman to win an argument with a manager. Going 'outside the house' is usually mortifying for a manager and no inconvenience for a shop steward. The serial process of negotiation produces a situation which is never static and not always predictable. For example, in November 1969 Imperial Chemical Industries gave a 5 per cent salary increase to their 43,000 staff, who had no negotiating body. At the time, this was a reasonable award in the context, but the context was about to be changed by the unofficial dustmen's strikes which were harbingers of the rapid wage inflation of 1970. By February ICI found themselves negotiating a settlement of 10 per cent with their 65,000 'manual' workers' unions. In March they felt obliged to give a further 6 per cent to staff, and opened up the whole question of negotiating rights, whether through unions, or a staff association, or an extension of the existing staff committee system.

In 1969 one of three engineering firms in the same part of a North Midlands city made a productivity agreement with its 600 workers. The other companies were much the same size and required much the same skills, although they made different products for different markets. The productivity agreement gave a good deal more money to the workers involved in return for more efficient methods. There was no redundancy because the firm had heavy arrears of work. But the two other companies, with no time to prepare a proper 'productivity' agreement, were obliged to pay more to their workers on a basis which could be patched up to meet some criterion of incomes policy but made very little difference to practice. The first management presently came under pressure to restore the 'productivity differential'.

The Industrial Relations Act seeks to end this sort of thing by making collective bargains legally enforceable unless the parties explicitly say not. If the ICI staff had negotiated a 5 per cent contract in November 1969 they would have had to stick to it, and the three companies' different situations would also have been secured by contract. That is the rationale of the Act. What difference this makes to behaviour remains to be seen, but there are some broad general conclusions.

First, the behaviour of people, whether as managers or trade unionists, frequently conflicts with their stated objectives. Their objectives are normally stated in simple, exclusive terms ('My job is to make and sell cars . . . my job is to raise the standard of living of my members') whereas their behaviour and real accountability are complex.

Secondly, most people, including trade unionists, apply routine terms of commerce to their own organisations without making allowances for the different behaviour and relationships which they imply in the new context: 'growth', 'monopoly', 'power', even 'efficiency' and 'market'. True, the word 'conglomerate' moves easily between the two usages, presumably because in neither can one see an objective more rational than more money and more members respectively.

Thirdly, unions exist to inhibit managements, to give them something other than caprice as an instrument of accountability to workers. This makes unions essentially responsive rather than initiative organisations, but they do not merely respond directly to the behaviour of employers although recognition by an employer is far and away their most effective means of growth. They exist in society as a whole, and influences on the collective thinking of their members are not confined to contemporary or local affairs. Still, exotic workers' responses normally indicate a sour local and contemporary atmosphere, like mining and the docks in the brutal days. This means that conventional explanations of behaviour mean different things to different parties. Sometimes the same word is used by both sides to a dispute to summarise mutual exasperation. It is usually 'unfair', which is perhaps why the framers of the Industrial Relations Act have given the word a series of precise definitions in its list of 'unfair industrial practices', as bold a venture as defining 'pleasant'.

Fourthly, procedure is of much more consequence to managers – and usually of rather more consequence to union officials – than to workers in general. Orderly procedure is a natural objective of anyone whose job is to organise; one might almost say that management is procedure. The complication is that life operates on a basis of probabilities and humanity has developed a taste for exceptions. One man's orderly procedure is another's soul-destroying routine. Industrial relations can do no more than maintain a range of tolerance. And commentators predicting how a union movement will develop are wise to hedge their bets.

Large Claims and Small Gains

'The worker,' as A. J. P. Taylor says in *The Trouble Makers*, 'is by nature less imaginative, more level-headed than the capitalist. That is what prevents his becoming one. He is content with small gains. Trade union officials think about the petty cash; the employer speculates in millions.'

This is true up to a point; but trade unions use terms and behave in ways which are influenced by the state of feeling in society in general. Craftsmen base their exclusivity on the model of the professions. In 1969 the Boilermakers refused to accept a construction site agreement at Grangemouth in Scotland which involved other unions' representatives in settling issues to which boilermakers were a party. In 1970 the British Medical Association resisted a recommendation by the Commission on Industrial Relations that medical practitioners should join ASTMS like other scientists employed by the Medical Research Council. No doubt a majority of members at least of manual unions and a huge majority of activists would profess some form of socialism or non-capitalism or co-operative system as their ideal of how things should be organised. But they must operate in the existing system and have some yardstick for measuring the value of their activities, setting immediate objectives and making decisions.

Trade unions cannot depend on anything so simple as profit, which is not a completely satisfying measure for an employer and is meaningless for a trade union. Certainly unions seek higher pay for their members, either by forcing it out of employers or co-operating in new techniques at a price. One that relied solely on the first method would earn the title 'militant', one that relied wholly on the second the title 'responsible', at least among non-members. However, there are no such absolutes in the obscure and complex dealings of the workplace. At times when prices are rising workers naturally demand more money. At times of growing unemployment they are reluctant to accept improved techniques that would put some of them out of a job. Recent experience shows how unpleasant it can be to suffer both pressures at the same time and how inadequate mere public machinery is to solve the problem. Although unions now habitually claim higher wages this was not always so, and there is no theoretical reason why employers should not claim wage cuts as they used to do or pre-empt union demands (now habitual only among companies which pay a bit more than the odds as part of an overall strategy to avoid trade union representation). The objective of maximum pay for individuals may conflict with the objective of keeping as many as possible at work. In engineering shops where piece-work is normal, work groups regulate maximum earnings so that high pay for some will not mean the dole for others. There is probably no workshop practice which generates more middle-class indignation than this one, if one excepts the rare phenomenon of political strikes, lately reactivated by the controversy about industrial relations legislation. Nor do unions brag about the total earnings of their members or even make much attempt to collect the figures, although employers can always tell you, usually with distress, the size of their total wages bill. The two meet like gearwheels, the trade union counting the petty cash of, say, a wage increase of five new pence an hour, the employer realising that, spread over a thousand workers, it becomes a year's interest on more than a million pounds.

Inter-union Competition

Yet there is no question that this is an area in which unions compete. If more and more groups of workers come to demand tough action to match the successes of 'militant' leaders of other unions, even 'responsible' leaders will be obliged to concede it. The remarkable sequence of 1970, when the teachers' first strike was followed by NALGO's first official strike and a series of official strikes by the sedate NUGMW, illustrates the point. Something of what a moderate union may face appears in the CIR report on Clayton Dewandre Limited of Lincoln. There were 750 members of the Amalgamated Union of Engineering Workers (AUEW) in the plant, 430 of the NUGMW and about 200 of the TGWU. Nearly a third of the workers had been with the firm for twenty years or more and nearly two-thirds were aged forty-one or more. The CIR found that competitive wage bargaining was common and workers might change from one union to another when they felt that one bargained more successfully than another, or sometimes when they felt that their present union was being unnecessarily militant. The TGWU gained members for the former reason and the NUGMW for the latter. The TGWU had twice the proportion of short-service employees (one to five years in the plant) as the overall figure and more than twice as many people aged twenty-one to thirty. They tended to be more pushful and less identified with the company than older men. Other people's grievances and claims were put off because the TGWU members might cause a stoppage if their problems were not resolved first. 'The other unions are pulled along in the wake of the TGWU pace,' the CIR said. 'Most employees do not like living and working in this continuous atmosphere of social turbulence.'

Now, whatever purpose this competition serves it seems to have little to do with the original protective impulse of trade unionism. Unions develop an institutional momentum of their own; they acquire different styles quite apart from their representative and service functions. They evolve different structures and some unions, especially general ones, have vast contrasts within themselves in different geographical and occupational areas. For example, most London dockers and all London busmen are organised by the TGWU, but the attitudes and behaviour of the trade groups are different in several ways. Road transport workers and warehousemen are also mostly TGWU, and yet under the pressure of technological change in packing and stowing, notably the use of containers, the definition of what is 'dock work' led to the conflict with the dockers which culminated in the imprisonment of five dockers for defying the National Industrial Relations Court, and their release under threat of a general strike, in July 1972. But we should remember that some *people* decided to introduce the technological change, just as employers, not workers, introduced the specialisation in crafts and processes which has since become a rod for their backs.

A consortium of large shipping companies, none of them with any legal responsibility as employers of dockers, introduced the use of containers without any planning to cushion its predictable effect on port employment: a reduction of about two-thirds in the number of dockers. The dockers' reaction was to fight whatever comprehensible offender they could find, and treated warehousemen employing non-dock labour to pack 'grouped' containers – made up of consignments from several sources – as they used to treat employers who used cheap labour to do dockers' packing work outside the harbour gates. The particular incident which led to the contempt charge was the picketing of a warehouse run by the Vestey family through nominees. Although the Vestey family have achieved a more than modest prosperity over the years while employing dock labour, they allowed it to get about that the pilfering and laziness common in the London docks had become too much for economic operation. For the dockers this was 'export of jobs' as surely as if the operations had been switched to a Continental port; besides, many of them are educated Marxists enough to answer points about pilfering with the adage, 'Property is theft'. They were also in two different unions and Vesteys had chosen to give negotiating rights to a third. This is not the place to go into the nightmare of the docks dispute, but it is fair to say that even if all the workers involved had been in one union, as so many people seemed to think that they were, including for a time the NIRC itself, it would have been sorely tried by these incidents.

This is a special case of demarcation, the 'who does what?' dispute which often causes friction. There are also demarcations among crafts – between plumbers and heating engineers, between boilermakers and shipwrights, between metal workers and woodworkers, among engineers, boilermakers and sheet meal workers. There are demarcations between craft skills – acquired by apprenticeship – and process skills acquired by experience or specific training in almost every industry where technology has overtaken traditional distinctions. There are demarcations between 'spheres of interest' where the best that one can say, often enough, is that custom and practice have drawn the line between one union's sphere and another's. Whatever the rights and wrongs of these situations, they are normally settled by compromise.

The TUC has developed a set of rules – the 'Bridlington principles' drawn up in 1939 – and its annual report records the principal adjudications by its disputes committee. The big general unions, the TGWU, AUEW and NUGMW, have had understandings intermittently for forty years to prevent the worst problems of friction. The Bridlington Agreement lays down that unions should require from applicants for membership full information about their experience in the trade union movement. Then:

'No member of another union should be accepted without inquiry from that union.

'No member of another union should be accepted where inquiry shows that the member is:

'(1) Under discipline;

'(2) Engaged in a trade dispute;

'(3) In arrears with contributions.

'No union should commence organising activities at any establishment or undertaking in respect of any grade or grades of workers in which another union has the majority of workers employed and negotiates conditions, unless by arrangement with that union. Each union should include in its membership form questions on the lines of the TUC model form in regard to past or present membership of another union.'

Certainly this limited workers' freedom of choice, although in individual cases the inquiries are often not made. It hamstrung small unions in competition with large ones and made breakaway unions in some cases impossible. On the other hand, it moderated the 'continuous atmosphere of social turbulence' and prevented too whole-hearted a belief that unions were competitors in a sort of industrial relations market like grocers or drapers in theirs.

One small union kept down before the War was the Chemical Workers Union, which year after year applied unsuccessfully to join the TUC against the opposition of the general unions. (A generation later, having been admitted, it almost merged with the NUGMW and has now cast its lot with the TGWU.) A *cause célèbre* was the Hull and Mersey docks dispute of 1954, when the 'blue union', the little NASD (National Amalgamated Stevedores' and Dockers' Union), recruited TGWU members who were in dispute with their own leadership about interpretation of an agreement. The TGWU ('white union') easily proved a breach of Bridlington. The TUC suspended the NASD's affiliation, but the dockers in revolt still objected to being ordered what unions they might join. Fifteen years later, although the NASD still has no negotiating rights outside London, you can find dockers with blue cards on Merseyside; indeed, there are several with both blue cards and white.

It is one thing to make a ruling about a whole plant, and another to hold individual members. The general unions have not made much progress in sorting out problems like this, but some of their agreements have had remarkable consequences. More than forty years ago the NUGMW, historically strongest in the north, agreed with the TGWU that in municipal transport in several cities the NUGMW would organise the trams and the TGWU the buses. At the time, the NUGMW was taking the bigger share of potential membership, but the future lay with the buses to the profit of the TGWU. There is even some straightforward 'commercial' competition. The TGWU has lower contributions than the NUGMW and the NUPE lower contributions still. There have been mergers determined by the possibility that a small union which is virtually penniless will have access to funds again.

If the TUC, by some miracle, were to develop the aspect of 'one big union' with authority over its constituents, some of these misdirections of energy of the union movement might disappear. Even as a voluntary association, the TUC has done a great deal to eliminate the worst 'demarcation' disputes, which seldom lead to strikes nowadays, by its inter-union disputes procedure. So far as it can, the TUC has encouraged mergers which cut out conflicts of function; although unfortunately some mergers have made the parties to demarcation problems members of bigger unions without eliminating the frontiers themselves.

New Law and Old Unions
Technically, the Industrial Relations Act affects these matters in several respects, although its operation has yet to make a pennyworth of difference. If a union is registered and unable to meet its obligations, the Registrar may apply to have it wound up under the Companies Act (although no doubt a solvent union proposing to merge with one of its weaker brethren could keep it alive for the present with a loan). The Bridlington Agreement as it stands is unlawful in part, because it prevents an employee's choosing which union he will join, if the prevention is 'by way of arbitrary or unreasonable discrimination'. The Act also provides for challenge to existing representation structures by methods outside the control of the TUC, although as we shall see in Chapter 5 the first challenge was something of a damp squib.

The Act not only installs statutory oversight which would effectively destroy the TUC's regulatory power as a voluntary association if the statutory processes became effective, but it could at least in theory give a splinter union the chance to compete and flourish, as a stimulus to existing unions to keep in touch with their members' real desires. It also makes illegal compulsory union membership at a place of work (the 'closed shop') unless employer and union together can persuade the court that it is vital to proper organisation; even this conditional recognition was written in as an amendment to the original Bill to meet the special cases of seamen and entertainers, and in the fullness of time the TUC suspended the National Union of Seamen and the British Actors' Equity Association for registering to take advantage of it.

These and other parts of the Act are an interesting mixture of commercial and political concepts. They imply the existence of widespread abuse, and apparently are intended to make the behaviour of British workers more orderly and more productive, to the mutual benefit of all classes and persons. By giving members new rights against the union and new rights against unfair dismissal and other oppressive practices, the Act may attempt to encourage in the average union member at least a greater venturesomeness in turning criticism of his union leadership into active campaigning, while at the same time reserving responsibility for the union's activities to the properly elected leadership. However, the scepticism remains among union members. If the unions are now predominantly powerful over employers (an intrinsically improbable thesis in the experience of most union members) why throw the power away with nothing to show in return except a recognition of their public spirit from those sitting above the salt? Perverse though it may be, there are millions of British workers who believe that they are more secure as individuals because they are in a union with 95 or 100 per cent membership in the plant or occupation, or with another hundred thousand or a million members outside. No amount of ingenuity will persuade them otherwise, since the whole point of unions is that many people of like mind have more chance of getting their way together than separately. Al-Ghazali, the medieval Arab scholar, summed it up precisely:

> 'When I have acknowledged ten to be more than three, if if anyone were to say, "On the contrary, three is more than ten, and to prove the truth of my assertion I shall change this rod into a serpent", my conviction of his error would remain

unshaken. His manœuvre would produce in me only admiration for his ability. I should not doubt my own knowledge.'

Another manager's aspiration which has had some vogue recently, and is to some extent expressed in the Industrial Relations Act, is to turn trade unions into labour contractors. Some unions in some countries, like the United Auto Workers and Machinists in the United States, come fairly close most of the time to meeting the requirements of a labour contractor. They provide labour in accordance with legally enforceable agreements. They exercise discipline in a formal, direct and managerial way. But they also exact a heavy price, not only in terms of wages but by a rigid seniority system. British unions do not normally behave like that. It is an expensive system, which is one reason why trade unionism is not nearly so widespread in the United States, rich though it is, as in Britain. The British system, subject to the revolution proposed by the Industrial Relations Act, is very cheap, very flexible and exasperatingly idiosyncratic and various. The US system is like a series of cities with suburbs: megalopolitan industries with titanic unions or staff associations, surrounded by suburban sprawls of small businesses and unorganised workers. Britain, where unions were firmly established before the days of conglomerates and massive enterprises, presents more the atmosphere of small towns and villages, some of which have come together. There are local quirks in large, unco-ordinated trade unions, sturdy and unexpected survivals, and a distaste for the law at least as old as Wat Tyler's revolt in 1381. That revolt followed a poll tax which brought to a head a whole series of grievances, including the Statute of Labourers, the first recorded incomes policy in Britain, passed after the Black Death to prevent inflation by fixing a maximum wage. By 1377 Parliament was complaining that villeins 'did gather themselves in great routs and agree by such confederacy that every one should aid other to resist their lords with a strong hand'. On their way to London the rebels fell upon lawyers and massacred immigrant artisans as well as an archbishop. Not all trade union orators go back as far as this in their references, but references to Tolpuddle martyrdom and other woes of the nineteenth century are a commonplace. 'The trouble with the trade union movement,' according to Mr Len Neal, chairman of the CIR, 'is that it is always a mass movement of historians. Like the Irish, they have such long memories.'

Our culture encourages this. As institutions, modern trade unions are based on the great Victorian settlement of 1867–75 which brought in electoral reform, local government reform, universal primary education, licensing laws, Factories Acts, Trade Union Acts and military and public service careers open to the talents. Compared with other countries' evolving systems, Britain's was peculiar in leaving both businessmen and trade unions more or less on a word of honour basis. A burst of inflation, like any other hurtful event beyond the control of a group, makes co-operation among them difficult. By distorting the expectations of managers, it first of all changes managers' attitudes to other workers and finally produces complicated changes within and among unions. We know that some co-operation becomes necessary when simple deference to authority or status declines. The increase of unofficial strikes in Britain after the middle 1950s (masked by the decline in mining strikes, which were mostly about interpretation of confused local pay arrangements) was the result of the independence of work groups from central union control, but they could achieve it only with the consent of managers. The same reasons which make an employer reluctant to recognise a staff union make him ready to do a deal with his own workers in general by way of bogus overtime or special bonus to improve on the national rate. This has been most common where there is a shortage of men with particular skills, although it can be maintained for other reasons, including tacit agreement about 'fairness'. It is for this reason that one can maintain that British inflation is made in Coventry, where the wage leaders of engineering are, and marketed in London, the centre of decision and still close to full employment when one man in ten or fewer is out of work in Scotland or on Tyneside.

We seem to have come a long way without greatly amplifying our first paragraph. Surely, 'to be convincing' by way of size or quality of membership is an unsatisfactory criterion? We do not say this about salesmen or barristers, or even managers, for that matter, although they spend most of their time persuading other people to do what they think that the organisation requires. An unconvincing union is an unsuccessful union, even if it is run by a band of saints, just as a company of objectively superlative producers is unsuccessful if it cannot sell the product at a price that allows for survival of the business. We should not confuse the marks of success with the value of objectives. Nor should we blame unions for failing to achieve what in the nature of things they cannot achieve, like model democracy or surges in production. Most trade unionists would like the latter and think that they would like the former, but model democracy is merely five impressive syllables and life is short. There is an old Gaelic proverb, 'The cat's delight is on the foreshore, but it cannot get it itself.' Cats love shellfish, but they cannot get them off the rocks and out of the shells. Both managers and organised labour are caught in this dilemma, and when the system of which both are servants fails to perform as they would like, it is easy to blame each other. Paradoxically, it is also possible for individual institutions – companies or trade unions – to grow proportionately stronger in a comparatively stagnant economy. The size of the cat makes no difference to the shellfish problem.

It is not difficult to see what is the shellfish in this analogy: the production of goods and services. It is more difficult to say which is the cat: management, with control of resources, information and decision-making, or labour which executes the decisions. The cat depends on a person with a tool, at the very least a knife; management and other workers are of course interdependent and both want a share in the eating. But workers want to know and control a great deal more than they used to; it is not reasonable to expect people to think in terms of twenty-five or thirty years about buying a house and in terms of a week and blind obedience about their work; to think in terms of representation and democracy away from work and submission to autocracy for the third of their time that they are there. They may be prepared to leave the large-scale bargaining and eloquence to specialists but like all normal people they want to have their direct surroundings to their liking, so far as they can. In an interview on Belgian television, Professor J. K. Galbraith was asked what he thought of the fashionable pressure for 'workers' participation'. He answered, with all the authority of a scholar who has a clear idea of the wood but does not bother much about trees:

> 'It's a pipe dream. I advise you to give up the idea of such a reform. The very nature of organised and bureaucratic management of a large concern concentrates the power in the hands

of people who share the information: specialists in technology and management. Neither the capitalist nor the worker has a part in it.'

There is, of course, a simple answer to this analysis. Specialists in technology and management may have all the information they require, except what the workers will do when the specialists act on the information. We have trade unions because the specialists are so often wrong, and current performance suggests that we shall continue to have them.

Chapter 2
Growth or Pseudo-Growth

'*As a man with an ulcered stomach spends all his thoughts on his stomach, so a society with a sick and aching economics is forever preoccupied with economics.*'
Lin Yutang

Peaceful Increase and Tolerable Change
In many respects managers and trade unionists are in broad agreement in Britain. By and large, they all want a peaceful increase in prosperity and social harmony. They also want to be effective. Yet as things stand we do not appear to be as successful in the matter of increase as other less mature and less complicated societies. Why not? The paradox is in the word 'peaceful' and the tension of choice between quantity and quality. Even if the currency is a less reliable indicator than it used to be, tons and minutes are constants. Quality is much more subjective; it is no use giving someone who has never been taught to read a library, or to expect a change of values automatically in someone accustomed to mere subsistence because of the mere accident of getting enough money to afford a fuller and more gracious life, whatever that means. What it means to the person with the choice is all-important; what it means to you or me may be irrelevant to most people, and although we are entitled to persuade people who disagree with us that we are right, mere assertion will not persuade them. Nor is there a solution in urging workers or groups of workers to accept a revolution in the working lives that they have been used to, arousing a perverse but natural suspicion in their minds that they must work harder for less or at least not more, with the mere promise that when the change pays off they will share in the profit.

There are very few people who will not, at least if they are able, work harder for less money in certain circumstances, and there are many privileged people who are able to make this sort of choice regularly throughout their lives. If they understood this as a privilege which is not available, at least in any way that they can see, to millions of fathers and mothers of families obliged to count their small change day by day, we could eliminate a great deal of moralistic nonsense which obscures the social context of our industrial problems.

As for 'peaceful', nothing wounds a person with a limited range of choice more than constant moralising on practical matters which implies, directly or indirectly, that he is to blame. I have never been more angry as a shop steward than on the two or three occasions when a manager in a temper said that the people I represented were 'no bloody good', or words to that effect. As a seasoned tactician, I have managed to conceal my feelings at the time, because losing one's temper with an angry man never achieves anything. Observation suggests that every leader of any group has had this experience at one time or another, and that sometimes the insult is passed on. It is even more often implied. Once, sitting in the Edwardian comfort of the Jockey Club in Buenos Aires sipping brandy after a solid lunch, a local businessman was deploring the 'laziness' of Argentine workers compared with British. Over his shoulder, through the great window put up by Argentine labour, a group of men were toiling in the sun on a multi-storey brick building with equipment so elementary that they were hauling barrows full of mortar to sixty feet above the ground with a rope pulley.

Some of them were no doubt lazier than others; but collectively they were giving as good as they had bargained for and were used to. We know how groups determine these things, and exert sometimes unspoken discipline over the member who works too hard, the member who works too little, and the member who goes running to the boss with tittle-tattle to the detriment of another member. This may be a frustrating quality about group behaviour for abrasive and innovative leaders, but it is a fact that cannot be avoided. Tranquillity is a matter of tolerance. Subordinates tolerate employers on certain terms, and a change of terms means a strain on tolerance, which fortunately is not an exact quantity itself. But you cannot have *peaceful* increase in prosperity if it requires intolerable change. Britain has long been a more than normally peaceful country; this does not mean that Britain must always have a slower growth rate than other economies which have come on faster with a daunting array of social problems and tensions building up at the same time. It does mean asking how can we have growth without discarding tolerance, and whether we are not whoring after false gods if we think that bigness of institutions – companies, trade unions, what you will – even of itself tends to increased prosperity. Big machines mean more efficient production, other things being equal, but all the evidence suggests that returns on human talents diminish rapidly as organisations grow. At the basic level, a tug o' war team of six strong men does not pull 20 per cent more effectively than one of five; and, to revert to our metaphor at the end of the last chapter, the bigger the shellfish operation the more fat cats.

Union Growth Points
That is why I have called this chapter 'growth and pseudo-growth'. All over Europe, as well as in Britain, companies have been merging and concentrating their resources of control. Not only by coincidence, during the past few years trade union membership in Britain has been concentrating fast and growing slowly. There have been more than a hundred mergers, large and small, in ten years. Large unions outside the TUC have joined it, and at the 1971 Congress the affiliated membership passed ten million for the first time. At the 1972 Congress, after an increase in unemployment, and the dissensions caused by the Industrial Relations Act (with the apparently inevitable result of a mass expulsion of thirty-odd unions), membership slipped again. The long-term effects of this unaccustomed intrusion on the organic development of trade unionism cannot be predicted yet except by observers with the simple confidence of partisans, one way or the other. But in British unionism as a whole there are clearly distinguishable natural 'growth points' as well as institutions which are inevitably static or declining. The growth does not always occur, or occur as rapidly as it might, partly because of the very slow incorporation into a movement originally of manual workers of modes of thinking palatable to the more complicated and less directly determined roles of white-collar employees (as we shall see in Chapter 5). The natural incentives to protective association are certainly growing for all employees because of the concentration of important decision-making in fewer heads, even if concentration of decision normally means only the power to say yes or no.

It is ironical, in view of the prominence that dockworkers, miners and railwaymen have had in the great national confrontations of 1970-2, that they are the most obviously declining areas of employment. The National Union of Mineworkers and the National Union of Railwaymen have been hard hit in numbers by the contraction of employment in the industries they serve almost exclusively. So have the smaller specialist unions of colliery overmen (NACODS) and locomotive engineers and firemen (ASLEF). In ten years NUM membership has fallen from 639,000 to less than 300,000, and NUR membership from 334,000 to less than 200,000. These were two parts of the famous 'Triple Alliance' which led trade unionism in the early part of the century up to the General Strike of 1926. The third part, the dockworkers, have been trimmed just as severely, from something like 100,000 after the war to fewer than 40,000 and with further decline technologically inevitable; but this does not show in the overall fortunes of any particular union. Most dockers are members of the TGWU. A few in the north-east are in the NUGMW, and a handful in the British Railways docks are in the NUR; the rest are in the National Amalgamated Stevedores and Dockers Union (NASD), whose attempts at giant-killing we noticed in the first chapter. The splinter Scottish TGWU returned to the fold in 1972 after a generation.

The TGWU itself is not only the biggest union in the country but the one growing fastest in absolute terms, if not proportionately. From 1,240,000 members in 1959 it has reached more than a million and three-quarters, fortified by a recent cluster of mergers – the Vehicle Builders (NUVB) (80,000), the Chemical Workers (16,000), the Scottish TGWU (23,000), the Scottish Commercial Motormen (21,000) and the Tugmen (3,000). The Amalgamated Union of Engineering Workers (AUEW), in second place, grew from 907,000 at the end of 1959 to more than 1,300,000 in 1971, taking in the Foundryworkers (44,000), the Draughtsmen (87,000) and the Constructional Engineers (27,000) and changing name twice in the process. The TGWU organises in almost all industrial classifications and its system of trade groups or industrial divisions (devised by the late Ernest Bevin and a model for the famous German industrial union system set up after the war*) has great advantages; for example, the NUVB

---

* One should remember that it was the *only* British model of its kind, and the British occupation administration had direct responsibility; in organic terms, by way of practical influence on German trade

could move smoothly into the TGWU automotive group and the NUVB leadership take a predominant place in the section leadership.

Still, about a fifth of the TGWU membership remains in the 'commercial group' of 'general workers'. The NUGMW has a structure based on areas and a single class of membership, although studies are under way to make it more flexible. The NUGMW has also been hit by a contraction in a specific industry, gas, and this was an important reason for the union's membership marking time for several years. Just as the dockers were a foundation group in the TGWU, the gasworkers were in the NUGMW. Obviously, at all events, general unions as institutions are able to weather a large reduction in some industry or occupation in a way that an industrial union cannot.

When the NUGMW was in merger talks with the Chemical Workers five years ago, it offered a semi-autonomous status with a special conference to the new chemical section. The merger was approved by the CWU leaders but turned down by the membership. In the much more consequential negotiations with the Electrical, Electronic and Telecommunications Union/Plumbing Trade Union (EETU/PTU, but still usually known by its old simplicity of ETU for Electrical Trades Union), the NUGMW is discussing, at least as a basis for the early days of merger, a quasi-federal divisional status. If it comes off, this will be an immensely important merger, producing a combined membership of 1,300,000, but as we shall see presently it is only one of a number of possibilities open to the ETU in its present pivotal position both in the functions of its members and the attitudes of its leadership.

The AUEW have been able to adapt their ancient constitution, developed by the Amalgamated Society of Engineers a century ago on the model of the American constitution, to give their new colleagues from DATA (Draughtsmen's and Allied Technicians' Association) the CEU (Constructional Engineering Union) and the Foundrymen what is almost federal status. Although the AUEW technically confines itself to the engineering industry, this is an extremely broad remit. Incorporating the Draughtsmen was a new venture for the Engineers into white-collar recruitment, the most promising field at the moment. Rather more than

unionists, the Swedish movement, organised in industrial unions since 1912, was just as much of a model and more persistently exemplary to the Germans.

half of 'manual' workers are in trade unions already; fewer than a third of white-collar workers are, and union membership is concentrated in the public service. Yet the total number of white-collar workers will probably exceed the rest, as it has already done in the United States, before 1980. The TGWU established its own white-collar section, the Association of Clerical, Technical and Supervisory Staffs, many years ago as an occupational and not industrial group, and has been emphasising its importance increasingly for a decade. It has a much larger membership than several independent unions. In the same way absorption has given the union a vital place in several industries: in building, for example, most bricklayers and most steelfixers are in the TGWU. Merger with the NUVB will mean that instead of the rough tripartite equality on car production lines of TGWU, NUVB and AUEW, the TGWU will outnumber the AUEW two to one. But this is only a generalisation of a random mosaic of local variations.

Paradoxes of Engineering
The AUEW combines the attractions of a general industrial and a craft union. It still bears the marks of its origin in the Amalgamated Society of Engineers, strictly a craft society which did not bend its exclusivity until the mergers in the 1920s which established the Amalgamated Engineering Union. Its field of operation covers all the 'engineering trades', which means virtually all industry that cannot be called something else. Thus the manufacture of machinery for the food and tobacco industry is engineering, but not the industry itself although it will employ some engineers to look after the machinery. Shipbuilding is not engineering, although the traditional shipbuilding crafts sometimes competes with traditional engineering crafts outside shipbuilding.

'Engineering,' as Arthur Marsh puts it in *Industrial Relations in the Engineering Industry*, 'is the least easily defined of all British industries. It is an area of industry primarily concerned with the manufacture of articles made of metal and makes use of a common range of basic skills, especially those of shaping, milling, machining and fitting. But the range of its products has no obvious limits; nor are the skills it employs confined only to engineering factories.'

Outside this wide boundary, AUEW members operate as craftsmen and craftsmen's mates in repair and maintenance work which gives them a vital influence. They do not have a monopoly of such skilled men. Just as the NUR has organised some dockers because they are in railway employment, so they have organised some skilled engineering workers in railway workshops. There are still several local and specialised engineering craftsmen who have either remained in independent unions or joined some other big union. Still, when the AUEW called its official strike against the Industrial Relations Bill in the spring of 1971 highly unionised enterprises well outside what could be called the engineering industry were obliged to stop work. Long before the merger with DATA brought an avowedly white-collar section into the AUEW, the AEU itself developed 'supervisory branches' catering for foremen, charge-hands, and other first-line managers grouped under divisional organisers and so passing by the normal district structure.

This separate representation of supervisors and rank and file is an advantage in seeking recognition, since no employer cares to have his supervisors potentially under discipline by subordinates. For the AUEW to recruit successfully it was probably vital. The TGWU did it already. This flexibility gives both of them an advantage over the NUGMW, whose membership moved only from 769,000 to 804,000 in the ten years after 1959. Apart from its unitary membership, the NUGMW has a regional structure which entrenches its historical bias to the north and west. Power is in the regions, not in trade groups. Although the union has many outstanding national officers and an exceptionally well developed education and research functions, specialised knowledge tends to become diffused down the line. During the abortive negotiations with the Chemical Workers the NUGMW promised specialist officers as well as a special conference for the chemical section. Since that venture failed the NUGMW has had a couple of conferences on structure and started a recruitment drive which lifted growth to over 40,000 new members in 1971. As a mature bureaucracy with a family tradition in elective office and a professional tradition in its service officers – the two boldest attempts to set up a national organisation of professional trade union officers both began in the NUGMW – it has had difficulty with its representative function.

Revolt at Pilkington's

Any large organisation with a democratic basis has trouble of this kind from time to time. The AUEW and the EETU are in a state of constant political argument; twelve years ago the TGWU went through a rougher patch of rank and file discontent than the NUGMW. But the NUGMW, sedate, stable and mistrustful of current slogans of workers' control and serial negotiation, has had particular trouble during the past couple of years. The most publicised was the unofficial strike at Pilkington Glassworks in Lancashire in 1970. Pilkingtons recognised the NUGMW in 1906 and no other union ever organised process workers there. The company dominated the town of St Helens and for years paid higher wages and offered better conditions than any other employer of local consequence. But neither the company nor the union was very responsive to social change and changing expectations among the workers. One NUGMW official was responsible for 9,000 members. New industry came to the area. workers became more mobile and the effective local working area grew with the availability of the car, and the age structure changed; the eventual outcome was a social explosion led by a highly militant group of shop stewards who tried to form their own union, the Glass and General Workers. Bridlington principles and the difficulty of sustaining fever heat put an end to that venture, although they might not have done if the full provisions of the Industrial Relations Act had been in force at the time. The GGWU withered on the vine, and the NUGMW set about putting its house in order again.* The company and the union together established effective consultation systems, replaced a decayed and inequitable bonus payments system with proper job evaluation, and generally did what the best textbooks require. Lack of contact and crazy payments are a common cause of labour trouble, but employer and union are seldom caught by it in the same way.

* The leaders of the 'revolt' were naturally disciplined by the union, and indeed the case of one of them was the first between a worker and a union to come before the National Industrial Relations Court (*Caughey* v. NUGMW). Mr Caughey demanded readmission to the union, from which he had been banned. There was no public hearing – at least, there had been no public hearing in the six months of 1972 after the application – but the union was represented at a meeting for directions. The union proposed a compromise of readmission but exclusion from office for a certain 'probationary' period. The next case of this kind before the court was *Goad* v. AUEW (see Chapter 8).

Apart from its local stimulus, the Pilkington strike (and others equally publicised at Lucas and GKN) had further effects on the union. Fifteen years before, all three major general unions had been under solid right-wing leadership. By 1970 this remained true only of the NUGMW. Yet after the Pilkington strike the NUGMW endorsed the unprecedented average of ten strikes a month, none of them very big or lasting but significant nevertheless. The burst of unofficial strikes which began in the middle of 1969 and fell away again at the end of 1970 was the result of national policies of restraint which were failing to achieve their objectives. The sudden increase in strikes came on top of the long-term trend of a general increase of unofficial strikes in other industries as the chronic level in mining fell away. The NUGMW suffered from particularly nasty ones because the leadership refused to condone as much local initiative as the leaders of some other unions did. At the same time, a competent recruiting drive began to show results, especially after the tripartite 'dirty jobs' strike of local authority manual workers in the autumn of 1970. But the main beneficiary of that strike, in terms of membership, was the National Union of Public Employees (NUPE), which increased its membership by more than a fifth as a result, pulled well ahead of the Union of Shop, Distributive and Allied Workers (USDAW) as the sixth largest union in the country and stood within reasonable distance of NALGO and the EETU/PTU, the fourth and fifth.

The 'Dirty Jobs' Strike
NUPE, like NALGO, is a sector general union in public service but recruiting only manual workers while NALGO recruits white-collar staff. More than half the members of NUPE are women; indeed, only the TGWU and NUGMW have more women members and a much smaller proportion. Under the autocratic leadership of Bryn Roberts from 1934 to 1962, NUPE pushed unashamedly for the highest possible membership in local government and the health service, with some adventures into related areas like the domestic staffs of schools and colleges. It kept contributions low and corporate enthusiasm high. It was perennially accused of 'poaching' members from the two big general unions, but poaching is difficult to prove in a field of employment where turnover of members goes as high as two-fifths in a year. One can derive some idea of the merry-go-round from the figures that more than 400,000 members have left NUPE since the end

of 1965 while total membership has risen from 250,000 to about 400,000. NUPE is a union catering for a specific sector of employment, and incidentally a growing area of employment, as a central concern and not a peripheral afterthought to catering for a hundred industries. NUPE is, besides, a co-operative union which does what it can to improve conditions for its members by the 'responsible' methods of work study, rationalisation and new techniques. Finally, its leadership has a considerable flair for publicity without giving the impression of dramatic combativeness.

All three unions had been taken by surprise by the outbreak of unofficial dustmen's strikes in the autumn of 1969 which buried the remains of the Labour Government's incomes policy in untidy piles of rubbish. The unions consequently shared a common interest in giving their members a militant lead in 1970, although neither NUPE nor the NUGMW normally behaved that way and the TGWU's militancy has usually been forced upon the leadership by the forwardness of individual trade groups. (No rigidly conservative leadership could have held the dockworkers and it is a fair guess that if Frank Cousins as general secretary had not been howled down by London market workers during their unofficial action in 1957–8, he would not have led the London busmen into their long, official and disastrous strike in the latter year.) The election in the interval of a Conservative Government pledged to hold down wages in the public sector for the private sector to emulate, but with no machinery to enforce the pledge, set the scene for the 'dirty jobs' strike. As strikes go, it was an unqualified success. Although it was as pure a money strike as one could find, the play on the 'dirtiness' of working in a sewer or on rubbish disposal or as a hospital porter maintained public sympathy. Even more interesting, it became NUPE's strike not only in the public mind but apparently in the minds of potential recruits, and the union gained 70,000 of them in nine months. A great deal of trade union recruitment and amalgamation is no more rational than this, but this does no more than match the irrationality of commercial and political decisions in a wider context. The temptation to expect trade unions and unionists to behave better than organisations with legal authority and control over material resources is one of the standing anomalies of our culture.

NALGO, taking office workers from junior clerks to town clerks, is NUPE's white-collar counterpart: larger, inevitably better funded and bureaucratically smooth. Other unions used to find NALGO exasperating; as Sir Harry Nicholas recalls of his days as a local official, he never knew whether he was going to meet the town clerk as an employer or a union spokesman, but he knew that he was going to meet the town clerk. With the spread of public service after the war, NALGO changed its range of interest, which now covers public utilities, privately as well as publicly owned, the staffs of such bodies as docks and harbour boards, and indeed every non-manual job in public service outside the civil service and the nationalised industries. It has grown from a quarter of a million in the late fifties to nearly 450,000 members, having joined the TUC in 1965. NALGO also had its moments of agony in 1969–70. First a negotiated agreement was rejected by its local authority members, and then the union had its first official strike, in Leeds, early in 1970. In 1971 the Leeds branch, the largest and most militant, went to court to restrain the union leadership from casting its votes at the TUC in favour of joining the Common Market on the terms negotiated by the Government. At the same time the general secretary, Walter Anderson, was telling the TUC that NALGO would not be dragooned into coming off the register of trade unions under the Industrial Relations Act if its membership preferred to stay on. The wider companionship of trade unionism has its interesting problems.

Electricians and Other Crafts
Twenty thousand members or so smaller is the EETU, rather surprisingly incorporating the PTU. Traditionally the ETU has been to its field of interest what the AEU was in engineering, but with a much clearer definition although the ETU itself was in the TUC's engineering group until the separate electricity group was created for it a few years ago. The ETU began as a simple craft union and made a conscious decision to 'go general' some forty years ago, taking on assembly workers on the one hand and specialised trades like lift and electric crane operatives on the other. It is now an industrial union in electricity supply and contracting, a general union in manufacturing with an electrical component, and a craft union across the board in anything to do with electricity and plumbing. There is probably no union now that is considered more likely to play a pivotal part in some historic merger: among the potential partners have been the AUEW, the NUGMW, the Boilermakers, ASTMS and other

smaller craft unions. The merger with the plumbers which made it the EETU/PTU was in 1968. Before that the tensions and particularity within the union survived for a long time. In 1959, when the late Sir Leslie Cannon was organising his campaign to unseat the Communist leadership of the ETU, one of the branches he persuaded to his way of thinking was the London Lift and Crane Engineers, who decided at a meeting in a pub on the Old Kent Road to appeal to the Chief Registrar of Friendly Societies to look into abuses in the union. There was nothing the Registrar could do, of course, but the resolution was good publicity and no doubt helped to water the seed from which the Registry of Trade Unions and Employers' Associations has sprung in 1971.

During the years of Communist leadership the ETU had no chance of expanding through amalgamation. The alliance with the plumbers in the lively atmosphere which there has been since the Trade Union (Amalgamations) Act in 1964 made mergers easier was a definite declaration of intent to play a part in building a rival to the giants. The PTU had also been wooed by the Boilermakers, who had brought off the amalgamation of the shipyard 'black trades', taking in the shipwrights and blacksmiths, under the more restrictive rules that applied before 1964. There was also a more natural, functional possibility of a merger with the Heating, Domestic and Ventilating Engineers, whose demarcation disputes with plumbers and electricians, especially plumbers, had been a cross for some industries to bear for many years. The 'HDV' are a small but widely deployed union; any building with a central heating system may have its handful. But in 1967 they joined the Sheet Metal Workers and Coppersmiths (SMW), who had themselves merged seven years before, and this new merger itself has become a focus for flirtation. Who will join whom? is one of the great guessing games of trade unionism. Looking back to John Hughes's paper for the Donovan Commission helps to show how difficult prediction is. Writing in 1966, he recorded that the Boilermakers seemed to be developing 'a dynamic' as a result of their amalgamation, and actively seeking to attract other unions, most recently the CEU, the SMW, and the PTU. Yet it attracted none of them. The first and last have joined giant partners and the SMW, although likely enough to merge with someone, is unlikely to choose the Boilermakers unless there is more to it than that.

Clerks, Supervisors and Technicians
When Mr Hughes wrote, the CWU had rejected the NUGMW but had not started talks with the TGWU, the union which more than most had resisted the growth of the CWU before the war. When he wrote, too, DATA was talking to the Association of Scientific Workers (ASCW) about amalgamating to form a wider-technicians' union, although he added a perceptive footnote about the renewed attractiveness for DATA of amalgamation with the AEU on the pattern of a separate section as had been given the Foundryworkers. Five years later DATA did of course become the technical and supervisory section of the AUEW. Another union which had been on friendly terms with DATA was the Association of Supervisory Staffs, Executives and Technicians (ASSET), whose rapid growth from trivial beginnings earned a nod from Mr Hughes. In fact it was ASSET which merged with the ASCW to form the Association of Scientific, Technical and Managerial Staffs (ASTMS), which in 1970 celebrated its 200,000th member within two years of celebrating its 100,000th. In 1961 ASSET had 24,000 members and the ASCW 12,000. In Chapter 5 we shall look at the context in which these and other unions like the Association of Professional, Executive, Clerical and Computer Staff (APEX) with 130,000 members and the other white-collar organisations in private industry seek or find their feet.

Here we have another of the anomalies of trade unionism in Britain. It became a power in private industry through the manual workers, but the white-collar unions have flourished most mightily in the public service (with special exceptions like journalists). This can be explained only by examining the underlying assumptions of the people involved. There has always been a prejudice among private employers against unions for 'staff' in that they tend to divert or dilute the natural loyalties of employees from whom the next generation of management must come. But they will admit staff associations, or some other form of staff representation, more readily so long as it keeps 'outsiders' out. In the nature of things a staff association in the civil service, and to a lesser extent in other public service, becomes a trade union in real effect. NALGO and the National Union of Teachers (NUT) began principally as bodies to get pensions, not to negotiate with the power tactics of workmen. In fact the NUT had its first official strike only a few months before NALGO at the end of 1969. The IPCS, which has not joined the

TUC yet, not only organises civil servants up to the level of assistant secretaries but has an enviable density of membership. Since there is no competing employer and a less obvious 'clash of interest' in the public service, anxieties about conflicting loyalty arise only rarely. Yet in private employment they are in fact arguments by analogy from the position of the Crown.

The Crown has prerogative; the Board must have it too. The Courtier next the Throne is in a position of peculiar responsibility and favour; the manager next the Board must be too. After the 1970 strike Pilkingtons recognised ASTMS to negotiate for their 4,500 'general staff', but insisted that although their 1,200 staff described as 'managers' might join a trade union, there would never be collective bargaining for them. The implication is that the Board's courtiers may bargain with the representatives of the common people, but the Board will never bargain with them. To see the absurdity of this, one need only look at how the public service actually operates, with a form of collective assessment up to the very top, for judges, MPs, senior civil servants, generals and medical men. It is a special form of collective provision with a special secretariat, and only the doctors have ever threatened anything remotely like disruptive action under the style of 'withdrawal of professional services'. They use a Queen's Counsel to make their case. For them, as for the public service generally, high required standards are matched by dismissal and disciplinary procedures far better than in private employment where they are necessary at all. The private manager has neither protection nor collective bargaining.

Although white-collar unionism generates great resistance, it has an increasing momentum as more and more workers find the prestige slipping away from 'middle-class' jobs and personal contact with the ultimate employer becoming more and more theoretical for most staff workers; meanwhile craft and process wages pull ahead of clerical wages and technological change threatens the clerk and the administrative factotum as profoundly as the labourer and more than most craftsmen. In fact, a clerk or a technician in middle life who has not been promoted is likely to feel a certain disappointment, and some of the eccentricities of white-collar unions, especially in their politics, are the result of this unnatural combination of the young and the frustrated, with the rules of courtiership depriving them of the influence on the union of men who have been promoted to real responsibility in their careers. The doctrine is presented in its full absurdity in a recent American textbook (Basil: *Leadership Skills for Executive Action*), as a statement of fact, let it be said, not an endorsement:

> 'Disloyalty is one of the cardinal sins of business, and is rarely tolerated. This reduces the options open to the man who is dissatisfied with the leadership provided him. He can create a crisis situation by demanding the removal of his boss, which usually has little chance of success. He can wait until it is obvious to everyone that the boss is incompetent, but he himself may be swept out with the broom of the newly appointed boss. Or he can decide that the situation is intolerable and seek employment elsewhere.'

Effects of Recognition

With this sort of thinking the norm, it is even surprising that white-collar unionism is not growing even faster, especially when one compares it with the comparative freedom of the shop floor from such curious principles. This is not to make a romance of the liberty of the shop floor, merely to record that in the comparatively harsh material and psychological context in which most manual workers do their jobs it is impossible to maintain the more colossal fictions for long. It is true that many eminent men at the head of large concerns may complain of the lack of loyalty of thousands of employees whom they have never met and who may not know who they are either; only the courtiers next the Board pay much attention, because whatever loyalty is, it is a personal quality and requires a known person, rather than a title or an image, to have real meaning.

This brings us to the other end, as it were, of trade unionism: the impulse to membership. In stable situations with mature trade unionism, there are thousands of workers who join a union because it is the normal and natural thing to do (and lots of others, of whom we shall see an example in the next chapter, who consider it the done thing even if they have not done it themselves). Nothing does more to bring about this attitude of mind, and the comparatively harmonious expression and resolution of difficulties, which it makes possible, than free and open recognition by an employer. There is probably no better reason than this for the strength of white-collar unions in some fields and not in others. Sociologically, journalists, actors and musicians are not a by-word for temperamental stability and tend to be more individualistic and even narcissistic than most workers. Yet nine out of ten or more are members of trade unions – in journalism largely because of the personal decision of one man, Lord Northcliffe, and the later realisation by most other newspaper proprietors that it would be unreasonable to have total representation for all other workers and none for journalists; in entertainment because public policy in checking the abuses of the industry required the co-operation of a strong and representative workers' organisation. These occupations have certain features in common: the difficulty of providing a normal qualification by way of training and apprenticeship (although all of them try) and a possibly unjustified eagerness by youngsters to enter them for the sake of their presumed creativeness, glamour and other qualities calculated to broaden (or 'blow') the mind. However, employers even if they wanted to, cannot exploit these qualities exclusively because of the regularity required of them. The show must go on, the paper must come out: the result is a comparatively dense but not obstructive trade unionism. If it is hard to break into these occupations, it is because of competition to get in rather than successful resistance by people who are in already.

Craft unionism is dense for different reasons. In the nineteenth century the unions consciously modelled themselves on the professions and so far as they could established control of their own mysteries, by way of apprenticeship. There was a time, when jobs were scarcer and money tighter, when they successfully established 'union rate' in many areas: that is, a craftsman's services were not to be had for less than the rate which the union determined. The phrase 'union rate' has been meaningless for more than half a century, since collective bargaining supplanted unilateral assertion of minimum pay. Indeed, the process has gone a step farther with local bargaining, plant by plant, developing on top of national agreed rates and leading to the sort of free-for-all that the CIR reported from Clayton Dewandre. (The realities of industrial relations outstrip the terminology, just as the industrial groupings in the TUC always seem to reflect the last state of affairs but one. Only ten years ago there was still a separate grouping for the cotton industry, with six unions but only 115,000 members.) In fact, this development from jealous crafts protecting the rate to industrial bargaining units was necessary for the emergence of the AEU and ETU as occupational-general unions. There are some industries in which this has never happened. The Boilermakers remain a craft union even although most of their members are in shipbuilding. The National Graphical Association has remained a craft union in printing, with a craft offshoot into telecommunications. The Society of Graphical and Allied Trades, a general process-workers' and clerical and ancillary workers' union in printing with some craft pockets, and a craft and general union in paperworking, is the one significant union merger of recent years which has split again rather than solidified.

We have seen that public service recognition never appeared as a threat to that prerogative which survives in practice only in private employment. Public service in hard times offered security and working conditions above the average in return for low pay. Apart from career men, it attracted older workers with stable and modest expectations and outlook, and in their early development public service unions or sections of unions reflected this. About twelve years ago Charles Smith, the late Lord Delacourt-Smith, general secretary of the Post Office Engineering Union until his death in 1972, called one of a series of press conferences in a long campaign for higher investment in the telephone service, then as now commonly mocked by comparison with the privately-owned Bell System in the United States. Then, as now, external critics inclined to blame the people who operated the system rather than those who determined its share of investment. Smith commented that his members were becoming impatient, and someone asked him whether they had considered industrial action. 'We are a civil service union,' he replied, 'and we have never had a strike.' In the absolute one could make a case for striking for higher investment to meet a clear public need, but the point is not about the use of power to meet a certain objective but the attitude of the union.

Attitudes have changed. With different expectations and improved state provision against the most desperate consequences of losing a job, the old definition of a working man as someone who could not afford to be without a job for a week has become outdated too. A generation of full employment, summarily terminated certainly by fiscal restraint and technological toughness during the past two years, has allied with better pensions and statutory conditions of employment generally to swallow up some of the advantages of public service. And the Post Office, of course, has left the civil service, on terms which helped to bring on the lamentable strike in 1971 of the POEU's sister organisation, the Union of Post Office Workers (UPW).

The Post Office Fiasco

The Post Office became a public corporation without union resistance, but with no positive steps taken to ease the change of status. The change raised high expectations among the workers, who looked forward to better pay and prospects in an efficient and autonomous commercial undertaking. Yet all the spadework was left until after the change, although it was made in the peculiarly delicate circumstances of the decline and death of an incomes policy; a leading part in the obsequies fell to workers in public service outside direct government employment, like the dustmen and teachers. The UPW had never had a serious rival for organising the workers in its field, but there is a small independent union catering for telephonists which was registered with the Chief Registrar of Friendly Societies but never admitted to the TUC (which, as we shall see later, does not normally admit non-member unions which are in direct competition with existing members unless there are exceptional reasons). The Post Office Corporation refused recognition to the Telephonists' Guild (now Telecommunications Staff Association) and also, in effect, helped the UPW with discipline of dissident members. One of the punishments provided by union rules is disqualification for a period from holding any office. At the same time, the Post Office allows certain lay officials full time off work with pay for union duties. Dissidents who enjoyed this privilege must automatically go back to the routine of the switchboard.

For want of any other standard of remuneration in 1970, the Corporation simply followed the old civil service formula. In August, the Corporation made an arbitration agreement with all its unions, but in spite of obvious breakers ahead and the certainty of a wrangle because of the conflict between workers' expectations and government policy to combat inflation, took no immediate steps to man the arbitration system or even agree on a chairman. The novelties of commercial operation, staff planning and the dismissal of the chairman of the Corporation by the new Government helped to accentuate the pattern of discontent. The postal workers clearly considered it only fair that their pay increase should be at least as large as that won by the 'dirty job' strikers. The Government was clearly determined that it should not be, and Bill (now Sir William) Rylands, the acting chairman, although an engineering civil servant by training and experience, was equally determined to see commercial good sense (as he saw it) prevail. The strike duly took place. Everyone had miscalculated. The immediate effects were not nearly so paralysing as the UPW expected, partly because the telephone service remained in operation through a combination of mechanical innovation and the defiance of strike orders by many UPW members as well as the splinter union. The Government and the Corporation underestimated the will of the strikers to hold out, although the UPW had no strike fund and very little other money. The strike failed in the end, and did great damage to the UPW and the postal service.

TGWU's *Bargaining Alliances*

Thus the UPW was humiliated within a few months of NUPE's success. Not only had the UPW its internal dissensions and lack of resources for battle, but in spite of abundant expressions of good will and a few interest-free loans it was isolated. The local government strike was sustained by three unions, two of them the richest in the country (although the NUGMW is now much smaller than the AUEW it is much better funded as well). For the TGWU in particular, as hostile to Government policy as any, the strategy of avoiding isolation is most important; only in the dock strike of 1970, within a few weeks of the Government's coming to office, was the TGWU virtually alone. That dock strike was the result of a series of miscalculations and a strike in which no person of major responsibility had any interest but to settle. In the major strikes in the motor industry, like the Ford affair in 1971, in the large, ineffective and unsatisfactory series of local battles in engineering in the early months of 1972 before return to national agreement between the Engineering Employers' Federation and the Confederation of Shipbuilding and Engineering Unions, and in the building dispute later in the year, the TGWU was present and influential but sometimes even inconspicuous. And when another dock strike developed out of the industrial and litigious confusion of 1972, there were so many cross-currents that there was no question of simple polarisation. Mr Jack Jones, general secretary of the TGWU, was running a joint committee with Lord Aldington, chairman of the Port of London Authority, to find a formula to which the dockers would consent.

As a result, the leaders of the TGWU came out of the dispute with considerably increased reputations. They had already been given expressions of sympathy by the National Industrial Relations Court, perhaps slightly to their surprise, compared with dockers acting against union policy. They were obviously trying to hold the union together, and inevitably became testy with other union leaders who exhorted them to absolute defiance of the court but drew the line at having the TUC collectively finance the defiance, which was the TGWU's condition for it.

The strikes emphasised that trade unions, like the bitter youth in the poem, are born into a world they never made. Whether or not a government embarks on major experiments with a 'framework of law' for industrial relations, its actions and the actions of employers effectively determine the context in which union members and eventually the unions themselves must operate. If the Post Office strike had come before the 'dirty jobs' strike instead of after it, the positions would not have been reversed exactly but the postmen would have done rather better and the dustmen and park-keepers rather worse. Later on we shall see some of the wide variations of pattern and aspiration from trade to trade and industry to industry in Britain, where collective bargaining directly or indirectly affects three-quarters of all pay slips; where there are between 175,000 and 225,000 shop stewards of varying degrees of training, shrewdness and activism, and only 3,000 full-time union officials; where there may be as many as 250,000 collective agreements of one kind or another in a year (the figures can be only speculative); where collective agreements until now have been legally enforceable not between the parties who made them – negotiators for employer or employers and for employees – but as part of legally enforceable individual contracts between employer and employee afterwards. The flexibility of the British system was a matter of national self-congratulation until about fifteen years ago, when publicists' alarm about 'stagnation' and 'restriction' picked up overwhelming momentum. In fact the stagnation in the movement itself had begun to break up, but not fast enough or in the right way to prevent the most determined assault on trade union privileges and immunities for a century.

The Improbable Legal Intervention
The Industrial Relations Act is so radical and by British

standards so improbable* that it will take years to determine whether the new system has taken root. What is certain, as we have seen, is that if it does the TUC's potential as an effective 'government' of a voluntary trade union movement has been set back, perhaps irretrievably. Jurisdiction for an external Registrar, industrial tribunals and a new Court takes invigilation outside the family circle. At the 1972 Congress, as the National Union of Seamen and the Confederation of Health Service Employees stumped out of the Dome auditorium in Brighton, there was still an atmosphere of an angry member of the family about the matter; no doubt, if the pressure continues, this will go. These unions and others opted for registration because they felt that they could not go on without it. There are, in fact, bigger unions which would readily organise some or all of their members. The Registrar is given oversight of registered unions' general behaviour, and in particular of the rules they make and the manner in which they implement them. The political subtlety of the Act is that the rules required of registered unions are in the principles for all organisations of workers, whether registered or not, which it is an unfair industrial practice to break.

There is nothing in the prescribed rules for registered unions which should make much difference one way or the other to the growth and development of individual unions. The pressure of legal norms about membership, voting and so on enforced by the Court and tribunals would also be a slow force because someone has to take a case to court. By the end of 1972 this had not been a cheerful experience for anyone, nor had the imperatives of establishing its authority allowed the court to do much in the way of elevating good practice to an enforceable or even comprehensible norm. The point about the docks dispute was that it developed out of a coincidence of bad practices, beginning with the shipping industry's decision to cut job opportunities for dockers without telling them (and they had no legal duty to tell them), which in the end produced a situation where no one was clearly to blame, except perhaps for lack of imagination, in specific disputes. However, as lawyers often are, the Court found itself obliged to pronounce on the rights and wrongs of a small incident of strife which was symptomatic of

* This is not the place to analyse the Act; I have discussed these points at length in *The Times Guide to the Industrial Relations Act* (Times Newspapers, 1971).

the major problem – the 'blacking' by dockers of certain transport undertakings. Judges referred to the 'spread of containerisation' as if it were a natural phenomenon or an act of God, not the result of commercial decisions whose consequences for workers all responsible parties should have considered. As a result the country temporarily faced within a couple of months the prospect of the country's largest union deprived of control of its funds for defiance of an interim order in a case involving a small part of the business of a small company, and the TUC prepared to call a general strike to get five dockers acting in breach of union policy out of prison. At the first hurdle the TUC gave in a little, and allowed unions to defend themselves before the court. At the second, the Official Solicitor was available with a formula for the men's release.

These dramatic distractions from notions of peaceful increase also prejudiced the humble, necessary cultivation of good industrial relations expected of the Commission on Industrial Relations. The Labour Government established the CIR in 1969 on the recommendation of the Donovan Commission to investigate and report on general questions of principle and on such individual problems as the Government referred to it. The reports were well received except by people who might have to act on them. The CIR was doing its job, but was not being effective – not necessarily because 'reform through inquiry' is a faulty principle, but because in individual situations a few people have the power to take initiatives, and if inquiry does not persuade them they must either go or be persuaded in some other way. This is true whether it refers to a powerful manager who expects the CIR to see the 'real facts' as he sees them, or a union in a competitive situation led by men with the same egocentric attitude. The Industrial Relations Act gives the CIR wider functions and the backing of authority, as well as the right to take ballots of union members on democratic principles. It is another example of the social asymmetry of our commercial life that these principles cannot in the nature of things be applied to the other side.

The powers of the CIR to establish bargaining units, to consider the competence of unions to represent individual workers, to make awards between one union and another which the court is virtually obliged to endorse, and to ignore or override existing union pretensions and arrangements if it pleases constitute a total novelty in this country and an unusual and distinctive feature of labour law internationally. The CIR need pay no attention to 'Bridlington principles' which have not prevented poaching and shifting of membership but at least set a standard of good practice and prevented annexation of whole plants by one union from another. In theory this becomes possible under the Act although not easy. The external system is given effective oversight of both straight recognition disputes – one union and one employer – and competition among unions.

'Process of Mutual Intimidation'
Before the Act, recognition was a matter of persuasiveness and strength. One not wholly frivolous definition of collective bargaining is 'a process of mutual intimidation'; more often than not a union felt that it had to prove its power before getting recognition, although this is not always true and need not ever be true. Recognition itself is the greatest stimulus to union organisation and if an employer concedes it freely the union may never acquire the habit of 'intimidation'. In matters between union and union such arbitration as existed was exercised by the TUC Disputes Committee. Once, or if, the CIR's enhanced functions begin to take effect, the TUC's role will decline. It is true that instead of maintaining the Bridlington agreements, unions may make contracts with one another, but they could not maintain contracts if they ran clean contrary to CIR recommendations, or excluded workers from unions which they wished to join, or obliged them to join particular unions. Besides, unions who make a point of excluding legal enforceability from agreements with employers will presumably do so among themselves. In any event, a union has not traditionally been an institution with members as clients, maintaining a formal professional relationship with them, as the Act implies. A good deal of trade union growth and decline has been as casual as that of a village cricket team, depending on having one or two volunteers available in a work group to do the thankless jobs.

For seventy-odd years commentators in (or on) Britain have blamed the restrictive practices of trade unions for the country's declining competitiveness, first with the United States and Germany and lately with most of the advanced industrial world. They have criticised the unions' resistance to change, and everyone from the late Ernest Bevin to the latest Secretary of State for Employment has emphasised the innate conservatism of the British working man. This may be a misconception. Resistance to change in the absolute is not a natural human attribute, nor do the run of young people nowadays cling obdurately to the standards of their parents on life in general. Resistance to *imposed* change is natural. The working-class movement has had a hand in tremendous social innovation, but can hardly be expected to welcome industrial innovation without some guarantee of a share of the profit and compensation for lost security. Hence the anomaly that some of the most stubborn defenders of protective devices as trade unionists are politically advocates of the revolutionary left. One cannot say in the absolute that a Marxist or a Maoist resists 'change' as such. There is another anomaly. Although the trade unionist will stick to his last rather than do work which would cost another man his job, the movement is also the greatest single channel of voluntary service in Britain, and trade union activists often find themselves drawn into other forms of voluntary service as well. The Industrial Relations Act is to some extent an attempt to professionalise it – to shift authority from the shop steward to the permanent official and to subject the voluntary work-group leader to the discipline of the permanent official, the employer and in the last resort the Court.

There are those who believe that legislation of this kind and the consequent discipline are necessary for the improvement of national economic performance, healing the ulcer of low productivity and a low increase of production. The Act is not purely a restriction on the worker and his organisations, of course; it places duties of good practice on employers as well. In theory it should produce a transformed trade union movement requiring performance from both managers and its own members – purposeful, dynamic and a force for economic innovation and increasing prosperity in a competitive world. This would indeed be revolutionary change in a society where the earned income component of the gross national product appears to have remained roughly constant at some 42 per cent for a generation, rain or shine, until the growing incidence of taxation at the bottom range of wage-earning increased militancy in support of maintaining 'total take-home pay'. Besides, collective organisation is a shield against the arbitrary exercise of power, principally by employers, sometimes by Government. It is questionable whether in the nature of things it can be much more, or that it would be desirable even if it were possible for British unions to take on some of the qualities of labour contractors. Besides, common observation shows us that many of the assumptions on which such policies are based are not valid in individual cases. A person gives up defensive subterfuges when he is confident of his security. An individual's eagerness to work well does not appear to have any direct relation to his pay; changes in his pay requirements have more direct relation to the cost of living than to his level of productivity. Besides, a man may work the shirt off his back and still have more demanded of him. Perhaps the saddest effects of the recent shake-out in Britain have been the closing of little plants which are themselves profitable in a small way to release orders which will restore the profit at large central plants where there is unused capacity. One may say that the man in the small plant in the backwaters of British industry must be realistic and become mobile towards where the work is going. It is quite another thing to moralise about his reluctance. Perhaps instead of seeing Britain sinking giggling into the sea one should instead see it engaged in a perpetual orgy of finger-wagging and homilies, most of them based on increasingly ludicrous preconceptions rather than examination of what is really happening.

Electricity and Gas Disputes

Towards the end of 1972, there was another crisis of bargaining: in electricity supply. Four unions are involved, and they make a formidable quartette – the ETU, the TGWU, the AUEW and the NUGMW. For several years they had operated a national agreement under which numbers of employees declined and pay went up. Productivity increased very rapidly, and of course it would not have done without heavy investment. Since electricity supply is a nationalised industry and the Government, by and large, both puts up the money and exercises some control over tariffs, there is no real market guidance about allocation of reward to capital and labour. What the men knew was that over the period since the original demanning agreement, their standing in the table of average earnings among industries had declined. When the miners made a stand against a similar decline in similar circumstances in the spring of 1972, the electricity supply workers accepted a comparatively modest pay increase. Yet by the autumn the electricity cuts caused by the mining strike were being referred to by motor industry managers, of all inflationary people, as 'electricity strikes'. In a work-to-rule in 1970 electricity supply workers had discovered the ferocity of public reaction to power cuts, but felt that compared with other workers they had nothing to show for being temperate – and the four biggest manual workers' unions in Britain were spitted on the problem at a time of grand strategy talks on incomes policy among the Government, the Confederation of British Industry and the TUC. As institutions, they had no 'growth' interest in electricity supply since employment was declining; yet they were in a situation so complicated and contentious that the only way to remain convincing was to emphasise their power to cut off supply.

The grand strategy talks failed, in the habitual wave of competitive diagnosis of the reasons why. It would have been a remarkable novelty if they had succeeded on any basis of actual bargaining; as their final statement showed, the Government were in fact reserving their powers on several matters which affected the cost of living, such as the policy of accession to the European Economic Community on certain terms and the enforcement of a new policy on municipal rents. The participants in the talks agreed on the need for them, or at least on the need to reduce the hurtful processes of inflation. But they did not agree on detail, and the TUC refused simply to endorse a traditional exercise in wage restraint. Immediately the talks ended, the Government brought in wage restraint by law. A number of union negotiators, including those in electricity supply, just had time to squeeze in a settlement before the term of the 'ninety-day freeze' began. But some equally worthy categories of worker were caught: the National Health Service ancillary workers, normally settling for the same as local authority manual workers, were caught by the arbitrary date; so were the farmworkers, although they had already settled but the effective date fell in the standstill period; and bitterest of all, gasworkers were restrained from even negotiating on their claim, although their rationalisation and redundancy record was quite as good as that of electricity supply, and the prosperity of the industry and productivity increase for each employee were considerably better. The NUGMW leaders once again found that there is no gratitude for past temperance, and as working restrictions began at local level the automatic process of denunciation slipped into full voice.

A refusal to carry on working normally is in the end the only persuasion that a union or one of its constituent parts can use that is not either bluff or a statement of good intentions. If all bluffs have been called and good intentions have been honoured at least as well as could have been expected, and better than in many other occupations – which undoubtedly happened in mining, the railways and electricity supply, and certainly in parts of the docks – the final overt confrontation will be all the more bitter. 'Growth' of any kind ceases to matter. A work force becomes an angry crowd. Most seasoned union leaders have had experience of angry crowds of their own members, as we shall see later on. Few of them can take it lightly.

Chapter 3

Commissars and Fixers

'Charles V, when he abdicated a throne and retired to the monastery of St Juste, amused himself with the mechanical arts, and particularly that of watchmaker. He one day exclaimed, "What an egregious fool must I have been, to have squandered so much blood and treasure in an absurd attempt to make men think alike, when I cannot even make a few watches keep time together."'
Colton's *Lacon*

'Emotion often makes madmen out of the wisest of men, and often makes the most blockish guileful.'
La Rochefoucauld

What Determines Leadership?
Circumstances give play to an appropriate kind of leadership. If we take the principle far enough, we can all realise this: for example, if a sailor from Devon behaved now as Sir Francis Drake behaved four hundred years ago (if indeed he could) he would certainly become a celebrated figure and in the end there would be novels and films about him, but he would not be a national hero knighted on the poop of his flagship. We are much less ready to admit this in small, but important matters of degree, so that you will find many people who consider so characteristic a product of English circumstances as, say, Jack Dash to be an 'un-British' figure and deplorable in a general way. Accepting that not only Rupert Brookes are by England shaped and made aware, one may go on to reject the crude, deterministic statement that a man is wholly the product of his environment. What is true, given the inevitable responsive quality of trade unionism, is that a manager will get the reaction from his workers that they consider appropriate to his style in

the context of previous experience. A tough management style will produce tough shop stewards if it is not dominant enough to produce subservience or guile. Unfortunately for managers, the response from their subordinates, at least to begin with, often springs from the activities of earlier managers who may have had qualities of character and habits of mind that have conditioned the workers in ways that his successor can learn only by experience. As if that were not bad enough, a dramatic change of style is likely to produce dramatic and upsetting consequences. These general principles are as true for leaders of trade unions as they are for managers, but as we have seen the criteria for success for trade union leaders are somewhat looser than those for success as managers.

In industrial relations you must make sure where you are, and test the springboard before taking a great leap forward. It is, no doubt, some consolation for disappointed English innovators that even the Chinese in their immemorial wisdom have been known to make the mistake of not doing so. But so much discussion of human behaviour is argument by analogy, that one must be particularly careful in this respect lest our thinking should degenerate into a series of bad puns. The resulting paradoxes may produce satisfying closed systems of words, like 'the conservative working man' or 'trade union mentality' which we noticed in the last chapter. Unless they are checked against reality they will not help us very much in choosing our own courses of action or understanding other people's.

The British trade union movement is immensely various. There are more ideologies, attitudes and whimsicalities in it than in most comparable movements, simply because it has developed from the mass upwards. Inevitably there are two common tendencies of leadership: the autocrat who considers as a rule that the workers' interests are too important a matter to be left to the workers, and the greaser of wheels, the master of compromise who may have strong views of his own but prefers to achieve them by side winds and persuasions. I have called them – not being original – the commissar and the fixer. There is a bit of both in most successful trade unionists, perhaps in most successful leaders, but the character and style of different unions and different occupations favours one or the other. It would be unnatural to expect long-distance lorry-drivers, as a class, to have the same outlook as draughtsmen in a shipyard, or park-keepers, or tally clerks in the docks; it would be unnatural to expect any of them to develop the same collective habits as factory workers on an assembly line or pen-pushers in a government or municipal office. The predictable level of participation in joint activities is different, even the understanding of words and phrases can be different. Besides, inside the labour movement as among managers in general there are gradations of status, class and expectation. Finally, the development of trade unions as institutions has its effect on the habitual behaviour of their leaders.

Ernest Bevin at the peak of his career, when he had forged the merger that became the TGWU, fixed it in handsome quarters in Transport House and accepted the message of 1926 that influence over broad ground was a better strategy than mass strikes, was perhaps the most formidable example of a trade union autocrat. He was a man of great vision, personality and organising ability, but he cared so little for expounding what he was about that suffering reporters trying to record his speeches were in much the same state as Carlyle trying to make sense of Cromwell's. Like Cromwell's, Bevin's speeches excelled human belief in their unlikeness to all other speeches, in their utter disregard of all standards of oratory and logical sequence of thought: 'agglomerations of opaque confusions, of darkness on the back of darkness'. Yet both of them were influential in much the same way on their followers. One might also say that a measure of a union leader's authority is his ability to make an incomprehensible speech and nevertheless retain control of his hearers.* Some of us might prefer a liturgical oratory of this kind, demonstrating a relationship, to a commoner kind of oratory which appears to be a reasoned and logical sequence but implies and stimulates dark and divisive behaviour. Lucid poppycock is a bane of western society, especially at these delicate communications frontiers like industrial relations when the same words may mean different things to different people beyond the minimum level of tolerance to keep them out of conflict.

When Frank Cousins succeeded Arthur Deakin and Arthur Tiffin as general secretary of the TGWU about twenty years after

* Of course, Bevin knew perfectly well what he was about. Sir Frank Roberts tells the story of Bevin's reading a brief carefully prepared for him when he was Foreign Secretary. 'Well, it's a very good speech,' he said. 'Yes, it's excellent. You won't mind if I take it away and de-grammaticise it, will you, because it's not me?'

Bevin moved into government, he had something of the same oratorical style but distinctly less command of his audiences. Besides, he was not the architect of the union but an unexpected inheritor of the principal office because of Tiffin's untimely death; partly from pressure within the union and partly from wider political considerations he followed a policy of decentralisation of power and local participation in decision-making. In the docks and the motor industry, for example, there was not much choice. In general the developments of the past twenty years have made autocratic union leadership more difficult although some notable examples have survived. In the Iron and Steel Trades Confederation Dai Davies carries on the tradition of the late Sir Lincoln Evans: during the war the Government suggested that its appeal for co-operation in the productive effort should be relayed by union leaders at their conferences, if necessary special conferences. Evans replied that his union was not due to hold a conference that year (or indeed the next) and would pass the word on by normal channels. There are other unions which exist in a state of almost permanent election fever. In the AUEW every officer comes up for election every three years unless he is within five years of retiring age. At national level this makes little difference from unions where appointments are for life. At district level in troubled times it may make important differences in election year. The EETU also requires periodic elections for all its principal officers. Indeed it was this provision that made possible the celebrated revolt against Communist leadership of the union in 1955–62. If the general secretary had not had to stand for re-election, there would have been no occasion for fraud and no remedy.

The Informal System

Although the unions are representative institutions, participation in their affairs becomes progressively less dense the farther away from the work group the affairs are. The highly charged political election for general president of the Engineers in 1967 produced the 'unusually high poll' of 14 per cent. Most shop stewards, even if they are in some constitutional sense elected, emerge informally rather than systematically. Theirs has become the basic office in the trade union movement and where they do not formally exist something else develops, like the unofficial liaison committee in the docks before the Devlin Committee recommended a shop steward system. Although dynasties develop in some unions and in the labour movement generally as it matures (just as they have done in other occupations and political movements) the road from work group representative is still the normal one for a career in the movement. I use the word 'group representative' because the office passes under many names – shop steward, collection steward, corresponding member, chapel officer – and may develop its own institutional momentum which works to subvert the formal influence of the union itself. Pilkington was a case in point. There have been many others in the motor industry. At the many unconstitutional meetings of dockers between 1950 and 1970, irrespective of changes in attitude both at the head of the TGWU and among employers, the militant oratorical styles, the typical responses of members, and the leaflets, broadsheets and periodicals that littered the ground at the end bore little relation to the formal representative dealings between union and employers and developed in their own way, influenced but not determined by national union policy.

The same general principle is true of work groups which do not even have a trade union: or may even have a strong collective prejudice against trade unions. In certain circumstances leaders of such a group may resist employers' decisions in a way which a trained, conventional shop steward would not dare (or perhaps care) to do. This phenomenon is particularly common among women workers. I recently came across a clerk in an industrial plant who had informally become spokeswoman and interceder for the dozen or so women in her section. She is a naturally helpful person with a 'mind of her own' and the confidence and standing which come from long continuous service where most of the other women had changed jobs or were likely to change jobs for family reasons or mere whim. She finally led them into a boycott of a work study and evaluation exercise which the management had agreed with a white-collar union that she had left. She left because the union had never been well organised in the company or done anything useful that she could see or kept in touch with members, and she did not much care for unions anyway. The exercise also had the approval of a staff association of which she and the other women were automatically members. The consultants arrived with their questionnaires. She asked what it was all about; because nobody had really explained what the forms meant or what the managers would do with the answers, and she felt that she was wasting a lot of time, she said simply that she would not fill up the forms and none of her girls would either. The boycott spread to other sections. This mildly right-wing lady put paid to the whole venture with an effectiveness that a militant rebel inside the union would envy.

There is in fact no 'line of authority' in the trade union movement or on the workers' side of industrial relations in general. (Prudent managers should not depend too much on it on their side of the business either.) Of course, trade union leaders at all levels frequently get their own way, may as a rule dominate individuals or groups by virtue of their office when they have to, and generally exercise leadership in a way that appears to have 'authority' about it. (Others may sometimes refrain from giving the normal guidance that leadership requires, for fear of giving an 'authoritarian' impression.) But the trade union movement does not put people 'in power' as political elections do. The commissar style therefore has its limitations and is always an uncertain inheritance. A new official should not assume that he is really in his predecessor's shoes. No doubt a new manager should not either, but managers do have at their disposal against subordinates formal sanctions which they can initiate personally with accountability only to a superior. In initiating sanctions against individuals, as in other matters, a trade union official is accountable to the membership as a whole. The machinery of accountability is frequently inadequate and the membership may condone sanctions which are gratifying as punishment rather than necessary to preserve the union's function. Both points are equally true of management and the second comes up more often in management, if only because trade union leaders do not normally see any need to exercise day-to-day discipline and many managers do.

Triangle and Circle
Mr John Garnett, director of the Industrial Society, makes the point by describing managements as a triangle, with authority delegated from the ultimate manager at the top corner. The union, by contrast, is a circle with diffuse authority concentrating at the centre. It is a useful concept for making the particular comparison (one should be careful not to extend it and assume that management in every aspect is, as Caesar said of Britain, 'by nature a triangle' or representation by nature harmoniously rounded); it also helps to illustrate how different attitudes

develop. The way of the permanent official is often difficult in breaking in new recruits to the necessity of formal organisation, especially if managers are unsympathetic.

A major company with national agreements with several unions established a plant on Merseyside. Each union recruited as the plant expanded. The managers were preoccupied with the task of bringing 'green' labour up to the necessary technical standard and hardly considered that of bringing a green industrial relations system to the mature level of the parent plant, although as rationalisation progressed a stoppage on Merseyside would quickly affect the parent plant as well. Local trade union officials, with other responsibilities on their hands, had not the time to make good the deficiencies. In the nature of things, there was no question of the company not recognising unions. What was lacking was any company policy to ensure that the unions had all the help they needed to do their job properly in this large, new plant employing men with a tremendous mixture of industrial experience but few of them with any to speak of in a large engineering works. Within their limits, the managers' attitude was perfectly understandable: they had their own job to do without helping the unions to do theirs (and no doubt many of them thought the union an unproductive nuisance anyway).

There was particularly a shortage of experienced shop stewards. One section of fifty-odd men elected a new steward, young and untrained but anxious to make his mark. He was a member of the AUEW. He called a meeting and proposed that they have a closed shop and everyone agreed. He formally told the responsible manager, who said not to be silly. A couple of days later the company sent to the section two men who were not members of a union. The steward called for a show of hands on strike action to protect the closed shop, and the men unanimously agreed to walk out. The management, realising a little late that there had been a serious failure to exchange appropriate messages, called in the shop steward convener, an old hand at the game. He spoke kindly to the young steward about his intentions, but suggested that before going into a dispute they should have a card count. Of the fifty-odd men, 10 were members of the NUVB and 32 were members of no union at all. The young steward lowered his sights to the humdrum job of recruiting, and was no less successful because of his gaffe. It is difficult for people to refuse to join a union when they have voted unanimously for a closed shop, and some men who were not AUEW members had already discreetly applied for membership at the branch although the whole affair had lasted only a few days.

That is the clue to a situation which was certainly ludicrous but not simple. There is a strong psychological pressure to do the right thing in a group. Until the convener called for the show of cards, presumably no one knew what the level of union membership was in that section, but several of the 'nonners' would simply not have bothered to join, or would not have got round to it, and facing the sudden unconstitutional initiative of the steward decided that they had better go along with it. The managers concerned should have taken the situation less lightheartedly before work stopped in the section. However absurd the behaviour of the steward, he was in a position to cause trouble without any guidance from anyone, and with no obvious idea of what his responsibilities were.

Some union members in really complicated multi-union situations may not be able to tell you off-the-cuff what union they are in. They may have joined because of the persuasiveness of a particular person, a visiting organiser or more likely a steward. In the Victory Café in Dagenham in 1958 a Briggs Motor Bodies striker told me that he was 'in Kevin's union – him over there – because we're both in the party': perhaps he was in the Communist Party because of Kevin's influence as well. Kevin Halpin, whom we meet again in the next chapter, is a very persuasive man if he has some basic point of agreement to work on. Equally a union without competition in a plant, and sometimes even enjoying limited recognition, may find its organisation atrophy and its membership fall away before a proper routine has been established. The departure of a couple of enthusiasts prepared to take up the drudgery of branch meetings and section records in the plant may be enough. Without doing anything positive, unenthusiastic managers may deal the final blow. It is startling to find the number of managers, especially in the white-collar field, who do not know what unions operate in their plant and in particular do not know how many of their subordinates are union members. They sometimes sound like considerate neighbours refusing to intrude into private grief: 'I assume some of my people are in a union. I don't know and I wouldn't ask.'

Roots of Authoritarianism

Group psychological pressure is the only reason why one can have a commissar style of trade union leadership at all. Indeed, I suppose it is what makes possible any kind of authoritarianism. What determines whether a commissar or a fixer comes to the top, or that a union leader shows more of one quality than the other? We have seen some of the influences already, and it is difficult to put them in any order of importance. No doubt the most diffused is the pattern of society as a whole, since certain dominant trends are bound to affect everybody. Everyone has his own view of social change in Britain, but no one denies that it exists. The decline of deference, or obsequiousness, or common courtesy, or knowing one's place, whatever one cares to call it, has affected all kinds of leadership, including leadership of work groups and trade unions. The heavy, dominant figure, benign or not, has a harder row to hoe because what was once upon a time menacing or charismatic has become simply unconvincing. However, the process has not been uniform throughout Britain or throughout industry. One must not underestimate either regional and occupational variations or metropolitan trend-setting. The effects are conflicting in a number of complicated ways. Obviously new methods of communication have increased the centralisation of control in London (or, for that matter, Detroit or New York). Enterprises and their owners, often sons or grandsons of the founders, tend to move southwards or at least take their cue from London. Most great mergers, of unions as well as commercial enterprises, tend to find their centre in London. There are exceptions, of course, like USDAW in Manchester with the Co-operative Movement which provides the great bulk of its membership, and the Boilermakers in Newcastle-upon-Tyne near the centre of gravity, in more ways than one, of shipbuilding. There are large and small regional survivals like the Scottish Typographical Association, the Birmingham and Midland Sheet Metal Workers, and the variety of small textile unions in Lancashire and Yorkshire. But the union growth points are in London; being in Newcastle is one reason why the Boilermakers' overtures to craft unions outside shipbuilding have not come to anything. In commerce and government, concentration of control has meant emphasis on control. This has not happened in the unions precisely because they lack a line of authority based on real sanctions.

But the emphasis of commerce and government obviously affects the unions' context.

In late 1972 London still enjoyed virtually full employment, while the effects of restraint lashed remoter parts of the country. The outlying areas are disproportionately hurt by such policies because they stop sooner and go more slowly. This emphasises the existing difference between comparative urbanity and steady expectations in the south and rougher styles of management and the readier prospect of distress in the development areas. In general in the north strife is more painful. With shining exceptions, both managers and workers think in tougher terms, having fewer marginal resources to cushion industrial relations and being more vulnerable to the mutual desperation of a change in the economic climate. They work harder for less. (This is another respect in which conventional terminology is inadequate. By a sort of pun, people tend to think that an employer squeezed by 'fiscal discipline' will resist inflationary wage demands to avoid going to the wall. In practice, he may calculate rationally that to resist a wage demand and precipitate a strike may mean going to the wall next month, whereas keeping production going, even with an inflationary settlement, will at least save his bacon until next year and then there may be a turn for the better. Unhappily, not enough managers have the training or constructive imagination to take advantage of a turn for the better to improve their industrial relations, so that there can be some basis of trust for mutual concessions if there is another recession. Better industrial relations in any event has a tonic effect which may make the next recession less wounding.)

If the fieriest spirits all stayed in their native provinces, the position there would be even more contentious. But enough of them move to man the barricades in the south. A roster of names is enough to make the point. Johnny McLoughlin ringing the bell that set off the Dagenham strikes against Ford in 1958; Sid Maitland at the head of the BOAC maintenance strike in the same year; Ian Stuart (admittedly an Anglo-Scot) leading the London Airport shop stewards' combine in 1970; Hugh Cassidy, Matt Lynch and Brian Behan expressing the public noises of the South Bank strike in 1958-9, and several others before and after; Jimmy Black from Renfrew in the airport firemen's strike in 1970; Ralph McBride taking the heat of the GKN-Sankey strike in Shropshire later in the year. Sins against the fathers are often avenged by the children, perhaps not to the third or fourth generation but for long enough. Among trade union officials too, London is probably under-represented – certainly among those who capture most public attention.

Words and Attitudes

All this helps to shape a man's view of the world. Perhaps an extreme example would again help to illustrate the point. About twenty years ago a Highland building worker in a tavern on Clydeside was telling about his brother in the hospital, come down with pneumonia in dirty spring weather on a construction site where he was a probationary foreman. He had the prospect of staff status and security after a season's trial. His brother said:

> 'He was ill, too, before. You could have fried an egg on his forehead and his face was like the heart of a fire. And it was plod, plod about in the mud with just a cloth jacket. I asked about oilskins and the man said, "Oilskins? Canna a grown man buy his own oilskins?"' 'Was it Rannoch?' asked the landlord. 'Aye, Rannoch, God bless him,' said the man.

Rannoch was the site manager, a hard man apparently. But what struck me about the sick man's brother was the perfectly impersonal attitude he had to the manager, who was just an unpleasant natural phenomenon that no one could do much about. 'The man' is the phrase used among Negroes in the American South for the white boss, and 'God bless him' sounded exactly like an incantation against mischance that you might expect from someone in the bush who had accidentally mentioned the storm-god. I heard afterwards that the sick man was in fact taken back when he recovered and did become a staff foreman, which is not surprising. Anyone who could go on working with incipient pneumonia at least showed an impressive appetite for the job. Rannoch probably considered it a tribute to his powers of leadership and the loyalty they induced, and for all I know it was.

There is another point about the style of the foreman's brother. A relationship, or lack of relationship, like this is often accompanied by great circumstantial eloquence. At one time or another it has been common in the mines, in the docks, and in construction; it is almost as if the remoteness of 'them' when these industries were at their toughest permitted a line of rhetoric more appropriate to an old man in Hemingway's boat, say, than matters of what we now call 'management decision'. This is natural enough. Exaggeration compensates for lack of substance, just as ceremonial will plump out time that would otherwise be unoccupied. One finds a slipping away into procedural jargon when casual work changes to regular, where workers' representatives develop habits of negotiation, where frequent experience of managers' company inhibits the natural desire to turn a phrase or makes a workers' leader anxious to avoid a solecism. Not that acquaintance necessarily means harmony, merely a different quality of language. One detects the same quality in the increasing abstraction of unions' own titles as they spread wider. In the broad commonalty of the Transport and General Workers' Union, for example, are buried innumerable little bodies like the Cardiff, Penarth and Barry Coal Trimmers, whose ten dozen members merged with the big battalions in 1968. Sometimes a union does the same thing to itself to meet with changing times, as when the Stove, Grate and General Metal Workers decided that the time had come to change to Domestic Appliance and General Metal. There are survivals, of course, especially in general metals and textiles, like the Chain Makers and Strikers' Association (the only union with 'strike' in its title), the Sheffield Wool Shear Workers' Trade Union, the Military and Orchestral Musical Instrument Makers' Trade Society, and local spinners, twiners, twisters and overlookers.

The nature of the work makes a difference to leadership styles as well. If a union is to hold together at all in dispersed or transient work like transport or building, the officials have to take a dominant position. At national level industrial relations in construction are good; on many celebrated occasions, of which the South Bank strike was one, they have exerted discipline against outrageous breaches of procedure and agreement. At the same time, they have special problems at a time of full employment when 'high fliers' will take the chance to earn a bit of money autonomously by labour-only sub-contracting. In factories and offices members may work comparatively all on top of one another, with lively group relations and opportunities for rapid and informal collective action. In theory this ought to make the job of managers easier, if they are adequately qualified, organised and trained; it makes the job of union control more difficult without management co-operation and gives more scope to the talents of the fixer in either collective or individual cases.

Finally there is the style and structure of both management and trade union. Leaders of the AUEW may, and usually do, behave autocratically in some respects once they achieve office, but they cannot readily achieve high office without being accomplished conciliators or at least election campaigners. There are some unions (and pockets of all unions) where autocracy survives. The late Jim Matthews, national officer of the NUGMW, was a stout anti-Communist and upholder of agreements. His wilfulness eventually brought him the censure of the TUC, and he actually damaged his own union's prospects at London Airport in 1958 when he took the lead in denouncing the unofficial BOAC strike. The only shop stewards involved over whom he could exercise discipline were NUGMW ones. When the strike ended the inter-union combine remained powerful and only the NUGMW members suffered any penalty. The net effect was to make membership of alternative unions appear more attractive, lamentable though this may appear to an orderly observer. Fishing for membership among the free-wheeling and highly-paid airport workers required a different style. In any event, the commissar touch is usually appropriate only in a single-union situation, and even there it can come unstuck as it did at Pilkingtons. The most disconcerting moment for Harry Norton, NUGMW official in St Helens, was when a mass meeting flatly refused to accept his advice for the first time in his many years' experience.

Any form of collective organisation may be both irrational and ungrateful. A union leader, full-time or lay, pays the penalty for losing contact with his members as harshly as anyone else. An apparently apathetic rank and file may become stirred up in a week if a hot enough grievance emerges, often a grievance which the leader can neither predict nor remedy and may not be qualified to interpret. Change may build up by degrees over months or years, and both the shop steward and the manager are better placed to observe it than a union official not in daily contact. However, self-righteousness or grievance may well have unmanned them both by the time the union official arrives; the steward will be calling for 'fair do's' and the manager for enforcement of procedure. The commissar always has a question mark against his authority, especially if managers insist in public that he should exercise it. The fixer may have to deploy his talents at short notice in a crisis that he did not see in the making. His perplexities multiply in an inter-union situation.

Ford, for example, have 26 locations in Britain, and one national joint council with 15 unions represented on it. All have different spheres of influence and different strengths from site to site. The TGWU dominate the process workers at Halewood, the AUEW at Langley, the NUVB at Thurrock, but everywhere there are some minority pockets of other unions. There are four unions represented in the joint negotiations for National Health Service laboratory technicians: the ASTMS has five representatives and the NUPE, NALGO and COHSE three each. No one knows exactly how many members in the service each union has. In engineering it is not uncommon to find a plant of, say, 2,000 workers with 10 unions operating. The obstacles to personal domination are formidable.

Circumstances of Leadership Style
We can now hazard a summary of the situations which favour one kind of leadership or the other:

Commissar: Primitive industrial relations or naïve membership; single-union situations; conflict (either with managers or within the union, usually in the latter case matters of politics); dispersed or transient membership; depressed industries or areas; unions with a hierarchical rather than specialist structure; emphasis on national settlements as determining practice rather than providing a loose framework.

Fixer: Well-established industrial relations and knowing membership; multi-union situations; abrasive and competitive situations without major conflict; concentrated membership; prosperous industries and areas; flexible union structure; emphasis on local and plant bargaining.

Stable situations with little change or development favour whatever is the established style. Craft unions or craft sections of unions habitually give more discretion to their officials because their members are more secure and their habits of thought are longer established and more systematic, emphasising routine and service. There is a class element in this as well as one moves into white-collar and professional organisation. This leads to a formality and confidence of officials' behaviour which has something of the commissar style about it; but of course its basis and limitations are different from those of authoritarian handling of naïve membership, where the leader takes discretion without such tacit understanding.

As we have seen, the notion of authority in the trade union movement is precariously based. As a matter of observation, a man's hold on office when he reaches the level of general secretary or thereabouts is pretty well invincible, unless he is unusually eccentric or reaches active enmity against important colleagues, whether he is subject to re-election or not. The ETU case was unique. But of course a man's leadership habits will have been set much earlier, and countless other influences and experiences will have played a part. All trade unions and other workers' organisations have something in common, but it would be a bold commentator who would say precisely how much. Although the vogue for writing books is growing among trade unionists, they are practitioners' books as a rule. A movement traditionally understaffed and, in proportion to the number of people it caters for, operating on a shoestring, does not provide much scope for sheltered reflection. One effect of everyone's having so much to do is that the movement has many publicists but few philosophers, generators of fresh objectives and contemporary synthesis in a wide context. Karl Marx, the Webbs and G. D. H. Cole were really extraordinarily unworkmanlike people to exert the influence that they have done on what workers think that they are doing. When a TUC delegate (especially at an emergency Congress like the one at Croydon in 1971 on the Industrial Relations Bill) goes back to history he may not be making a contemporary and relevant statement but he may be stimulating what he considers to be the appropriate response among mass membership. Mr George Woodcock, the previous general secretary of the TUC, is something of an exception. His famous comment that before restructuring itself the TUC should decide what it was there for is still reverberating. The answers range from 'Reform the world' at one end of the spectrum to 'Provide a contract-labour service for employers' at the other. Let us look at the major roles that a trade union performs, either individually or collectively as part of the TUC:

voluntary service organisation;
representative institution;
bargaining and advisory agency;
conciliation agency;
political propagandist and lobbyist;
education and training unit;
deliberative assembly;

joint legislative and regulatory body;
benevolent society;
social club.

There are many possible variations and additions. Some unions do very little in certain fields. Others do a disproportionate amount of one thing, like the regulatory work of British Actors' Equity; education and training have their ups and downs. People often say that a union is 'not doing its job' or should have its performance measured by the same standards as a commercial organisation. For trade unionists it is easier to see that there is a flaw in the statement than to say exactly what it is. From what we have seen in the first chapter of the dynamic of trade unions, we can say with confidence that it is as sensible as saying that all flesh is grass, and reaching for the lawn mower to remove some extra weight. If one tries to run the lawn mower over one's stomach, the effects will be disastrous. If, however, one uses the lawn mower properly and takes the necessary steps about diet, the exercise will be a useful supplement to them. To say that unions have a lot to learn from the best companies about running their affairs efficiently is quite a different thing. There is an analogy with the comment made by Mr Jeffrey Archer MP, the well-known fund-raiser, who said in a newspaper interview in 1970 that if an organiser raised £25,000 and were paid £2,500, he should be proportionately rewarded ten times as much for £250,000, as if tapping the reservoir of private generosity were a legitimate field of operation for private profit.

What Rate for the Job?
In this country we do sometimes go too far the other way. When Dr (now Lord) Beeching moved from private to public employment with British Railways, there was great uproar about the salary the Government gave him to keep his standard of living at the Imperial Chemical Industries level. When the pay of leaders of great trade unions moves up to the level of obscure academics, a reasonably successful headmaster or an indifferent company secretary, grumbling begins about feathering of nests. This is certainly preferable in important respects to excess in the other direction. In the United States the executives of some trade unions are more nearly on a par with the executives of great corporations. Whether as a result, or a parallel symptom, of other causes, they also behave more like corporate executives.

The unions are commercially more efficient, as a rule, than their British counterparts but this does not necessarily help with industrial relations. Contractual necessity obliges the union leaders to follow the commissar pattern, yet they find it more difficult than in Britain to develop relaxed, informal social dealings with managers for fear of the suspicion of a 'sell-out'. In wider social terms the American movement has had a less persuasive emollient influence than the British. This is partly because of the intensively individualistic ideology of the United States and the survival of various ethnic, religious and other assumptions which have either cut across trade unionism or limited its appeal. It is also to some extent because of the concentration of organisers on areas which produce the 'best results'. An American trade union official once showed me figures which indicated that the US trade union movement 'absorbed a higher proportion of gross national product per member' than the British, although having proportionately about half the membership; there is always some criterion for success.

There are no appropriate terms for comparing the efficiency of an employer and a trade union. Once workers acquire the habit of trying to compare them, they are much more severe in judging the employer. This is natural enough. A worker's direct stake in his job is much greater than his direct stake in his union. He is normally in some fairly continuous personal contact with a supervisor, but he may never meet a full-time union official. A shop steward, although a union official, is a workplace person. So far as the individual's direct interest is concerned, the activities of his managers are more important than the activities of his union leaders. Indeed, what he most wants of a union is a desirable effect on the primary relationship with the employer, because it is in that relationship that the continuing satisfactions of day to day, real money for the individual, and often a host of other particular habits and interests are involved. In trade union administration there are not many £100,000 decisions and they are usually uncomplicated ones. In plants of a certain size or level of technological development they happen continuously, and in a real sense they happen publicly. If responsible managers do not circulate the truth, the 'grape-vine' will carry a series of wounding approximations. One new, idle vehicle or missing set of spares can keep the grape-vine buzzing. It is much more difficult to arouse interest in the fact that the union pension fund has performed at 3 per cent when most private pension funds manage better than 7 per cent. There is a perfectly natural double standard for judging managers and union leaders as a class; it does not necessarily exist for judging individuals, because that depends on whether the individual manager and union leader are successful in personal dealings with people. The double standard may help us to understand why the comparison is meaningless. One can, perhaps, compare the efficiency of a doctor and a dentist, because their occupations and their benefits are roughly similar. It is more difficult to compare either with a lawyer or a space scientist or a managing director. It is also difficult to compare the efficiency of a shop steward and a supervisor, largely because one looks at them from a different point of view. No doubt it is recognition of this that makes most shop stewards say that they would not expect promotion in the particular plant where they work. It is not unusual to hear a manager say that a shop steward is too valuable where he is to move into management, although often this is a rationalisation. Having agreed that comparisons of a specific kind are worthless, one may then venture that set against the best practice, whether in government, management or, no doubt, private housekeeping, the detailed operations of large parts of the trade union movement lose by casualness some of the advantages of economy and flexibility.

Science of Solidarity
This chapter has been mostly about circumstances which tend to promote one kind of leadership or another. Perhaps it would be useful to end it with a word about symptoms, following the fashionable model and borrowing from the findings of ecology – 'the science of solidarity', one might call it, since it treats of the interdependence of all living things. Ian L. McHarg, an American scholar, has drawn up a table of symptoms of ill-health which seems to me to have a clear lesson for industrial relations, as well as dealings among people and between people and the world about them in general. He uses the concept of 'entropy', which means the measure of thermal energy which is not available for conversion into mechanical work. There could hardly be a better analogy. Dealings 'become heated'. People 'working to rule' to cut back production may very well expend more energy than they do on normal working. In an engine unnecessary friction develops unproductive and eventually damaging heat. In a living system high entropy is a sign of ill-health –

fever, decomposition and, by extension, misdirected aggression. Most people understand this intuitively although they do not use a fancy word for it. What is less obvious is what goes with the diseased state, or the light which a mere list of them may shed on matters of rationalisation, control and individual initiative. We know that society is forever setting norms which mean that success in one generation would be obloquy in another, although it may remain enshrined in the history books as heroic. One thinks, for example, of Richard the Lionheart, the parfit, gentil Crusader knight, who lost his temper with a bishop so menacingly that the poor man died of fright. The ecologist's list of qualities may be unexpected and tend to uneconomic conclusions (for the personnel man they may even seem conflicting) but here they are:

ill-health and regression	*health and evolution*
simplicity	complexity
uniformity	diversity
independence	interdependence
instability	stability (steady state)
low number of species	large number of species
high entropy	low entropy

The commissar should be happy that every problem is different; it indicates the human inclination to sanity. The fixer should perhaps curb his energy a bit in case his activities increase expectations, a great source of psychological heat, beyond the means to meet them.

Chapter 4
Prejudices and Politics

'*As a rule it is not the alleged reasons that lead people to their statements. . . . Not only is the wish father to the thought, but all the feelings and habits and ways of thinking are fathers to the thoughts. A man who knows life, knows how little possibility there is of convincing people by logical grounds and argument.*'
Rudolf Steiner

Parochial Concerns in Politics
Trade unions as a whole reflect one basic prejudice – against unfettered unilateral action by employers. Perhaps it is the only prejudice that all trade unionists have in common, but it is of course a very powerful prejudice and it is not surprising that employers, universally a century ago and in large number still, have considered it subversive. The record suggests that its institutional form, the trade union, has not been subversive. We can see one indication why from McHarg's table in the last chapter. Collective movements are a constant reminder of complexity, diversity and interdependence in an innovative society. The Labour Party is certainly the political stepchild of the trade union movement, and has been committed in principle to apparently drastic change. But in sum, it has not made changes more dramatic than the Liberals did when they were on the progressive side of the two-party see-saw. Trade union activists certainly include a disproportionate number of people with revolutionary ideologies of one kind or another, although their behaviour as individuals may bear remarkably little resemblance to their dogmatic ideas of what behaviour ought to be when the world is put to rights. In fact, their union activities rope them in; they have things to do for people which complete consistency would prevent; in the end the extreme militant either drops out of the main stream of trade unionism and finds some eccentric

pocket for his talents, or he confines his politicking more and more to matters in which as a trade unionist he has no particular standing, like nuclear disarmament, peace in Vietnam and joining or not joining the European Economic Community.

How else can one explain the particular atmosphere of public debates at the annual gathering of the TUC? Would Frank Cousins have been able to swing the entire TGWU for unilateral nuclear disarmament when Nye Bevan was against it, or Lord Carron dispose of the whole block vote of the AUEW as he pleased on large international questions if their members and the Congress had really felt that it was their immediate daily business? At the 1971 TUC nobody even bothered to call for a count on whether the terms of entry to the EEC were acceptable, and what was billed as an 'historic' decision was taken as casually as the re-election of an unopposed shop steward. But where the intimate concerns of the movement were at issue, on whether or not to register under the Industrial Relations Act, only one union took an unequivocal stand for disciplining any affiliated organisation which dared to register – and that union was not in itself remarkable for discipline. The TUC is a political assembly attended by people whose reasons for being there are not primarily political. Of course there are individuals whose objectives are primarily disruptive. The psychological set of trade unionists makes it possible to turn a fairly small grievance into a fairly large stoppage. It also means the rejection of exotic ideologies from real power in the movement. It would be naïve to suppose that all the political expertise in trade unions is on the side of militancy. Only two actual members of the Communist Party have ever won a seat on the TUC General Council, although former Communists do. And a Communist of any stripe – official, Maoist, Trotskyite – is always conspicuous and closely watched.

The activities of the trade union movement in general cannot be called revolutionary simply because the basic prejudice against unfettered discretion for employers is almost universal. This year's intolerable intrusion on the rights of property is next year's statutory requirement. Governments of all parties have consistently chipped away at the liberty of employers to do what they will with what they call their own. There has always been an element in the Conservative Party anxious to curb the full excesses of the free play of market forces. Reputable men in government become joint parents of legislation which would have prevented the accumulation of their family fortunes if they had been in force when the fortunes grew. Through the TUC and other political contacts the trade union movement is a diffuse and important lobby on such matters. There is no reason to suppose that it is a particularly powerful lobby, although it is very widely reported. The reasons for this paradox are complicated and various, and indicate as much about the peculiarities of public communications and their agents as they do about the unions themselves.

At the root is the fact that the trade unions are not 'political' and 'economic' in any grand sense at all. The bulk of their work is practical and parochial – what Cowper called the 'servile drudgery of friendly offices'. Cowper was making the point that once a man got into his head that he had genius, he would discharge himself from drudgery and concentrate on what he did best (or with most 'genius'). Of all pretensions this is the one that trade unionism most abhors, sometimes to the extent of penalising harmless individualism. In principle, trade unionism favours a man's doing his work diligently and well, so long as he does not do another man out of a job. In practice, a man who works for an employer as long as he likes, as hard as he likes at what he does best for as much as he can get is in danger of doing precisely that. There are always 'cowboys' and 'high fliers' in any occupation, and more in some than in others; but the general principle of the movement is to hem them in, either by allocating piecework earnings or overtime or by bargaining for standard pay and hours. There are, of course, exceptions in individual work groups, especially those with tight control over entry and habits of continuous haggling, but in every case the pay is related to the job not the man. The trade union does not cater for the extraordinary talent, let alone the genius; on the other hand, it does not necessarily circumscribe him either, since in the unlikely event of his being obsessed with money he will find better ways to earn it than putting in excessively long hours with one employer. There is no room in the work group for concepts of marginal utility which would allow members to compete for any available extra earnings in proportion to their eagerness to make more; but there is usually a certain tolerance, a recognition that a young man with a young family is able and willing to work all the overtime that he can get while a grandfather twenty years older may need more rest rather than more money. Besides, in a modest way that the 'natural leadership of society' does not commonly do, the movement provides something else. 'Not geniuses . . . but average men,' John Collier says, 'require profound stimulation, incentive towards creative effort and the nurture of great hopes.' The movement may indeed provide this, and then ropes in an activity to the servile drudgery of friendly offices. It may not work forever, but it has worked for a long time.

Filters of Union Influence

Classical economics is thus not much help in analysing the situation, but conventional politics is downright misleading. Anything that narrows the context of human behaviour and makes people's motives appear simpler and less complicated than they really are produces inaccurate judgment and eventually distortion of action. It also limits sympathy, usually by emphasising small grievances and grudges, but sometimes expressed in spacious absurdity, like the comment of an American industrialist recalled by the consultant Bill Paul. Finding himself on the same platform with a trade union official with whom he had had a particularly rancorous negotiation, the industrialist said: 'My main concern is to do my duty to my shareholders; that son of a bitch is interested only in money.' Demands for money may be, and usually are, the conventional expression of a range of other aspirations and grievances, money being the only simple token of compensation that society universally provides. We do not consider a widow greedy or venal if she sues for compensation for the death of her husband. What is equally true is that potentially at least relations between managers and other workers in an establishment are more intimate and of greater personal consequence than relations between managers and shareholders or relations between workers and their trade unions. But the intimacy and personal consequence are not uniform, since his job means far more to an individual worker than any individual worker means to an employer, and frequently are not recognised. Given the extravagance of political and economic dogmas, it is surprising that so many managers and managed rub along as well as they do. What is even more consoling is how often people behave in ways which, according to their political dogma, are almost treasonable but, according to a sane reaction to given events, the best that a man can do.

Because of the political and social history of Britain the trade union movement is, of course, inextricably wrapped up with the political Labour movement. The unions are the party's paymaster, and individuals move between the two parts of the movement freely and frequently. Members active enough to become full-time union officials are almost automatically active in Labour Party politics – or, for a small minority, Communist Party politics – as well. Occasionally leadership of important unions falls to men of great political fervour; but since anything political which union leaders wish to achieve has to be filtered through the TUC and the Labour Party conference (and even after that the Parliamentary Labour Party refuses to be bound by resolutions of conference), one can almost say that the direct political influence of the trade union movement is small and specialised. The Parliamentary Party is influenced in turn by the collective atmosphere of Parliament itself and, especially when in office, that of the great departments of state. The TUC has to haggle as hard with a Labour Government as with any other on regulatory legislation on safety and health, for example, although one can say on the basis of a fairly brief effective experience – 1945–51 and 1964–70 – with somewhat greater satisfaction. On great affairs of state it has very little influence as a body.

Illusions of 'Revolution'
However, illusions persist. One serious flaw in the image of the trade union movement comes from uncritical reporting of the agenda for union conferences. A typical example was that of the Edgware gasworkers in 1970. They are members of the NUGMW, collectively the most cautious and law-abiding of the large unions. The Edgware branch put forward for annual conference a resolution calling for a general strike if the Government persisted with its proposals for legislation on industrial relations. This resolution had no hope of being passed but the Edgware men had the right to put it on the agenda. Its terms found their way on to the front pages of many newspapers, with the technically correct but substantially misleading headline that Britain's third largest union was to discuss the proposal for a general strike. Political talk at conferences is often widely reported if the contributions are startling enough, and naturally the most startling ones tend to be made by people with wayward views. But if one looks at the great public debates between left and right in the Labour movement, it is hard to see any substantial victory for the left; it is equally difficult to see

systematic 'revolutionary' activity that adds up to much for long, although it may fog issues and disrupt the thought processes and public appeal of Labour as a political party. There used to be much more talk of revolution; there was more of it in the Labour Party fifty or sixty years ago, before the Communist Party was founded, let alone all the hilarious or sinister variants that we have seen since, than there has been in my lifetime. This has produced some remarkable reactions, none more notably wide of the mark than the last two paragraphs of Clive Bell's *Civilisation*, published in 1928:

'The government of England is based on a precarious alliance between great wage-earners and small. It is plutocracy tempered by trade unionism. In politics the plutocrats have slightly the better of it at present; and in life they call the tune. What the tune is anyone who studies the daily and weekly illustrated papers knows only too well. It is what the people want; also, it is what they call civilisation. It is what they fought for to please the plutocrats, and what they may fight for again to please themselves. For this jolly alliance of great and small money-makers is precarious. The small will always be breaking the tenth commandment; hence this incessant talk of revolution. And the odd thing is there are always philanthropic optimists who of such a revolution expect some good. Positively they upbraid me, because I am disinclined to let go such good as I possess in the hopes of getting what they think may be a means to better. "If only," they assure me, "the people were to come by their own, all your dreams of civilisation would come true in a moment. The people, you must know, have always loved the good and the beautiful – the highest when they see it: here lies the road you seek."

'If, so adjured, I have not yet abandoned the study for the tub, that is because I have not yet noticed that the soon-to-be sovran proletariat, the working men of old England, manifest any burning desire to avail themselves of such means to civilisation as they already dispose of. Rather it appears to me their ambitions tend elsewhither. Far from discovering among them any will to civilisation I am led to suspect that the British working man likes his barbarism well enough. Only he would like a little more of it. He has so little fault to find with the profiteer's paradise that he would like it for his own. His notion of a glorious revolution is not the reshaping of life to bring it nearer the ideal, but a slipping into some rich man's shoes. The fact is, wage-earners and capitalists agree very well on all questions save the division of the spoils. The revolutionary coal miner conceives no better life than that of the reactionary owner; rum and milk before breakfast, and breakfast of four courses, a day spent in pursuing and killing, or in some bloodless pastime, champagne at dinner, and long cigars after, an evening at the movies or music-hall, with an occasional reading of Miss Corelli and Michael Arlen, *The Mirror, John Bull,* or *The Strand Magazine,* and all the time a firm theoretical belief in the sanctity of the marriage-tie and a genuine detestation of foreigners, artists and highbrows. That is a life that would suit Bill Jones just as well as it suits Lord Maidenhead. It is the life he admires and understands: which not unnaturally, therefore, he desires for himself. And that is why he is revolutionary. One appreciates his position; one quite sees that he would willingly change places with his lordship. Also, one sees no reason why he should not. Also, one sees no reason why he should. Above all, one sees no reason why he should expect sympathy and admiration from anyone who stands in for no share of the swag in what he loves to hear called his "fight for freedom and justice". The pull-devil-pull-baker between Jones and his master for the plums of barbarism is their affair entirely. No impersonal issue is at stake to agitate those who stand outside the ring. Who gets the cars and the cocktails is a matter of complete indifference to anyone who cares for civilisation and things of that sort. The trade unionist is as good as the profiteer; and the profiteer is as good as the trade unionist. Both are silly, vulgar, good-natured, sentimental, greedy and insensitive; and as both are very well pleased to be what they are neither is likely to become anything better. A will to civilisation may exist among the Veddahs of Ceylon or the Mege of the Gold Coast, but no sign of it appears on the Stock Exchange or in the Trades Union Congress.'

We can afford to be more subtle in our judgments now, not necessarily disagreeing with Bell's value judgments although wondering whether 'insensitive' is not the pot calling the kettle black. He must have seen very little of revolutionary coal miners, and indeed there cannot have been all that many reactionary coal owners who took rum and milk before breakfast. But there are two common British prejudices which stand out in the passage. The first is that dealings between wage-earners and employers depend on 'division of the spoils' and that attitudes to the spoils are similar. We have already pointed out some of the differences but there is another which strikes the observer very forcibly: some developments of fortune are psychologically inconceivable to ordinary people. They may, for example, consider it conceivable that they may win a six-figure fortune on the football pools and inconceivable that they could become chairman of one of the top 100 companies. This is very sane of ordinary people, although statistically the chances of anyone's achieving either are about the same. 'Bill Jones' also sets himself limits, and experience draws them tighter.

The second prejudice is to see some kind of equal balance of forces. All British legislation has patiently put the trade union and the employers' association on the same level. Commentators also tend to write about the 'power' of trade unions as if it were a positive power which, as we have seen, it is not. Unions have power to resist, to hold off, to disrupt the initiatives of employers and (in certain circumstances) governments. But they do not command great resources and politically they are weak. This has been amply demonstrated since early 1969; the TUC successively won a deceptive victory over a Labour Government and totally failed to deflect a Conservative Government bent on legislating about industrial relations. For four years the Labour Government had behaved in an unusual and rightist manner. The four previous royal commissions in the field were all appointed by Conservative Governments at a loss what to do, and three of them produced fairly widely accepted bases for legislation. The Labour Government first appointed the Donovan Commission in 1965 and then, when it reported in 1968, decided that it had not gone far enough and introduced a Bill providing for penal sanctions against unofficial strikers. The trade union movement put paid to this idea by successfully exploiting division in the Labour Party, and then spent another nine months expunging from the proposed legislation all powers which were unacceptable. A TUC-approved Bill was on its way through Parliament when the Conservatives returned to power in 1970.

At this point TUC calculation went adrift again. Apart from reflex action to the General Strike of 1926, followed in 1927 by an Act which made political strikes illegal and inflicted a couple of small nuisances on the political activities of the trade unions, Conservatives had not passed major restrictive legislation in the field for a century. Although the party had established a policy committee and produced a policy document, the experts were inclined to write it off for all practical purposes. Although disconcerted by the election result in 1970, the trade unions were still feeling their oats and did not expect to be simply overridden, but they were. The Conservatives had made 'doing something about industrial relations' a main plank in their election platform, and it was the first piece of at least apparently straightforward legislation that they could put in hand at once. In spite of the TUC's absolute boycott, an Act was on the statute book within fourteen months. Obviously the trade union movement is not able to prevent a determined Conservative Government, even with a small majority, from passing the legislation it requires.

Has the TUC *'Political Authority'?*

The events of 1969-70 had concealed this weakness, and revived some of the more consoling myths of the trade union movement – which is certainly older than universal suffrage, older than the Labour Party it helped to found, and an autonomous representative movement: odd and irregular in its operation, certainly, but an estate of the realm in its way. Walter (later Lord) Citrine's rejection of a place in the War Cabinet in 1942 was recalled. Citrine had co-operated as general secretary of the TUC in surveys of productivity which had greatly impressed Winston Churchill, looking for all available talent. Churchill offered Citrine the post of Minister of Production; Citrine, after some hesitation, refused. He said that at a time of political truce the TUC was the only independent representative of workers' interests and that he felt it his duty to stay there. After the war Citrine became head of the nationalised electricity industry. His reason for turning down a place in the Cabinet became part of the mythology of the trade union movement and was quoted in support of the battle for autonomy and freedom from statutory controls. It is, of course, a highly political piece of mythology, running counter to the Woodcock theme of 'What are we here for?' and an outrage to political constitutionalists. Against the TUC's pretensions they set the British tradition as a law-abiding country with a sovereign Parliament.

In fact, there is reason to believe that Citrine's statement was mythological: a rationalisation of his position rather than the reason for it. Perhaps many large political principles are born like this, just as Magna Carta was in its day a successful exercise in forcing privileges for the barons out of a reluctant king, and went on to become the cornerstone of liberty for orders of society on whom the thirteenth century bestowed no rights at all. Citrine had in fact been sardonic about the venture into government of his old associate Ernest Bevin, general secretary of the TGWU, and he felt that neither of them was particularly well qualified for parliamentary politics just by long experience in the other part of the Labour movement. Besides, he had been in charge of the TUC for nearly 20 years and had set the pattern for the job. So that although his political reason for turning down the Ministry was dignified and plausible, it may well have been illusory. There is no doubt that the concept of the TUC as a political authority outside the political system is illusory, and it was not difficult for the Conservative Government to call the bluff once it had made up its mind to do it. But the Government itself miscalculated, because although the movement is weak in terms of initiative and active politics, it has a tradition and capacity for dragging its feet. The Government believes that just as the movement could not prevent the passing of the Industrial Relations Act, it will eventually come to heel and help to make the new system work. The Government may be right, but it will be right by coincidence, since the two considerations are different in kind.

We have already seen what the issue is about: the exercise of authority, and whether it should lie within or outside the trade union movement. It is worth repeating that if the system works, the evolution of the TUC as arbiter and governor of dealings among its members, painfully slow now, will come to an end. The trade union movement, now representative in a clumsy and combative way, may become less representative as external criteria and systematic competition begin to affect the shape and growth of representation. The progress of the legislation has had some unintended effect already, causing a number of political strikes, a field day for left-wing opinion in the labour movement, and a state of affairs more contentious than it was already as a result of the 'break-out' from severe economic restraint.

Internal Controversies
So much for the trade union movement in politics: active, extensively reported, wielding a huge vote at the Labour Party conference but institutionally a step away from determining

anything of consequence. Equally important, and a good deal cloudier and more controversial, is politics within the trade union movement. There are several well-known paradoxes. Most trade unionists are politically inactive. They vote, no doubt, but do not canvass or organise. A significant proportion, and even more of their wives, vote for Conservatives or Liberals (or Welsh or Scottish nationalists). But activists bust out all over. If they are committed politically, they are likely to be more single-minded in their trade union commitment. The institutional politics of the movement clearly do not coincide with the collective political allegiance of members and minority persuasions like Communists, Trotskyites and for that matter Roman Catholics are over-represented. Whether extremists are the leaven in the lump or a dangerous source of discord is a matter of opinion. Certainly when they are wearing their political hats they are not primarily interested in the harmonious regulation of differences between employers and workers. This has not prevented many of them, especially orthodox pro-Soviet Marxists in the established CP, from behaving in a solid constitutional manner when they are being more union officials than politicians. Indeed, they may have less room for manœuvre than their brothers who have declined to become comrades.

The wilder variety – the Internationalist Socialists, the Socialist Labour League, the International Marxists and the Communist Party of Great Britain (Marxist–Leninist) – are obliged by their anti-bureaucratic principles and doctrines of continuous revolution to be forever running after trouble. Like bacteria in a wound, they are often able to make a bad business worse. Whether they can or do ever create conflict by moving into a harmonious or viable industrial relations system and subverting it, I do not know. I have never seen a convincing case study. On the other hand, when things have gone wrong, where there is a gulf of misunderstanding, inconsiderateness or lack of communication, one is likely to find Communist or Trotskyite intervention. Upper Clyde Shipbuilders may be the great example of the decade, yet Jimmy Airlie and Jimmy Reid, the two Communist leaders of the shop stewards who organised the 'work-in' against the closing of the yards, were indubitably native Scottish products in an indubitably malignant state of affairs which aroused genuine indignation among staunch anti-Communists. There is normally a strong anti-Communist movement where the party is strong, and even where it does not keep Communists out of positions of consequence it may act as a brake on their behaviour. When Frank Foulkes, Frank Haxell and Bob McLennan, all Communists, held the three top offices in the ETU they had to be very careful about keeping to a bargain. They were lost if they did not, and eventually they were lost anyway.

To make a judgment in an individual case you must know your man. At one time it was commoner for activists in the coal mines of South Wales and Fife to become members of the CP rather than the Labour Party. Often this was in reaction to what seemed to them an intolerable system. If their individual efforts produce improvements within the existing system, they may remain Communists but will put more emphasis on what they do successfully within the system than on their ideological objective of destroying it. They may cease to be members of the party but remain committed to varieties of militant socialism. Some of them come clean round the Horn and develop into committed and diligent anti-Communists, like the late Sir Leslie Cannon, a former protégé of the ETU leadership who when he died was General President of the union and a lion of the trade union right wing.

Why Be a Communist?
A relation of mine who worked in the Admiralty dockyard at Rosyth joined the CP during the depression because he felt that a system which caused good tradesmen to despair was too rotten to survive. He used to describe the effect on him of walking past the pawnshops in a city like Glasgow and seeing the array of proudly maintained tools in the windows. He left the party early, a couple of years after the war, when it seemed to him that the Labour Government was introducing a better era. Frank Foulkes used to say that when the Labour Party broke up in 1931: 'Ramsay MacDonald went one way and I went another.' In certain workshops party membership was taken as a guarantee of stubborn leadership; if a steward was tough enough to hold a party card he was tough enough to stand up to a hard master in hard times. He would also put in a power of work on the job and even where his long-term objectives were disruptive might be able to point to considerable practical achievements on behalf of his constituents. Often Communists consolidate their position while leaving to colleagues the blessings and curse of publicity. It was Johnny McLaughlin who rang the bell in the famous strike at Dagenham in 1958, but the real organiser

and the man who ran the lottery which gave the Briggs shop stewards their unusual capacity to make trouble was Kevin Halpin, then a member of the National Council of Shop Stewards and now of the Liaison Committee for the Defence of Trade Unions, one Communist organisation succeeding another. In the interval Halpin left the motor industry for the ship repair industry.

At any given time there is a host of fringe organisations fishing for conflict. The period between 1956 and 1958 was particularly active because of the split in the CP over Hungary, which caused defections to both left and right. It also included a number of episodes in individual industries where traditional industrial relations were under strain through expansion or technological change. The motor industry was one; London Airport was another, and particularly interesting because industrial relations and information systems in this rapidly growing, inchoate and essentially anarchic industry had been left to look after themselves. Many operations were on a cost-plus basis, there was no clear central authority and the fascination of the commerce and its machines pushed man management to one side. In 1958 the chief shop steward at the BOAC maintenance base was Sid Maitland, an Ulsterman who had served his apprenticeship as an electrician in the Belfast shipyards, a Communist and leader of a remarkably successful team of negotiating stewards. Jim Matthews, whose Pyrrhic victory in the strike we noticed in the last chapter, told a court of inquiry that the CP had set the following objectives for stewards at the Airport:

(1) Their power should be increased;

(2) The principle must be secured that shop stewards are immune from dismissal from their ordinary employment;

(3) Negotiations between employers and union officials should be short-circuited and employers forced, under threat of strike, to settle the question on the spot;

(4) Every shop steward must demand ample time off to conduct trade union business and conveners must insist on freedom to go anywhere in the factory at any time;

(5) Funds should be established to enable shop stewards' committees in the factories owned by one firm to meet on a national basis, whenever it is deemed necessary, and to associate with other committees on the National Council of Shop Stewards;

D

(6) Shop stewards must be used to communicate and explain important decisions to meetings of factory workers; and

(7) A strong Communist Party must be built in the workshops as this is an absolute necessity if shop stewards are to use their power to the maximum effect.

The odd thing about this shocking list of objectives is that during the past few years several of them have become accepted by most unions and many employers. In most West European countries by law and in many United States industries by negotiation, the second principle is inviolate; in Britain now it is unfair to dismiss a worker because of trade union activities alone (so long as they are lawful in themselves). The third principle, of settling a question on the spot if possible, is accepted without the implication of a strike; but we know as a matter of real psychology that a dissatisfied work force can do a lot short of a strike (or even of irregular industrial action short of a strike) to compensate their feelings for unresolved grievances. To quote John Garnett again: 'The difference between obedience and co-operation is usually the difference between profit and loss.' But the fact that some of these principles are good in themselves, or good in themselves in part, also illustrates the way in which alienation and frustration leaves the way open for perversity. In its report the court of inquiry commented:

> There is good ground for the view that the dominant figure in the joint shop stewards' committee and on the workpeople's side of the local engineering panel was Mr S. Maitland who was, and is, a member of the Communist Party. . . . We are satisfied that the Communist Party does not hesitate to act in a disruptive manner, and we are satisfied, too, that Mr Maitland's activities were of this kind.

The ETU *Scandal*

Yet the next year the engineering panel led by Sid Maitland concluded a pioneering redundancy agreement with BOAC. As his later career shows, he is in fact a tough and resourceful negotiator on either side of the fence. I first met him on the day that the BOAC strike began. The airport, as usual in time of dispute, was buzzing with cross-fire of indignation. At the pub at the north end of the airport there were shop stewards who professed not to talk to the capitalist press. There were time-served RAF flight engineers who found when they were demobbed that union seniority kept them from exercising their full skills in civilian life. There were worried and sometimes mystified managers and trade union officials. There were others, particularly officials like Clive Jenkins, who had come to terms with this curious environment and flourished in it. There were procedures apparently reached to be ignored. At the centre of this confusion Sid Maitland was an assured and somewhat withdrawn figure. With the heat off, he would rather talk about O'Casey's plays than the latest turn in the union power game, and in his time at London Airport he was certainly a strong case history against the generalisation that a shop steward is likely to be a highly sociable person. But he was not at all embarrassed in talking to the capitalist press and he was a deft controller of a mass meeting. He had been a member of the CP for a dozen years and was then in his thirties. He was also intimately involved in the great ETU scandal which was then beginning to pick up momentum and ended in the dislodgment of the Communist leadership after a High Court case in 1961. Bill Blairford, one of the legion of former Communists in the union, recalled in evidence at the trial that there was a party committee for the union including the three senior officials, Leslie Cannon, Peter Kerrigan (the national industrial organiser of the party) and Maitland. It has always seemed to me significant of the partial and impatient coverage of these matters that in the index to C. H. Rolph's little book on the trial he appears as 'Maitland, Mr'.

Hungary split the Communist leadership of the ETU, and of certain other institutions, wide open. Leslie Cannon left the party then and lost his post as education officer. Blairford left as well, and Mark Young, now a national officer, and Frank Chapple, now general secretary, as well as dozens of others. The union had been under Communist control since 1948 and party membership had been a natural route of advancement. So what happened afterwards was the dissolution of a power elite which was associated with an external ideology. Since the ETU is a union given to faction, the process continues in different forms to this day. In 1971 Mark Young emerged as a left-wing challenger for leadership after the death of Leslie Cannon, with Frank Chapple and the 'Cannon executive' holding power on the right. Yet it is doubtful whether employers found Cannon a softer man to negotiate with than Foulkes had been, although he was always readier to do a deal in a businesslike way and if it had not been for him the famous trade in electricity supply for higher pay in return for reduced manning would not have been achieved so soon.

An exception to the left-wing establishment was the late Jock Byrne, an Irish-Scots Catholic, who was firmly in control of the Scottish area and stood for general secretary against Frank Haxell. Allegations that the leadership rigged ballots had been in the air for years. Cannon and Young began to organise an opposition movement all over the country. Chapple remained on the national executive. A lay member in a south-west London radio factory called Dennis Kingston followed up allegations in the *New Statesman* with a press statement denouncing the leadership for fraud in the elections to the executive; within a year he emigrated to Australia. In Manchester Ernie Pinner, a former shop steward whose views were old-fashioned partisan Liberal with a touch of nineteenth-century authoritarianism, had been trying for nearly a decade to organise 'Pinner committees' to push out the leadership. To find out even what people were alleging involved plodding round Mitcham in the rain, finding Pinner's little terrace house in the Mancunian fog, and standing by and putting two and two together on the fringe of branch meetings and local political gatherings. If any members knew the full story, they kept it very much to themselves. Frank Foulkes as late as 1971 (in a letter to *The Sunday Times*) denied that he had known anything about ballot-rigging – after the High Court case the Communist Party officially disowned Haxell and said that his activities had 'brought it into disrepute' – and put down the whole affair to the desire among party dissidents to achieve power in the union, using Hungary and voting irregularities as a pretext. Anyone who knew Foulkes, with his diffused amiability and desire to be liked even by right-wing employers, could just believe that at least he believed that he did not know what was going on.

In Glasgow Jock Byrne sat tight and smoked his pipe. 'I don't need to tell you the position I'm in,' he said, 'I don't mind how much you find out and print, but I can't let you find out and print anything from me.' A series of rules revision conferences had made the discipline for breach of union confidences more severe, and there were many supporters of the leadership who believed that copies of the executive minutes which reached *The Daily Telegraph* from a Yorkshire branch had come from Glasgow. In 1958–9 the TUC had a long correspondence with the ETU asking unsuccessfully for explanations of the growing tide of reports of fraud and authoritarianism, and in spite of 'loyalist' invigilation, more and more accounts of branch meetings reached the press. One of the quaintest was the meeting of the London Lift and Crane Engineers. The pub in which it was held was built like a horseshoe with the meeting room upstairs from the public bar. Between the public bar and the saloon bar and the saloon bar and the private bar were little corridors with lavatories. Since the whole place was on the open plan, the 'observers' and the press could watch each other wherever they went, and even in the crowd that came downstairs from the meeting anyone could spot the tall figure of Leslie Cannon, who was exercising his right as a union member to attend and speak at any branch meeting. Yet the press got the story, a slightly fatuous one, as we have seen, because it asked the Chief Registrar of Friendly Societies to do something he was not empowered to do. Yet Cannon was still in the public bar with a pint in his hand when the journalists left with the report – given to one of them during a prearranged 'casual' meeting between bars.

I first met Cannon just before that, in another pub in Dalston with suitable precautions. He had already decided that the likeliest way to dislodge the leadership was through the courts, and he laughed at the idea that for a member to sue the union would be a breach of historic principle that would bring his career in trade unionism to an end. He also had evidence that there was cooking of books other than registers of votes. One of the ironies of the situation was that only in a union which required regular re-election would the situation have arisen at all. In 1969 Haxell faced defeat by Byrne but was declared elected after the executives had disqualified the votes of more than 100 out of 700 branches. Whoever controls the scrutineers controls the manipulation of fine print, and it had taken the opposition some time to perfect the exact compliance with every voting regulation which would ensure that their votes counted. In the end Byrne and Chapple sued for a declaration either that Byrne was validly elected or that there should be another election. The case was heard in 1961. Byrne won, and in the autumn anti-Communist candidates were overwhelmingly successful in the elections for the executive. The TUC, which had expelled the ETU in September, readmitted it in 1962. In due course Cannon beat Foulkes in the election for general president, and the coup was complete. Chapple succeeded Byrne, and a rules revision conference disqualified members of the Communist Party from holding office in the union.

It had been an odd case. Success would still have been possible, but less likely, if the opposition had not included so many former Communists with access to so many secrets. The course of the trial itself was peculiar – discontinuous, with fresh material facts becoming available more than once to keep the case going. The final result was as well documented a case history of the CP in trade union power politics as we are likely to get. The struggle continues. One possible effect of the Industrial Relations Act is to make disqualification from office on political grounds an unfair industrial practice, if the new Court should consider that 'arbitrary or unreasonable discrimination'.

During this purge Sid Maitland was elected a London area officer of the union, but he did not stand for re-election and took instead a job with a private company. He is now in charge of industrial relations for the London Co-operative Society, and ready to drive quite as hard a bargain for the LCS as he ever did for the BOAC stewards' combine. One of Maitland's contemporaries as an apprentice on the Queen's Island in Belfast was David Bleakley, the member of the Northern Ireland Labour Party who was six months Minister of Community Relations in the Northern Ireland Government in 1971. One difference between the two men is that Bleakley is a devout Anglican; another, that Bleakley has always maintained his roots in the Belfast dock area where he was born. As a bright lad in the union he went to Ruskin College, where he fell under the spell of G. D. H. Cole. Then he won an adult scholarship to Queen's University, Belfast, and after taking his degree had a job in adult education and a successful career in local Labour politics, almost as frustrating, from the point of view of winning seats (although Bleakley had a seat at Stormont for one period of comparative communal tranquillity) as running on the Communist ticket for Westminster. When the troubles began in Belfast in 1969, Bleakley organised the peace committees which helped to prevent disorders in his part of the town. When he joined the Unionist Government as the crisis deepened, Sid Maitland was one of the people who wrote to congratulate him. There is nothing particularly 'typical' in the contrast between these two careers, but there is certainly something instructive. It takes a bold or an ignorant man to generalise when he is faced with the interplay of individual political motive and collective political behaviour.

During this unhappy period, although ETU membership continued to grow, merger was unthinkable. The TUC is an anti-Communist organisation and block votes for the General Council go against active party members who are well respected. Year after year the representative of the North Wales Quarrymen was elected for the mining and quarrying group against Arthur Horner, the miners' secretary. Will Lawther, the union president, was on the General Council for years and became one of the first trade union knights. Being in origin a federation and a law unto itself, the NUM often had this balance at the top. Will Paynter and Sir Sidney Ford came next, and now we have Lawrence Daly and Joe Gormley. Although Daly left the CP before he became general secretary, and Paynter remained in the party until he retired, Daly remains a 'militant' and is proud of it. Yet under this balance of leadership, with a strong Communist element always present, the NUM has not only made successful arrangements with other unions for agency negotiation but co-operated with the National Coal Board in cutting out an irrational payments system which made it the most disorderly industry in the country. From logging the overwhelming majority of unofficial strikes, mostly about interpretation of complicated local pay arrangements, mining has moved to a strike rate below many other industries and less than a thirtieth of the national total, while reducing the labour force by more than half. Probably no single person had a more important role in this process than Will Paynter, but in any event the NUM is very much a closed union and there is no reason why it should merge with anyone. The ETU is an open and pushful union with an occupational base, and there are few really interesting major merger prospects in which it is not potentially involved.

Advocates of the Barely Conceivable
The Hungarian split of course affected CP operations in every industry. It not only provided the occasion for people moving to the right for various reasons to make the final break, but it gave a stimulus to members of more exotic views to go striding off in equally subversive and more anarchic directions. Scratch a bureaucratic Communist and you often find a hankering for authoritarian guidance of any kind. This may help to explain why the largest Communist parties of western Europe are in

France and Italy, nations with an equally strong tradition of devout Catholicism, and why there are such personal odysseys as that of Douglas Hyde from editing the *Daily Worker* to the comfort of the confessional. One is reminded of James Joyce's comment through one of his characters that it was one thing not to be a Christian, but he could not imagine anyone being a Christian and not being a Roman Catholic. There are obvious psychological disadvantages in living in a world of mere probabilities, but that is the world we do live in and the absolutist is out of touch in proportion to his absolutism. On the other hand, we also live in a world of order and the scales of probability range from the almost certain to the barely conceivable.

The Trotskyites and their variants set their standards close to the barely conceivable. The choice of Che Guevara as the archetypical figure of certain vague revolutionary aspirations is indeed appropriate. The last time I met him, at the United Nations in 1965, he spoke about his 'policy' of subverting the regimes of Argentina and Brazil with a rural uprising from the heart of South America. He was a small-city Argentine himself, and he certainly had a great deal of practical experience to suggest that fortune favoured the rootless young Latin bourgeois in search of a revolution. What he could not appreciate was the improbability of his own experience in arriving in Mexico just in time to meet the Castro brothers and set sail with them in the yacht *Granma* to their sojourn in the Cuban mountains, waiting for a uniquely gutless dictatorship in an unusually fragile society to fall apart. Argentina and Brazil contain some of the world's greatest cities: Buenos Aires is bigger than Paris and Sâo Paulo has a more diversified industry than any other city in the Americas. I thought his ideas bizarre and said so. 'The revolution is by nature bizarre,' he said. That he should not only have tried to put his ideas into action, but chosen as his base the hook-thorn jungle of Bolivia, hemmed in by some of the most catatonic peasantry and difficult territory in the world, was a measure of his oddity. Yet until he came to grips, unsuccessfully, with the problems of being a real administrator in an actual government in revolutionary Cuba, Guevara had had success well beyond the normal expectation of an Argentine petty bourgeois with a medical degree and picaresque revolutionary ideas. Latin America is full of lads like him. Only Guevara maintained his quixotry till the end. There are others who were with Fidel in the mountains or soon after who are working now in more substantial ways to make their continent a little more humane.

Trotskyites, *fidelistas*, Maoists and their competitors do of course believe that the 'capitalist system' is falling apart and that they will inherit the governance. Although no British Trotskyite has anything like the Guevara experience to buoy him up, there are a lot of niggling disruptions on the credit side, a certain amount of public attention and a long history of survival, sometimes in petty union office, but naturally no institutional development. A personal quarrel or horrific experience is enough to break a group apart, even with all the psychological solidarity of being one of a gallant few with powerful enemies in a misguided world. Peter Fryer left the *Daily Worker* after seeing what happened in Budapest in 1956. He became editor of *The Newsletter*, a publication for the alienated masses which gave a new dimension to many notable squabbles during the next couple of years: the sequence of disorders in the London construction business, for example, from the Hammersmith Flyover to the Shell headquarters on the South Bank and the first steps to the Barbican development. The construction industry was an easy target, because a long period of full employment had cut away the unions' control of members although industrial relations at national level remained good. Neither the left-wing agitator nor the high flier in search of big earnings felt the urgent need for union support which he had in the hard times before the war.* The London Building Workers'

---

* We have seen in Chapter 1 the part played in the 1972 building strike by the need for the new merged building union (UCATT) to show that it could negotiate basic rate to something less hopelessly out of touch with real earnings. There are difficulties about organising building workers in all countries. In Germany density of membership is as low as 13 per cent, not much more than 40 per cent of the national average. In the United States, organised building workers are the highest paid manual workers but outside the big cities and big sites there is very little union organisation at all. George Meany, president of the AFL/CIO, the US central trade union organisation, is reported to have said that he does not care how many workers are unorganised so long as the plumbers' union runs the hiring halls. Mr Meany is a plumber. Although the Taft-Hartley Act of 1948 outlaws the pre-entry closed shop, the US Supreme Court held that this did not outlaw an agreement which required employers to recruit labour in a certain place, a union 'hiring hall', a system which another US union leader observed was 'the closed shop with fancy fixings'.

Joint Sites Committee and the labour-only sub-contractor flourished in the same untilled garden.

One factor in these strikes was the aspiration of steel-fixers, the men who put the metal in reinforced concrete, to be recognised as a skilled group. Most of them were in the TGWU, but some were in the AUBTW, and neither the general union nor the craft-based union had done anything to humour their desire for status. Steel-fixers particularly resent, as dockers do, the common assumption that they earn very high wages for very little skill. They went on strike at the South Bank at one point because the contractors employed a non-union worker. Matt Lynch, a massive and intimidating man who was their chief shop steward, pointed to a passage in the TGWU *Record* which said: 'Negotiating for you is hard work, and makes our officers very tired. But negotiating for non-unionists makes them even more tired. See that there are no "nons" at your place.' Lynch said that since the union did nothing four days after they had reported the employment of a 'nonner', he assumed that he could go ahead and call a strike. This was stretching the truth a bit, of course. Lynch had bent and fixed steel all over Britain and the Commonwealth, and had been a shop steward for years. He knew that he operated in a world where action to get what he and his men considered 'fair' might be in breach of agreement. (With the passing of the Industrial Relations Act, a nonner's 'right to work' is enshrined in law.) But if steelfixing had been recognised as a craft with criteria for training, the men might not have pushed so hard; they might not have had to. A closed shop always seems more attractive, and a nonner more of a threat, where workers as a group feel insecure or uncertain of their status.

Matt Lynch was an interesting study in other ways as well. He was a byword for toughness; indeed, they tell me that contractors liked to find a firm site manager if they knew that Lynch and his colleague Hugh Cassidy were to be on the job. When I first met Lynch he gave me a rough welcome as a fancy hack for a boss's paper. Yet after a few days, when he realised that I was writing reports and not polemics, he began to unbend a bit, and said something which I have always remembered as typical of a dominant but not sophisticated man: 'What we want are men with brains who can go and argue with these men with brains over there.' Perhaps he was too set in his ways at 50 to respond to changes in management style, but I have often thought that if Matt Lynch had not felt outsmarted so often, employers would not have felt the need to stand toe-to-toe with him on the site. There was something of the same feeling in the docks. A group of dockers were on strike for some preposterous bonus claim for work which was covered by bonus already, on the grounds that the cargo in question was such a bad example of dirty work that the bonus for that kind of dirty work would not be adequate compensation. Bob Garner of *The Daily Telegraph* said to one of the men (what was no more than the truth): 'You know you can't win.' The docker answered: 'If we can't win, we'll make sure those bastards don't.'

Mr Justice Winn commented in the ETU case:

'Only a recluse in an ivory tower would fail to appreciate the tendency of all forms of single-minded devotion to an ideology, whether religious, political or economic, to degenerate into fanaticism, and a state of obsessive delusion that the only criterion of good and ill in conduct is the utility for the development of chosen ends. Such a state probably develops where a vacuum exists owing to the lack of any other faith.'

But there are countless collective situations where a vacuum develops for lack of common feeling. It is no accident, for example, that companies where management has a Quaker background tend to enjoy better industrial relations than the average. The founder might become as rich as the flinty materialist down the road, and indeed he usually did, but he gave tangible evidence of concern for his workers' welfare as part of his human duty, not by rationalisation that put investment in contentment on the same level as investment in lathes. Such an employer would certainly be 'paternalistic', and that has become an offensive word. It has not necessarily been an offensive fact. Hugh Cassidy was a more ideologically minded theoretician than Matt Lynch, but when he was leading an outrageously unconstitutional strike for the appointment of a safety officer in the same sequence of uproars, he said: 'We admit our lads do foolish things. We want a man who will stand at their elbows and prevent it.' Indeed, the history of safety legislation shows that one generation's paternalism is the next one's statutory duty.

Socialist Labour League

Behind *The Newsletter* was Gerry Healy, a seasoned Trotskyite who came into his own in those times of disintegration on the left. *The Newsletter* ran a rank-and-file workers' conference at the end of 1958, and from this enterprise the Socialist Labour League developed the next year. Fryer, an idealist and no conspirator, grew tired of the business and broke with Healy not long after, but the SLL survives as one of the principal channels for Marxist/anarchic enthusiasm. For a while it even had an organiser called Peter Kerrigan, and this identity of name with the CP organiser compounded existing confusions. Another notable figure was Brian Behan, the playwright's brother, expelled by the AUBTW for his red-haired Irishman's oratory and subtle provocations on the South Bank. He also became bored in the end, left the SLL and wrote an entertaining book, *With Breast Expanded*.

The SLL remains the most conspicuous of the Trotskyite groups in Britain: its particular strength is in recruiting youngsters from the universities and other hothouses and although the turnover is rapid, a few of them stick. The principal rival is a group called the International Socialists, originally a breakaway from the United States Trotskyite movement which made progress in Britain somewhat later than the SLL and has been particularly active in the docks and among left-wing teachers. The Communist Party of Great Britain (Marxist-Leninist) is a pro-Chinese and pro-Albanian splinter led by Reg Birch, a member of the AUEW national executive expelled by the CP for his advocacy of Peking policies. Birch has been an AUEW official for a long time and his political views have become increasingly individual and eccentric. He applied to engineering negotiations the Maoist doctrine of permanent revolution, which certainly makes it difficult to abide by strict procedure but is as much a rationalisation of life in the motor industry as a doctrine sprung fully armed from the thoughts of Chairman Mao.

All these groups are in constant competition wth occasional *ad hoc* alliances in particular disputes. They also fight for control of their own creatures. The Institute for Workers' Control, for example, was founded by Ken Coates, a sociologist expelled from the Labour Party in 1965. But 'workers' control' can mean all things to all men. The vice-presidents include Hugh Scanlon, general president of the AUEW and a former Communist, and Jack Jones, general secretary of the TGWU and a lifelong socialist of a particularly systematic and logical stamp (once one accepts his premises). What they consider to be the objective of workers' control is different, and each is different from what Coates thinks. There are other bodies of shop stewards' co-ordinating committees, power workers' combines and docks liaison groups which flourish and wither in their season.

Political 'Rag Trade'
Compared with real trade unions they are rather like those small businesses, especially in construction and the 'rag trade' (clothing) where the entrepreneurs remain the same but the companies are forever changing. Their titles and language are very much in the second phase of terminology that we noticed in the last chapter, being abstract and polysyllabic so that they may appear to have wide general associations. However, their information is frequently specific and detailed and just accurate enough to be convincing in particular situations. Workers readily accept that the boss has to hide something. If he never tells them anything, they are naturally inclined to believe that someone who knows a little bit and elaborates it has the full story. The activities of these various groups cause frequent alarm, especially among people given to conspiracy theories. They are forever turning up in industrial conflict and actually enjoy being given credit for it; if they are not active there is usually someone to infer that they are. But with the possible exception of the CP they are not really institutions at all. They work against rationalisation and harmony in the trade union movement just as they work against rationalisation and harmony in industry as a whole. We have already noticed that so long as the CP controlled the ETU, merger was inconceivable. So long as Communists and other eccentrics remain as influential as they are in the AUEW, the union will find it difficult to introduce the comprehensive reform which its ancient and peculiar structure requires to meet the pressures of the late twentieth-century. By definition their objectives are discordant with those of the ordinary citizen, who wants to do the best he can for himself, his dependants and his associates in the circumstances they are in.

The Douglas Hyde progress is of course not all one way, and it is not uncommon to find some who are as fanatical as their fathers but in a different direction. One of the most impassioned Trotskyites I knew on Clydeside was raised in a community of Close Brethren. A decently diffused sense of complementary tolerances and loyalties is a strong shield against any kind of fanaticism, and some British Communists have it just as some British Christians lack it. The trade union movement as a whole, in an imperfect and blundering way often enough, does correct really dangerous fanaticism. Sometimes this happens overtly, like the purge of CP leadership from the trades councils after the war. Sometimes it comes from the pressure of work and habit, and using a long spoon. This is not always possible. Two employers' practices are particularly helpful to the 'militants': the victimisation of a left-wing shop steward or other workgroup leader on the one hand, and the readiness to make quick concessions at plant level – often with a bogus reason to keep in line with national agreement – for the sake of a bit of peace on the other. A skilful manipulator of scapegoats and organiser of quick extortions can make a name for himself in these circumstances. He may even make his way up the union ladder to national influence. But it is possible for militants to make a career in this way only if they find the appropriate attitudes among employers.

The case of the Edgware gasworkers mentioned earlier shows how readily systems of public information can get trade union affairs out of context. This is very useful to left-wing freebooters and makes the job of moderates more difficult. One reason why so much of the 'underground' pamphlets, handbills, broadsheets and working papers that litter the ground after some unofficial strike meetings is credible, is that the encapsulated reports in the press and on the airwaves are incredible, either too brief to satisfy the people involved or to their way of thinking 'slanted' against them. Even here there is a curious asymmetry between managers and workers, both of whom seem equally dissatisfied with the performance of the 'media' when their own affairs are affected. The inclination of managers is always to withhold information until they can present it formally on their own terms as an accomplished fact. Confidentiality, like procedure, is most important to the people at the controls. Sometimes it is self-defeating, especially where people are competing for the confidence of others in their good faith and ability. Although it is seldom overt and for most managers unthinkable, many industrial disputes involve just such a struggle: there has never been such a vogue in Britain for the phrase 'incompetent management' as there is now, and militants are by no means averse to using it.

Opponents and Correctives

Apart from competent management and the general attitudes of respectable people in established institutions, these groups have their active opponents. IRIS (Industrial Research and Information Services) hunts out left-wing activities with the same diligence and perseverance as Aims of Industry and similar bodies display in protecting capitalism from adulteration. Society is full of Mrs Partingtons sweeping out parts of the North Sea with their various types of broom, while the untutored multitude learn to swim, generally a more hopeful activity, as best they can. Moral re-armament invites likely adolescents of all ages to be saved. The influence of the Churches is difficult to measure. There are certainly more active Christians than active Communists of any kind in the trade union movement. But they preach less and in trade union matters use the same language, which can be confusing. They are less regarded than they should be, not because they achieve less for the members they serve – they probably achieve more over time – but because they are unlikely to be in the lead in publicised conflict, and extremely unlikely to emphasise their religious interests when they are. Conflict attracts publicity and at the same time pushes moderate leadership out of the way. That Jimmy Airlie and Jimmy Reid, the shop stewards' leaders in the Upper Clyde Shipbuilders affair, should be Communists is not surprising. That Vic Feather, general secretary of the TUC and a Christian Socialist 'fixer', should intervene to try to persuade the Government to give the men alternative work was characteristic too. Extremism and irrationality take hold when there are no obvious alternatives; the distinctively human quality of making a tolerable choice (on which market economics is supposed to be based) is very often not available, or hardly available, to workers in a declining industry which dominates a community. The narrower the options, the more dramatic and exotic the symptoms of 'no choice but fight'.

In some senses trade unionism is highly political. The Conservative trade union group is as unconvincing in its way as would be a Labour free enterprise group. The behaviour of trade union representatives is often highly political in a different way, since it is the behaviour of representatives without authority. One central fact remains: the greatest single stimulus to trade union membership is recognition, and how recognition arrives makes a significant difference to the quality of membership and the sort of leadership which it generates. Respect for authority in many different ways has shaped trade unionism, although the basic impulse is to check or eliminate a certain kind of authority, that of employers to do as they please. Coming to terms with the ambiguities involved has never been easy. There is no want of advice to trade unionists at all levels about what they ought to do. It is not surprising and it is sometimes exasperating that so many of them have no clear idea of what they can do, or in fact are doing at any given time. The fault is not found only in trade unions.

Chapter 5
High Hats and White Collars

'*Experience teaches me that the number of semantic maladjustments, especially among the white-collar class, is very large.*'
Alfred Korzybski

'*We have quite a few words for hypocrisy, like tact, diplomacy, discretion – concepts which are dominant in public life, and which usually go unchallenged.*'
Bill Schutz

'*Braw Lad in the Office*'
In the first chapter we attempted a definition of 'white-collar worker' with which some people would not agree, but I have not found a better one: 'workers who are removed by one or more degrees from direct production or direct service.' Dress was never more than the slenderest indication; intellectual content is usually misleading; literacy is now irrelevant since it is virtually universal; status and terms of employment are arbitrary; hardly anyone outside the four foundation occupations of medicine, the law, the church and the Queen's commission in the armed services quite meets the total criterion of a profession which they have achieved; and proximity to authority, the other accepted mark, is illogical and uncertain.

Of course, some people are obviously white-collar workers and others are obviously not, if the distinction means anything at all. At the frontiers of occupations, the distinction is increasingly blurred, and because groups of workers have long collective memories we have to remember that it has been, and sometimes still is, a rancorous frontier. I have never forgotten the venom with which I once heard sung the old Glasgow street ballad:

'The toilers gone home to their slums in the gloom
From the pit, or the forge, or the yard, or the loom
Curse that braw lad, the clerk in the office.'

And at the Croydon special conference of the TUC to consider what was then the Industrial Relations Bill in 1971, Walter Anderson, general secretary of NALGO, made his celebrated speech saying that like any other union worthy of the name NALGO would make up its own mind about whether to register or not on the terms set out in the Bill. As we went out for the lunch break one miners' delegate commented to another: 'It's a middle-class union.' The other said glumly, 'Clerks'. Yet NALGO is the largest white-collar union in the free world, the fourth largest union in the TUC, and in the end its members decided to boycott the provisions of the Act like the great majority of TUC unions.

We noticed in Chapter 2 the anomaly of white-collar trade unionism in Britain – 80 per cent membership in public service, 10 per cent in private employment. Yet while the frontiers of white-collar employment are becoming increasingly vague and traditional white-collar jobs are under threat from mechanisation of mere checking and recording, 'non-manual' employment is expanding while 'manual' work is contracting in proportion. So far as the growth of the trade union movement as a whole is concerned, white-collar workers in private employment seem to offer the readiest ground for recruitment. The need for collective defence at ever higher levels of 'staff' employment is plain on the face of commercial developments, with the unprecedented scale of mergers during the past few years pushing the controlling apex of management ever farther away from local accountability, and creating executive and clerical redundancies. In fact, according to Professor Bain the density of white-collar unionism increased only from 28·8 per cent to 29 per cent between 1948 and 1964, while the density of manual unionism declined from 53·1 per cent to 51 per cent in Britain generally. The bandwagon may now be rolling a little faster, but not so fast as its wheels are going round. The 'white-collar explosion' is a fragmentary affair.

ASTMS: *Explosion in a Vacuum*
To match NALGO's membership in public service of 450,000, we should expect a union in private employment with a white-collar

membership of somewhere between a million and a million and a half. We have ASTMS puffing beyond a quarter of a million – an explosion in a vacuum; besides, its membership has yet to set into the solidity habitual in craft and industrial unions, in public-service unions and in the personal lives of white-collar workers in general by comparison with those of manual workers in general, at least below craft level. To guarantee stability, let alone growth, the trade union movement must recruit white-collar workers and bring the 'density' of their membership in private employment at least to the level commonplace in manual work and preferably to the level of public service.

'Density' is a simple statistical measure of the proportion of people qualified to be in trade unions who have in fact joined. It does not mean as much as 'quality', the word we chose in the first chapter. In a way it is a paradoxical word to use because a union could maintain density while having an enormous turn-over of individual members (as happens in some occupations) and an apathetic branch qualifies for density on the same basis as a brisk and active one, and entrenched and habitual branches qualify on the same basis as ones with shallow roots which may depend on a few eager individuals.

This last situation is particularly common in white-collar trade unionism at its frontiers of development. To be sure, there are tens of thousands of clerks, technicians and supervisors even in private employment to whom the union is part of the natural furniture of their working surroundings. But before accepting even the prediction of a 'white-collar explosion' we ought to look at the rich soil of prejudice, habit and even language in which white-collar attitudes to trade unionism grow. In many parts of British industry the initiator of trade unionism among staff meets the same resistance from colleagues and supervisors as the organiser of process workers did fifty years ago, and for more complicated reasons. The whole affair has been curiously circular. Craftsmen organised themselves on the model of professions. General workers picked up the lesson of collective power from craftsmen. But clerical and administrative workers remain in a conceptual limbo. They are seldom, as a rule, professional in any convincing sense, but many of them want to be. They tend to consider overt collective pressure on an employer, even if it is short of a strike, unworthy of the ambition to be professional and perhaps socially embarrassing (however justified the objective of the action may be; in the same way individual pressure, even if it is wrong-headed, is given high marks for courage, up to a point). But when the reality of special status has decayed, these workers often cling to a sense of personal contact with the centre of power, to the prospect of eventually running the show themselves, or to notions of 'loyalty' and 'order'.

Conventions of Office Work
Most of the order in a clerical or administrative worker's life is arbitrary and symbolic. Most of what he does and the times at which he does it are conventional, rather than dictated by any superhuman necessity. Even a great deal of the information that he handles is a conventional approximation, like the value of work in progress. Yet oddly enough this kind of order is fairly easily maintained, being attuned to the dominant conventions of society, and insulated from day-to-day change. Neither trade unionism nor equal pay will do much to change this. Ask a finance company whether they would rather lend money to an established civil servant earning £40 a week or to a construction worker of the same age earning £50 a week, both with a wife and two children. The civil servant would probably still get preference; he would get it without question if the pay were the same. He would probably get preference over his own counterpart in private employment as well, but his counterpart in private employment may already have favourable 'contacts' through his work.

However, even this advantage diminishes the larger the employer. In small communities with a number of small enterprises, even modest preferment may bring a white-collar worker into contact with colleagues in other lines who can put useful services in his way on an informal barter basis. But as companies grow and merge, ever larger pools of 'proletarianised' white-collar workers develop, all doing much the same thing and finding their occupational-social lives together. True, the big companies often provide substitute privileges to take the place of the friends who 'can fix you a discount' or 'know a chap who does it'. But the basis is different. Collective provision is natural, and no doubt collective bargaining would be natural as a result if it were not so distasteful to authority. ASTMS is now probably the fastest growing trade union in Britain. But underlying its success, and a drag on its success, is the series of agonising decisions by individual workers caught between two powerful pressures: they may not count for much individually to their employers and feel the need for mutual action, but on the other hand the risks of taking the lead in mutual action may appear too great and the example of trade unionism among other workers may involve a number of particulars which individual white-collar workers may either dislike or misunderstand.*

The higher up the scale of management hierarchy union membership goes, the more tempting it is for higher authority to work against it. Often enough, this is quite explicit, but it seldom needs to be. Many companies at a certain stage in an executive's career take stock of his 'loyalty' or 'company-mindedness'. If, as frequently happens, this means in effect 'loyalty' to the people at present running the company,† union activism may well seem an expression of dissent so grave as to be damaging; it is to allay this anxiety, I suspect, that some managers go to the equally odd extreme of refusing to inquire what members of their staff are in unions. Besides, there are shorthand terms for 'subversive', like that useful phrase 'socially aware' which has cost some militant sixth-formers a place in the university of their first choice.

Where management neither directly nor by nod-and-wink discourages union membership for any employees, white-collar unionism tends to grow rapidly unless the company is well placed and ready to pre-empt trade unions by treating its staff as well as they could reasonably expect without them. (Some companies, especially American unions, take this line with all their workers; indeed some US authorities say that the ideological distaste for trade unionism was in fact a spur to good management in that

---

* Every so often bodies come into being which attempt to cater for workers (usually white-collar workers) who feel 'squeezed' between the structural power of top management and the bargaining effectiveness of traditional unions. The latest of these, the Confederation of Independent Staff Organisations, includes among its sponsors bank staff associations and staff associations of companies like Commercial Union Insurance, Kodak and ICI which do not recognise trade unions for white-collar workers.

† In a column in *The Times* in 1972 I asked, intending it as a rhetorical question: 'Who would come into a room and say: "I am a member of management and I propose to communicate the intentions of the company" Then why write as if one might say it?' Among several letters, most of which implied that I was playing at literary criticism rather than practical communication, was one from a very senior manager who said that he had 'used that very phrase, with considerable effect, at a critical staff meeting only a few days ago.'

country for most of the first half of the twentieth-century.) The present figures suggest that prejudice is still alive and strong. The TGWU has a white-collar segment, Association of Clerical, Technical and Supervisory Staffs (ACTSS), which at 120,000 is nearly half the size of ASTMS. More recently, the NUGMW has separated its white-collar section, Managerial, Administrative, Technical and Supervisory Association (MATSA), with about 40,000 members. The AUEW has its technical and supervisory section, TASS, with over 100,000 members and once the independent DATA. TASS in turn, partly to compete with ASTMS, has concluded a loose alliance with APEX (now at some 130,000 members) to seek recognition as negotiator for supervisors and technicians while APEX organises clerical and administrative staff. All five are very much concerned with one another, and with other unions that have some white-collar membership like the Iron and Steel Trades Confederation (ISTC), or industrial white-collar membership with marginal membership outside it, like TSSA which is squarely based on railway clerks but has widened its horizon to other clerical workers in transport. TSSA in turn has marginal problems with the NUR, which has some booking-clerk members employed by London Transport. All the printing unions have some white-collar members and both SLADE and the NUJ are exclusively white-collar. Faction develops readily among clerical and professional workers and, as we saw from the quotation about 'disloyalty' in Chapter 2, is taken for granted among managers.

In all industries and in government white-collar workers spend their time manipulating symbols. Since manipulating symbols is so far as we know the distinctively human activity, there is a great advantage in such work. But since there is no limit to the nonsense produced by confusing symbols at different levels of abstraction, or by depending on symbols without matching them to reality, relations among white-collar workers are particularly vulnerable at times of rapid change. As things stand in Britain at the moment, survey after survey has shown the common problem of drawing the line somewhere. Given the intense feeling against trade unions above the most modest level, it is not surprising that the collective idea commonly expresses itself in terms of a 'professional' pressure group rather than a functional trade union. Bodies like the Association of Official Architects, the Association of Professional Teachers, and the United Kingdom Association of Professional Engineers hope to seek recognition as trade unions in bargaining units; others like the Institute of Work Study Practitioners are thinking about it. The Industrial Relations Act gives a special nod to professional qualifications, and the code of practice to behaviour in accordance with professional standards. A great deal of earnest thought has gone into these provisions and no doubt into the development of these exclusive unions. Yet in terms of trade union development they appear to be primitive in conception, as we shall see presently in looking at the growth of the present large white-collar unions in the private sector. This is perhaps not surprising, since the personal situation of a pioneer trade unionist is always much the same, and pioneering trade unionists in the real sense are now at managerial and professional level.

Narrow Objectives of 'Professionals'
Their objectives are likely to be narrow and call for close support among their nearest colleagues. Some unions grow no more: there are a dozen in the TUC with membership smaller than 1,000 and some with fewer than 100. No doubt at this size they achieve what their members want, or at least as much as they will put themselves out for. But unions which do grow generally abandon the early limits on their recruiting, and as their attitudes as institutions mature they take a wider interest in the world. When they join the TUC their range of interest becomes wider still. It may seem a paradox that a body representing comparatively well educated workers should enrich its concerns by joining another still predominantly composed of manual workers, but this seems to be what happens. The case of NALGO is commonly cited. Since joining the TUC in 1964 NALGO has taken a considerably greater interest in questions of general public policy as well as establishing the pay and conditions of an important part of the work force who carry it out. A union which is too specialised is likely to have difficulties with other unions and is bound to limit its effectiveness. If its limited area of interest declines, the union movement as a whole is likely to suffer because the advantages of experience are lost to it. One need only look again at the fortunes of the Triple Alliance unions of the 'twenties: the Mineworkers' TUC affiliation membership was 273,927 in 1971 compared with 602,274 in 1951; the Railwaymen 198,319 against 391,799 and the specialist Locomotive Engineers 29,277 against 68,752. Of the dockers, the NASD was expelled from the TUC after registering

7,000 members in 1951; in 1971 it claims 4,000 members. Dock labour as a whole is down from about 100,000 to 44,000, but most dockers are in the broad bosom of the TGWU (although a few are GMWU and Railwaymen in railway docks).

TSSA was different; the very name is a rejection of the narrow cell of the Railway Clerks' Union which was their old name. As a result of seeking recognition in whatever fields its new title could cover, TSSA still retained 75,194 members reported to the TUC in 1971 compared with 85,216 in 1951. In the same way the Association of Shipbuilding and Engineering Draughtsmen broadened into DATA, a general technicians' union. Their membership advanced from 42,048 in 1951 to 105,418 in 1971, just before the merger with the Engineers as AUEW/TASS (a coincidence of initials with the Moscow news agency which, because of the perpetual control of the executive by a chaplet of left-wingers, became one of the smiles of the year in the labour movement). APEX began as the National Union of Clerks and flourished a while as the Clerical and Administrative Workers' Union; it did even better during the 20 years – from 33,150 in 1951 to 125,541 in 1971.

The senior progenitor of ASTMS, ASSET, was a minor union in engineering in 1951, with only 11,623 members. By 1961 it was more than double the size at 24,351, but vigorous growth became spectacular after the major merger with the weakly Association of Scientific Workers (12,360 members in 1951, 12,000 in 1961). Apart from insurance workers, the MPU (a small body of doctors at 5,500) transferred their engagements to ASTMS in 1970, and ASTMS remains the only general white-collar union which offers convincing shelter in a storm to managers without a professional protector.

Membership of ASTMS had passed 200,000 by the end of 1970 and although the pace slackened in 1971 as it did for other white-collar unions, its growth continued. Pilkington Glass, for example, after the damaging strike by its manual workers in 1970, reviewed its relationship with the GMWU and recognised ASTMS for its white-collar workers in an unusual and candid bargain in which the union openly admitted its weaknesses as well as strengths in membership. At the same time, two significant references to the CIR involving the union met resistance. The Commission recommended that ASTMS should have bargaining rights for doctors working for the Medical Research Council as well as for other scientists. The recommendation ran into the powerful opposition of the British Medical Association, and later the Industrial Relations Act provided for a special register on which the BMA could qualify as a trade union for the purposes of the Act, but without the indignity of opening its books to the Registrar. In another reference the CIR recommended that the Commercial Union Assurance Company should recognise ASTMS as joint negotiator with its large and heavily subsidised staff association. Mr Eric Orbell, then managing director, who had agreed to the voluntary reference under the Labour Government with explicit confidence that the CIR would give clearance to the staff association, refused to accept the recommendation and waited to see what the implementation of the Act would do. Another incident, an unequal passage of arms between ASTMS and DATA in a provincial engineering works, led in the end to another significant foretaste of the implications of the Act for white-collar unions. DATA had long organised white-collar staff at C. A. Parsons of Newcastle-upon-Tyne, with a preponderant but not exclusive membership. An ASTMS group with a comparatively small membership challenged for recognition and lost.

The Parsons Case

A group of engineers with professional qualifications joined the fledgling UKAPE when the competition between the two TUC unions became disruptive. In March 1970, DATA called a strike and in May the company agreed that after 12 months all members of the staff below the rank of head of department who had not been members of a union affiliated to the TUC at that point must join DATA. Thirty-eight professional engineers refused and were given a month's notice on 30 July 1971. One of them appealed for an injunction against dismissal to the High Court and lost. In November the Court of Appeal reversed the decision in a remarkable judgment which anticipated the implementation of Part II of the Industrial Relations Act (which had been passed in August but came into force in stages; Part II, which gives protection from unfair dismissal and makes it unlawful to require union membership as a condition of employment, was still more than three months away). Lord Denning, the Master of the Rolls, said that in their original letter in May the company seemed to think that they could change the conditions of the engineer's employment without his consent. They could do no such thing. He added that they also had no power to terminate his employment on one month's notice. The appellant, Mr J. W. Hill, was 63 years old and had worked for the company for thirty-five years. Lord Denning considered reasonable notice for a professional man of his standing and length of service would be at least six months and maybe twelve months. Because Part II of the Act would presently come into force the length of notice mattered. Damages would not be an adequate remedy and the notice was far too short. Quoting the fundamental principle that whenever a man had a right the law should give a remedy, he said that that principle enabled the court to step over the constraints of previous cases and to bring the law into accord with the needs of today. Although Lord Justice Stamp, in the minority, stuck to the established rule that no court could require specific performance of a contract of employment, leave to appeal was refused.

As a foretaste of the challenge to existing unions under the Act, the case was startling. Obviously the sense of a small group of 'professional' men standing up to a 'powerful' trade union catches the imagination of important lawyers. Yet the issue at Parsons was the inevitable one of union security which can be achieved in one of only two ways – complete and co-operative recognition by the employer, or the imposition of exclusive bargaining rights which traditionally leads to a closed shop either by forced agreement or custom. As we saw in the introduction, the Act provides for an 'agency shop' instead of a closed shop: this means, bluntly, that the union may have subscription money from all the employees in the unit of employment but not title to control them. Why should Mr Hill and his colleagues object so much to becoming members of DATA? Their main reasons, no doubt, were that DATA's tactics of traditional industrial action, its left-wing leadership, and the minimal qualifications of some of its members made it an inappropriate union for people like them. It is true that DATA has a left-wing leadership, although three out of five members do not pay the political levy, and that in spite of its recent spreading of its wings it is dominated by men with modest qualifications. Yet it is trapped in a vicious circle. Managers originally resisted DATA because managers were traditionally recruited from the drawing office. After recognising the union, they kept it firmly in its place, and this had an inevitable social effect on its membership.

The Parsons problem came before the NIRC a few months later. The company asked the court to take account the union representation controversy. The court referred the question of who should represent whom at Parsons to the CIR. The CIR recommended that TASS should continue to be the bargaining agent for white-collar workers (other than ASTMS's supervisors) up to the rank of head of department, and to make no recommendation for bargaining above that rank. This disregarded the claims of UKAPE and other 'professional' unions for some overriding title to challenge from a minority base a mature bargaining situation. There was not much that an expert body like the CIR could recommend, and the case subsided into the habitual anti-climax of a working compromise.*

Bankers, Teachers and Union Security
There are very few unions which do not have at least a small fringe of white-collar members, but the trade union movement as a whole still shows no inclination to make any kind of concerted recruitment drive. ASTMS uses most of the techniques of publicity to sharpen up its image of cheerful expansion and, considering the speed of its growth, is fairly successful in keeping members; it has the difficulty that as a result of various minor transfers of engagements many of its members are still paying a lower subscription than the normal rate, and some of its members join in a crisis and leave soon afterwards before their membership can be consolidated – like several members of the staff of the London School of Economics after the dismissal of a lecturer in 1970. Another union with an embattled history is the National Union of Bank Employees (NUBE), which bears the marks of a long struggle for recognition against the bank staff associations which was extraordinarily bitter and mistrustful. In 1951 NUBE had only 29,622 members; by 1971 they had reached 89,144, with joint recognition from the major banks. The Industrial Relations Act set NUBE an unusual problem; not only were they threatened even more than other unions by staff associations which were themselves strong and wilful institutions, but an active minority and almost certainly an overall majority of their members considered the Act in general a good thing.

* There is even dispute about whether TASS, officially boycotting the institutions of the Industrial Relations Act, actually obeyed an NIRC order. NIRC at one time expressed satisfaction that TASS had obeyed its order to abandon a boycott while the matter was before the CIR. TASS claimed that its acting in conformity with the order was a mere coincidence, since the particular point in question was settled at about the time that NIRC made the order.

The NUT, who had joined the TUC only the year before, a year after the National Association of Schoolmasters, faced similar problems. One can hardly say in 1972 that the development of white-collar unions seems likely to be systematic, orderly or on a broad front. NUBE in the end was among the 32 unions – and one of the largest – which put registration above TUC membership.

The NUT, who had joined the TUC only in 1970, a year after the National Association of Schoolmasters, faced similar problems. But neither the NUT nor NALGO were in the peculiarly perilous situation of NUBE. They were so big and so secure in their representative position that the development of 'registered' bodies presuming to cater for borough surveyors of 'professional' teachers represented an irritant but not a mortal threat. One might almost say that the great surprise of 1971–2 was that so many trade unions which so many people considered were not properly trade unions at all actually behaved like trade unions in the event; although some of them, like ASTMS, did so only at the last moment. ASTMS avoided suspension by the 1972 TUC only by sending a letter to the Registrar a couple of days before stating an unequivocal intention to de-register after months of squirming on the fence.*

The pressures on white-collar and manual unions – and the assumed perceptions of their members – were so different that at one time predictions of a white-collar 'secessionist' TUC were not uncommon. Fortunately, nothing so time-wasting and purposeless has happened. As we shall see, by the mere fact of TUC membership and co-operation, trade unions and trade union officials become bound together regardless of the composition of their membership. The thirty-two unions suspended by the 1972 TUC were an extraordinarily mixed lot, catering for occupations from health service porters to airline pilots and West End celebrities: the peculiarly poignant thing about these departures was its family flavour. When Bill Hogarth led out the seamen, or Frank Lynch led out COHSE, their bearing was for all the world like that of spirited young brothers. This may not last –

* This provoked a complicated joke: 'What is a mugwump? – A Welsh hiccup.' A mugwump is someone who sits on the fence with his mug on one side and his rump on the other. ASTMS is pronounced 'Astums' and Clive Jenkins's well-known Welshness completes the description. On the other hand, Mr Jenkins has also been called by a critic 'the only man from South Wales who thinks of Rugby as a town in the Midlands of England'.

but then, the arbitrary advantages accorded by the Act to registered trade unions may not last either, since it does not seem to have had any effect that its framers intended.*

The TUC no longer has a miscellaneous category of 'non-manual' unions in which it used to lump together show-business associations (including the Footballers), CAWU, NUBE, insurance, the MPU and the ASCW. Now we have 'professional, clerical and entertainment' and 'technical, engineering and scientific'. But of course a gap still survives, and it may widen if there is a rapid growth of little 'professional' unions whose members will certainly not care to join the TUC even if the General Council and Congress drop their policy of inflexible opposition to the new system of labour law. We may even find 'professional unions' as ubiquitous as the Plumbers (now merged with the ETU) and the HDV (now merged with the SMW); one or other of these unions is likely to have a little band of members in buildings with central heating systems and contractors who install them, but with total numbers before merger of some 50,000 and 20,000 respectively; if the new professional unions are exclusive enough they will average no more members in a plant. In the nature of things they will find it more difficult to merge than bodies with less advanced pretensions, especially if the prospective merger is with these bodies. Before the Industrial Relations Act the CIR normally preferred the standard of similar services in similar parts of an establishment for bargaining groups rather than the standard of original training. The code of practice incorporates the general feeling that bargaining units should be as wide as possible. In fact, there is good reason to believe that they function best when they include a significant range of both skills and status, so long as senior people in the employers' structure are not subject to union discipline by their subordinates.

'Service' or 'Nuisance'?

Whether trade unionism continues to expand in Britain or starts to contract in a year or two with the comparative drop in the number of process and production workers depends on white-collar recruitment. In ten years the NUM and the three railway

---

* This is not unusual in legislation of this kind. The Taft-Hartley Act in the United States was aimed principally at the operations of the Teamsters' Union; but the Teamsters' Union has continued to put on membership and acquire new sources of strength – even while Jimmy Hoffa, the union boss, was in prison.

unions have lost more than twice as many members as ASTMS has put on, and nearly twice as many as the TGWU has put on apart from mergers. It is possible that the engineering industry reached a total of workers employed in 1969–70 which it will never reach again after the dismissal of thousands of them in the economising days of 1970–1. This is an unfamiliar situation for Britain, and it is not clear how British people and their organisations are going to meet it. The easy road will be the American one of developing a superstructure of profitable 'service' activities as production recovers, and taking for granted a higher level of unemployment or potential unemployment than Britain has become used to. But since this involves elevating to the title of 'service industry' a number of occupations which are more like 'nuisance industry', since the 'right to work' in Britain is coming to mean the right to an opportunity for a job rather than the American concept of 'the right to work without belonging to a trade union', and since the American system itself, like most industrial relations systems, is under challenge and strain, the easy road is both unpleasant and unlikely. The harmonious development of white-collar unionism ought in reason to be a part of a better answer. As things stand it is more likely to be narrow, vocational and with limited, material objectives for a few years at least: a response to a threat rather than a positive drive towards wider solutions.

There is something of this quality in all trade unions, which seldom find it easy to marry the objectives of high standards of performance and security and good conditions for their members. Indeed, they cannot do it alone even if they want to, and there are very few unions – probably no unions – whose members have not at some time or another tried, even to the point of industrial action, to maintain what they believed to be high standards. The loss of control over what they do and how they do it is obviously one of the influences towards restlessness and cynicism among employees. 'Professionalism' in the best sense is a natural and humane aspiration. The danger is that it should become identified in practice with special skills and certificates which are not important enough in themselves to carry the weight of respect that 'professional' status requires. It is a contradiction in terms to accept that someone is a 'professional person' simply because he says so. Besides, too great an emphasis on special qualifications disrupts the process of improved understanding which society requires, being essentially divisive, self-centred and confusing. As we have seen in earlier chapters, whatever turn thinking takes at a more educated level will be reflected in the attitudes of the main line of the labour movement. Since white-collar workers do manipulate the symbols of our society – much more important in human terms than the mechanical techniques of production – a collective misreading of the symbolic relations among people, their functions and their aspirations by white-collar workers will set the pattern of the future even if white-collar unionism remains as hesitant as it is now. If anything, the pattern is at present more confused than usual.

Tensions of the Supervisor
Against this background we can see some of the tensions involved in white-collar trade unionism. The body of recorded knowledge is doubling every few years and machines are capable of annexing an even greater proportion of routine functions. Clerks, supervisors, untrained managers and their peers have become vulnerable to technological change and lost their sense of 'staff' security (or, if they have not, they have at least seen others lose it), and they are increasingly likely to see the formal authority in the organisation they work for pass to strangers, either because the organisation is taken over or because someone is appointed from outside as it struggles to survive. The mere change will disrupt and may destroy a network of practical dealings which are not expressed in any formal rules and have never been made explicit, let alone recorded; yet when they are distorted the workers concerned have lost a natural means of maintaining collective harmony. The pretensions of the stranger may never gain acceptance and he may be obliged to rely on regular statement of his formal authority to compensate for the lack of real persuasive power. If his policies fail he can hardly expect his colleagues to share the responsibility and help to mend matters (although they often do) and a search for scapegoats becomes inevitable.

Against threats like these protective association is bound to develop. Where some form of organisation already exists it becomes more militant. Only the crudest conspiracy theoretician would try to explain official strikes of, say, teachers, journalists and local government officials by a decay of moral fibre and sense of responsibility. They may (in so far as one can define 'moral fibre' and give a specific application to 'sense of responsibility') be associated; certainly having been on strike once makes going on strike again seem a less horrifying prospect. Most people who have worked out the complicated interdependance of wages, prices, money supply, material costs and effectiveness in work and the organisation of work know that 'fighting' is the last way to mend matters; deliberate strife makes as much sense as treating a car that will not go by kicking the wheels, or attempting to exert personal authority over an unlubricated transmission. Yet very often authority is the only instrument of innovation which senior members of private organisations consider reliable, and junior managers and specialists are left with the difficult problem of translating authority into terms which will produce the behaviour required to make the undertaking work.

At the forefront of the effort stands the worthy but often frustrated and even more often untrained figure of the supervisor. Sometimes he is undefined as well. The position really is very difficult to define,* and a comprehensive definition is usually a statement of the impossible, like the one in the Government's *Classification of Occupations and Directory of Occupational Titles* ('Codot') in 1972:

'Directly supervises and co-ordinates the activities of a group of workers (unspecified). Considers the work to be undertaken by the group; determines work priorities and procedures and assigns duties to workers; ensures that the quantity and quality of output of individual workers and the group as a whole is satisfactory and re-allocates workers and duties as necessary; maintains record of output; assists workers who encounter difficulties; keeps workers informed of management policies and

* A panel at the 1971 conference of the Institute of Personnel Management grappled with the task of definition like this: Mr H. G. Smyth of Sheffield Rolling Mills called a supervisor a first-line manager who has a group of twenty to sixty men 'under his control' and is normally subject to a manager; Mr H. McK. Simpson of John Laing Construction called the supervisor 'the first organised line of management' such as a foreman or site manager; Mr I. G. Ellis of the Central Electricity Generating Board said that the supervisor is in some circumstances a foreman, in other circumstances a charge hand, a draughtsman group leader, a project leader, a site manager or some similar title according to the work. Mr Anthony Donovan of MSL has written a whole book on *Management of Supervisors* (Macmillan, 1971) which does not define them at all but uses 'foreman' interchangeably and sees for them a 'new, positive role' demanding 'many special personal qualities and many complex skills'.

ensures that company and other regulations are adhered to; informs manager of problems and suggestions arising from the work and advises on or effects the engagement, transfer, discharge and promotion of workers; liaises with other supervisors; trains workers; estimates, requisitions and inspects materials; confers with shop stewards or other workers' representatives to resolve grievances; ensures that plant or equipment is in good working order; progresses output on production, assists with rate-fixing, liaises with, and oversees the work of, specialists and performs tasks similar to those of workers supervised, as required.

'Additional factor: number of workers supervised.'

These tasks are achieved only by sharing them and the most fascinating part of the study of industrial relations is watching the immense variety of habits, assumptions and ruses that go into the achievement in different social, economic and technological settings. 'Individual control', in which one 'boss' invigilates the behaviour of many persons in detail is a fiction; but it can be a commanding fiction, in the sense that a 'boss' may be such an overwhelming influence that workers come to do what they assume he would have them do. So long as they are about right in their assumption, and he is about right in his judgement, the work goes on satisfactorily, but it may become abruptly unsatisfactory when the dominant figure departs in the due process of time. 'Boundary control', where the relations within a work group are so constructed that a supervisor can treat with its members as a group, or with its natural leaders, for common objectives is emerging increasingly clearly as the natural method of organisation. It is true that very large machines have a practical effect which masks the inadequacies of individual control and which may deceive managers and supervisors into believing that because 100 men work to a machine they can treat individually with 100 men. This is not the place to expound the dangers of machine-made illusion, except to say that this is a particularly offensive and dangerous one.

Changing Relations and Jobs
Supervisors apart, a complex of new white-collar jobs in production has developed with advancing technology and control: assessing, measuring, timing, recording. Functions become con-

fused: there are some plants where supervisors do less allocation of work than mere record-keeping. There are some where production workers themselves have jobs which are more like those of recorders or technicians than of traditional 'manual workers'; this is particularly common in large modern workplaces like power stations or chemical plants. The process will certainly continue. In parts of Europe where civilised arrangements have developed for collecting domestic rubbish the dustmen wear white coats and need not see the contents of the disposable bags at all. The more emphasis there is on getting things done in the most agreeable – or least disagreeable – way the less important the distinction of dress as the mark of status and literacy becomes. Besides, where 'clerical' workers move among 'production' workers as ancillaries in manufacturing plants, they are normally less well paid and campaign constantly to keep within striking distance (so to speak) of production workers' pay. They are seldom successful because they are weakly organised, dispersed where 'production' work groups are compact, and comparatively easily replaced.

White-collar workers' expectations have in consequence gone through rapid change, but this has not yet produced a general understanding of what this change means. Many clever people with amiable motives have recorded aspects of the change and brooded like Mr Donovan on special personal qualities and complex skills. This is not an appealing way to say that things are not what they used to be and will not be what they are. Most people are too modest or timid to recognise, let alone depend on their own special personal qualities and complex skills and would rather put their trust in 'objective' supports like certificates of competence. We must have such things, of course, and it would be unreasonable for a writer who spent much of his time up to the age of 22 collecting a hatful of them (although I do not know where any of them is) to criticise them. But far more important than emphasis on qualities and skills is emphasis on attitudes. I should like to see a joyful and optimistic recognition that our machines are now so effective that we can afford the time to co-ordinate the objectives of people in a patient and amiable way. The effectiveness of machines in matters of routine has left the way clear for this development as the principal concern of a class of worker still accustomed to putting routine first and fitting people into it. This rapidly becomes weary, stale, flat and unprofitable. Now we have job structuring, which is breaking a job down into a very short cycle, for example putting one piece on a product and leaving the next piece to someone else, and building it up again into a longer cycle with more variety in it: assembling a whole radio, perhaps, instead of only a sixth of it. We are on the fringe of job design, which in principle is taking a whole group of things to be done and putting them together to suit the talents and interests of given workers. Until the recent surge in unemployment this was required more and more by the shortage of highly skilled workers. There is a steady growth of ideas for increasing satisfaction and effectiveness. It is consequently disappointing to have them described as 'tools of management' or 'human engineering' or 'motivation systems', because all these phrases and their like are attempts to describe a new development in inappropriate language. Perhaps this is the natural fate of the white-collar worker – to make things work in spite of inappropriate language. No wonder the poor chap has semantic difficulties.

Large differences remain between the attitudes of different occupational and social groups. Neither trade unionism nor equal pay will do much to allay them. A process worker may feel that a clerk who earns less than himself is still substantially favoured, and the white-collar worker is often ready to talk about manual workers being 'overpaid' as if there were some absolute standard for totting up a man's worth. Partly, of course, this is the result of naïve interpretation of experience. The person chosen to be a supervisor has 'gone into management' or 'has prospects' or 'has bettered himself' – even if, as frequently happens, he earns less as a result. Clerical workers as a rule have rather more formal education than process workers, although not necessarily more than apprentices to a trade. There are long-standing traditions of separation both in the sort of work, the place of work and the style of work. Modern technology increasingly blurs the frontiers of these differences, but not always in conciliatory ways. A clerk with a stop-watch and a time sheet in the works can be a more painful spectacle than a clerk making his way to a separate block to do his separate job. On the other side of the relation, white-collar workers may believe that their pay and satisfaction are held back because the enterprise is 'held to ransom' by strongly organised manual workers with less elevated standards of conduct than their own. Prejudices like these frequently influence the behaviour of people who would deny that they held them, and they are constantly reinforced. If you think like that, it takes a powerful cultural shock to make you change your pattern, especially if it is complicated, as it usually is, by various occupational sub-distinctions too.

Miscalculations About Literacy

In our culture we still make large assumptions about literacy which are increasingly out of date. The ability to read and write is a commonplace, but not the capacity to read and write effectively enough to ensure that the required message is received. Anyone with the patience and wit to observe what becomes of his own messages can see this for himself; words mean different things to different people, and especially to different groups of people. This is particularly true of highly abstract words like 'fair', 'responsible', 'respectable', 'decent', 'intelligent'. 'humane'; it is also true of abstract descriptions of events, some of which are the common coin of public communication and yet virtually incomprehensible to a large majority of the people who listen to them and probably a significant number of those who use them. For example, Dr Hilde Behrend of Edinburgh University has twice put to representative samples of the British population the questions: 'What does the word "inflation" mean to you?' and 'What is the connection between wage claims and prices?' About two out of five could put no meaning at all on the word 'inflation' and only one in 200 saw 'manufacturing costs' and 'productivity' as essential parts of the connection between wage claims and prices; besides, hardly any distinguished between wage increases and wage claims. Although the samples were not very large and we know that pollsters can be fallible, even if we allow for a margin of error which would turn a large Conservative majority into a large Labour majority it leaves an uneasy feeling about how much we can take for granted – especially since the survey showed that 17 per cent of people in the AB class, which means managers, professional people and the like, were unable to give any definition at all of 'inflation'.

No doubt this means that if we must have such concepts as the shorthand of governing a various society in an acceptable way, we need a considerable effort of popular education. It emphatically does not mean that ordinary people are totally irresponsible or unaware of the idea of duty: we know by observation that this is not so, although observation alone cannot tell us why it is not so. There is some reason to believe that the strains of a complicated society governed by rule of thumb masked in incomprehensible jargon gnaw away the sense of duty. When there is a crisis which the majority of people have not been helped to understand, the jargon is supplemented by absurd simplicity. At the very least, one cannot demand indefinitely that people should freely accept responsibility for amending evils which are apparently remote from their personal thinking, have not been adequately explained and are thrown at them repeatedly as matters of trust by people with whom they have no personal connection. Naturally, we hope that people whom we do not know will give us the benefit of the doubt until they get to know us better, but we cannot expect them to trust us.

Professor Friedenberg put the problem neatly in his book *Coming of Age in America* when he wrote: 'Most of us will, I am sure, agree that here in America things have never looked brighter. It's the people who give cause for concern.' Another fashionable American scholar, Dr Herzberg, advocates job enrichment with the phrase: 'I'm doing a Mickey Mouse job; be careful how you speak to me.' Herzberg concentrates more on improving jobs than being careful about speaking. In the nature of things the second task is more important now, especially on these frontiers of management where supervisors talk to subordinates, engineers talk to accountants and directors talk to executives. These are points of conversation where clarity and simplicity are most deceptive and least productive. They call for a tolerance and understanding of ambiguity and diverse interests, because these interests may be more important to the people concerned than what the 'superior' considers the main purpose that they have in common. In countless enterprises many people are still employed sniffing about at the way that other people are doing their work, as distinct from coordinating, appraising and encouraging the processes that will produce good work. The trend of the times is against this waste of time, especially since machines record and retrieve controlling information so much more effectively than people can – or, to be more exact, make it possible for one man to perform the job much more effectively than many people without the machines. This is an important development because for the first time workers of moderately high status who have not had to get their hands dirty face the threat, long understood by the shop floor, of being made redundant by technology and can consequently understand the temptation to be a Luddite either by breaking the machines or overmanning them.

This is a form of insecurity different in kind from the traditional insecurity of managers as servants-at-will, who may be dismissed in accordance with their contracts at any time. You may still find many executives, especially in their prime, claiming that no manager worthy of his salt will want any more security than his skills and talents give him. Perhaps this happy breed is still in the majority among managers (or perhaps it is only that the majority whistle to keep courage up), but it is certainly some time since the notion commanded enthusiastic support among most clerks, checkers, supervisors and technicians.

Hatefulness of Computers

People may come to hate machines for various reasons. The most obvious is that machines may threaten their livelihood, a subtle combination of the money they earn and their social identity. The second is that a single machine is commonly more important commercially than large numbers of individuals, obliging the individuals to fit themselves to it. Another reason is that they do not own it and, as Marx remarked in one of his perceptive passages, it is a harsh thing to separate a man from his tools. For a great many people who have held the style of 'manager' or even 'professional' the machine has compelled recognition that in functional terms their work has been thin and unconvincing: mere checking and annotating. No wonder the computer appears a threatening and powerful monster. In fact familiarity with computers produces a modest confidence. 'Garbage in, garbage out' – there is absolute certainty that if you ask a computer a silly question you will get a silly answer. By contrast a silly question put to a person, with the great range and sensitivity of his reactions and his access to equally great ranges distributed at random among the other brains about him, may stimulate in the end a highly satisfactory answer.* A com-

---

* This reassuring fact of humanity, which most of us have used with diminishing eagerness since early childhood, is rediscovered several times a century as good for adults too. 'Brainstorming', 'bull sessions', 'lateral thinking', Zen, the theatre of the absurd and so on all show that if our thought is in a rut we can shake it free. Brains can take quite a lot of such treatment. Computers go off their poor, brainless heads rather easily.

puter can never find the right question. If you feed into a computer a question beginning 'If present trends persist . . .' it will tell you in a fraction of a second precisely when civilisation as we know it will come to an end. The computer is fast, accurate and stupid. A person is slow, often wrong, and brilliant. His mistrust of these blockish machines and resentment of their apparent greed for his job are only natural.

In particular, they imperil the steadiness of the clerical and managerial worker's way of life by comparison with that of a production worker. This is something of a paradox. Clerks' work, and that of many managers, is geared to conventions of accounting, not to spontaneous happenings. Traditionally a white-collar worker has regular hours, settles down early, and is insulated from such external difficulties as the weather, the state of the order books and the changing seasons. There are purely conventional times of pressure weekly, quarterly and annually concerned with making up wages, financial reports and the other calendar routines which the law or commercial habit requires. Besides, the white-collar worker down to a modest level may have some part to play in forward planning, the continuous business of keeping an enterprise going. He enjoys 'staff' status and has reasonable prospects of promotion if he has any significant capacity, and of keeping his place even if he has very little. These points are only indications of probability. Individual clerical workers may be much more erratic and uncertain both in their way of life and their expectations than individual production workers, but they are likely to be steadier. As we have seen, in public service the large trade unions developed virtually as staff associations. In private employment some of the more successful union expansion has recently been through merger with staff associations – notably the merger of ASTMS with the Prudential Staff Association which gave an extra thrust to the union's enterprise in organising insurance workers and was followed by merger with the Union of Insurance Staffs. There are union organisers who believe that a staff association may be no bad thing, even if it deters unionism for a time, because if the association's officers find that the employers are not playing fair with them they will be ready to throw the whole organisation and their own leadership behind affiliation.

There is some truth in this. If a staff association is just a front, a method of keeping people quiet with some show of consultation and procedure, union raiding will lead to conflict between the union and the association. If it is a genuinely representative body with officers who develop the normal commitment to the interests of their members, they will look for allies if they find these interests as they see them threatened. This is a perfectly natural course of events. We can expect to see it happen a great deal more often in Britain if the present disruption of the expectations of white-collar workers is carried much further. This is what has happened in the United States, for example, where teachers in the publicly-financed schools have become the most strike-prone single category of employee. There were good reasons for this. In all states but one strikes in public service are illegal under either statute or common law. Teachers' pay is set by local boards only partly financed by the state and making up the bulk of payments out of local property taxes; the boards are given to being a good deal less than generous. A similar system here would no doubt produce similar results, in spite of the tendency of teachers as a class to be orderly, unambitious and modest in their material expectations. At the end of 1969 the various tensions inside British school teaching – the difference of interest between career teachers with family responsibilities and young teachers with less commitment and fewer dependants, for example – and government attempts to keep a national settlement within bounds led to industrial action at national level. There were already rival unions for teachers, and the passing of the Industrial Relations Act has produced yet another one with an emphasis on 'professionalism'. This concept is a second significant element in white-collar attitudes to protective associations.

Notions of Exclusiveness
Notions of exclusiveness exist wherever men think that for some reason they are not as other men. We have seen it already in craft unions, some of whose members model their notions as squarely on those of the four senior professions as any specially qualified man in a suit who has taken his bank examinations or his institute diploma. In a real sense the consultant surgeon and the general labourer are at opposite ends of a continuum which is tight at the top and shapeless and diffuse at the bottom. To be a profession requires several clear marks: qualifications under the control of its members which are conditions for doing

the work; public confidence in the qualifications and in the standards of ethics of the profession; some form of discipline controlled by the profession, and some freedom from the ordinary norms of dealings between master and man, so that a professional person by title of his profession, not merely through his own personal standing and authority, has a right and a duty greater than that of an ordinary citizen to refuse the orders of the person who pays him with an appeal to the protection of his professional colleagues. This does not mean that any individual person who is a member of a profession is necessarily more courageous or necessarily sets himself higher standards than a person who is not; but he has collectivised his status in these respects and one can take it for granted that he is likely to be more dependable, other things being equal. This is naturally a valuable status to have, and the first step towards it is to make qualification as arduous as possible to carry conviction with the public and public authorities. Many thousands of white-collar workers have laboured over the years to attain professional standards, and the Industrial Relations Act now tempts them to consider equating their professional body with their appropriate collective bargaining agency.

At present people of many qualifications or none may become managers, sub-managers or other senior employees. In general, our culture will have encouraged them to exclusiveness. They are likely to have been selected for exclusive schools, or exclusive streams in schools, and to have had the notion of the old-school tie emphasised at an impressionable age. If they have attended a university or college afterwards, their expectations in after life are bound to be based on historical experience rather than practical probabilities. A university degree thirty years ago was rare enough in this country to make the appropriate level of employment afterwards fairly high. When graduates become thicker on the ground, the expectations tend to be maintained but not the opportunities. A working party of the Confederation of British Industry has at last recognised the lesson – that when the general level of education rises in this way, the general level of employment ought to rise as well to provide a reasonable opportunity for a highly educated person lower down the ladder of status. In reason, we ought to be seeing many more graduate supervisors as well as junior managers; the normal objection is that one cannot very well supervise people doing work that one knows nothing about, but to bring in graduates at a higher level then, surely has the double disadvantage that the fledgling manager may not know anything about supervising either. Besides, although the selectivity of an education system based on intelligence is no doubt gradually having its effects, there are still many managers who have worked their way up from the shop floor, redeeming an unlucky or uncertain start in life by 'drive' and ambition. There are plenty of ambitious men in the trade union movement, but their ambitions tend to be different from those of managers, and white-collar or managerial ambition is another significant point to consider.

If a white-collar worker sees his career developing satisfactorily he is likely to see it in terms of status, by one of two standards. Either he acquires command and control, and power of decision over other people; or he acquires autonomy and satisfaction in his special work and power of decision over his own time and projects. The first approach is 'managerial', the second 'professional and technical'. The diffusion of literacy and the multiplication of complex organisations makes the prospect of 'running your own show' in this way less likely; it makes less likely even the prospect of a major share in running the show. A foreman in a small plant may be the owner's right-hand man – more important in the total organisation than someone with years of experience and a string of significant letters after his name in an international company. We could not run large organisations at all if there were not an adequate supply of people prepared to live the kind of life required to get to the top and fulfil the functions required there. But only a few people get to the top, and those who do not are increasingly insecure if the people who do make a mess of their work. Every takeover means insecurity for someone. Generally speaking, mergers become acceptable to their employees only when they have achieved their objectives, and during the past few years they have seldom managed to achieve them without many dismissals, transfers or other measures which are unsettling in themselves. Disturbed expectations, disappointed ambition and loss of identity with a big enterprise as it gets bigger may be less calamitous than they seem, but they are bound to make employees think seriously about collective ways to ensure their security and a voice in their affairs more substantial than mere 'staff status'. Disturbance of habitual thinking is very important: the evidence suggests, for example, that interest among managers in joining unions is much stronger in British Leyland, the product of many mergers, than in Ford and Vauxhall, which have developed from a single stem although they are foreign-owned.

'Double Threat' of Management Unions

One curious result of the traditional ambition of the white-collar class makes the task of a lay trade unionist difficult. A manager faced with active shop stewards from the shop floor may feel exasperated, the victim of natural wickedness, or hounded by subversive conspirators; he may feel that the situation threatens his own future, as indeed it often may. But although some of the stewards may be comparatively powerful personalities and even more intelligent than he is, he will not see them as direct rivals. If he finds himself in dispute with a really obdurate negotiator or interceder for other managers on a level almost as high as his own, the situation is different. A trade unionist with the ordinary impulses of shop steward at a managerial level is unfamiliar enough to seem like a rival for authority. The concept of trade union organisation for managers is a profound threat to the assumptions of courtiership on which, as we have seen, private management still mostly operates. It also appears to threaten confidentiality. In general, experience suggests that managers underestimate the amount of substantial information available to intelligent leaders of rank-and-file workers, and overestimate the amount which is known exclusively to other managers. In any event, it is more the fear of personal challenge with collective backing than any actual experience of it that lies behind all the statements against collective bargaining for managers. On the face of it, the danger seems fairly remote. A managers' shop steward who uses his office for blatant self-seeking is as likely to be caught at it and flung out as a shop steward for any other group. Besides, there are other approved and successful ways of self-seeking and nobody with the traditional simple ambition would be likely to prefer the painful liberty of speaking for his colleagues. Still, in a different way it is a threat to a superior if it challenges habitual autocratic ways of doing things.

To conclude this chapter we might think about this statement of principle, which is undoubtedly commonly accepted:

> The status of management is the determining factor in business; for managers are not only the owners' representa-

tives in business, and sit in the boss's office, but even shareholders call them the bosses. . . .

Managers are rightly called called bosses, because they exercise something of the owners' function; if you consider the owner's prerogative, you may see how it is expressed in a manager. The owner has the power to recruit and dismiss, to promote or transfer at his pleasure, to give employment and unemployment, to assess the performance of his employees without being assessed himself or accountable to anyone for his business, to set new priorities and overturn existing ones as he wishes; the owner is entitled to both innovative and faithful service. And managers have the same power; they recruit and dismiss their subordinates, they have power of promotion and transfer, of employment and unemployment; they assess all their subordinates in all respects and are accountable only to the shareholders.

In language slightly adjusted for the circumstances and the jargon of modern enterprise, that is what James I told Parliament about the Divine Right of Kings. What his Majesty actually said was:

The state of monarchy is the supremest thing upon earth; for kings are not only God's lieutenants upon earth, and sit upon God's throne, but even by God himself they are called gods. . . .

Kings are justly called gods, for that they exercise a manner of resemblance of divine power upon earth; for if you will consider the attributes to God, you shall see how they agree in the person of a king. God hath power to create or destroy, to make or unmake at his pleasure, to give life or send death, to judge all and to be judged nor accountable to none, to raise low things and to make high things low at his pleasure, and to God are both soul and body due. And the like power have kings: they make and unmake their subjects, they have power of raising and casting down, of life and death, judges over all their subjects and in all causes and yet accountable to none but God only.

Modern capitalism is frequently traced to the puritans who cut off King James's son's head for pushing divine right too far. History has its little ironies. The language and concepts of the seventeenth-century do not survive only in Northern Ireland;

happily, commerce is slowly shaking off the autocratic assumptions of an earlier day. Some trade union leaders, who are not the best of employers, need to move as far as most managers in respect of their own subordinates.

Chapter 6
Birds of a Feather

The fittest survive in any case; but fitness is not goodness. It may be, but it may be badness. Fitness is only the capacity to fit – fit the environment. The society in which it is fittest to be best is safe; that society in which it is equally fit to be good, bad, or indifferent is doomed; that society in which it is fittest to be worst is already damned.
Caleb Saleeby

Industrial Unions in Other Countries
Once a trade union has become an institution, capable of surviving all its individual members, its future is limited only by the imagination of its leaders and the tolerance of outsiders who have to put up with it. Trade union development in Britain has been wayward and untidy. We sometimes envy the Germans, with their neat system of industrial unions (although it must be said that there are astonishing disparities in size and density among them, and the German conception of 'metalworker' is as vast and cloudy as the British conception of 'engineering'. As we saw in an earlier chapter, the rationalising of German trade union structure owed a lot to the British and American occupation authorities. At the end of the Second World War, new, 'organic', little unions were springing up all over West Germany, fragmented, separate and with the various confessional or ideological differences that had existed before the Nazi takeover. With the benign co-operation of the occupation authorities, who brought in advisers from the British and American movements, surviving German labour leaders managed to set up a rationalised structure from out of the chaos that Hitler left behind.

Equally, we sometimes envy the Swedes their highly mature system of industrial unions, dating back sixty years, and the solidity of organisation on both sides of industry (although this has led in times of trouble to a stand-off position between the two sides, with employers ready to lock out and impose discipline in a way that British employers have never been in a position to do; and Swedes sometimes become uneasy about the intense stratification of their society). We also sometimes envy the Americans their neat systems of bargaining units, and the arrangement within the AFL/CIO which excludes member unions from a plant where another member union has existing rights (although it must be said that American unionism covers a comparatively small part of the economy and that the departure of the two richest unions, the Teamsters and the Auto Workers, from the AFL/CIO has taken some of the firmness out of the arrangement; besides, the colossal trials of strength and the willingness of employers in certain circumstances to inflict mortal wounds on unions if they can appear unseemly on this side of the Atlantic). But all systems have two defects. The first is that the development of workers' organisations and employing institutions are always bound to be a little out of step, at least so long as the criterion for the employer is simply the profit in a new venture or acquisition – or even, which is to put it a different way, the 'productive efficiency' in a change. The second is that it is difficult to define an industry and once one has defined it the industry may very well be in decline, either in overall size or as an employer of labour or both. There has never been a political agreement underlying the organisation of labour in this country, as there was in the United States with the 'New Deal' culminating with the Wagner Act in 1935 or in Germany after the war, epitomised by the Works Councils Act in 1952. Until 1971, union growth in Britain was comparatively capricious and unregulated. This certainly brought flexibility, but it brought anomaly as well. Perhaps a situation so anomalous, in which the process of voluntary improvement through inter-union co-operation and the slow, ruminative processes of the TUC seemed always to be falling behind a world of hasty change and inordinate expectation, was bound to produce some unusually weird gesture of impatience. The Industrial Relations Act is the most elaborate single piece of legislation that any country has ever constructed in this field; the nearest counterpart is probably the Swedish legislation of 1928 in a small country not half way to the complexity of Britain in 1971. As Professor Bill Gould, Professor of Law at Stanford, comments:

The Industrial Relations Act of 1971 . . . is more comprehensive than all of the major labour legislation enacted by Congress in 1935, 1947 and 1959 viewed together. . . . Thus, from an almost exclusive reliance on 'voluntarism', i.e. the promotion of negotiating procedures drawing at most indirectly upon law, Great Britain has now imposed upon the conduct of unions and employers more formal and far-reaching regulations than those characterising the US system, a system which British experts traditionally regarded as excessively law-ridden.

It is fair to say that nothing moved politicians and other men in power more towards legislation than the untidiness of most British labour organisation and its assumed consequences of anarchy, inter-union rivalry, and 'leap-frog' bargaining in which one group of workers played off another's successes to the employer's detriment.

Specialists v. Conglomerates
As we have seen, the two big general unions each operate in more than 100 industries. The big craft-and-general unions, the Engineers and Electricians, have mass memberships in some factories and select memberships of craftsmen across the board. Only in mining, where the famous dual membership agreement allows the NUM to negotiate for engineers and electricians, but preserves their AUEW and EETU membership if they leave the industry, has this been avoided. USDAW, which is the Co-operative Movement's general union as well as a shopworkers' union, has been drawn into unlikely areas of organisation like chemicals, soapmaking and textiles in the wake of the enterprise of the CWS and Scottish CWS. There are dockers in the NUR because the railways own some docks (and there was even a movement at one stage among other dockers to ask that only goods carried by rail should be handled at these ports). Some industries have managed to amalgamate most craft workers (like the Boilermakers' Amalgamation of the 'black trades' in shipbuilding) without taking along the general workers. In others, like printing and textiles, craft and general workers have come together in separate unions. Yet in others, like building and engineering, union membership has developed in a hotchpotch of dissonant, diverse and frequently competing unions. Little unions may survive because they are strategically placed or undecided between two major suitors. Traditional rivalry may be as power-

ful a repellent as common interest is an attraction, and there have been some mergers which have made a demarcation frontier if anything more formidable because it is a frontier between two large groups instead of two little ones.

To put the American example in perspective we must remember that the TUC has done a great deal in Britain to take the heat out of demarcation disputes. The first method the TUC uses is to refuse membership to a group which competes with a union already in membership, just as the TUC threw out the NASD for breach of Bridlington and has refused to readmit it. For similar reasons during the last twenty years the TUC has refused admission to the Scottish TGWU, the London Schoolkeepers' Association, the National Union of Club Stewards, the Television Engineers, the Association of Broadcasting Staffs (in 1959, but admitted in 1963), the Water Works Employees (in 1947 and 1962, but admitted in 1964 after amalgamation talks failed), the National Union of Labour Organisers, the North East Tugboatmen, and the National Association of Licensed House Managers. There are other bodies like the Telecommunications Staff Association which do not bother to apply for an inevitable rejection. The TUC judgments under the Bridlington procedure are also normally respected, and both this procedure and the more recent experiment in industry committees have helped to reduce the number of demarcation and interunion disputes enormously. However, there is no TUC procedure which can deal with the other alleged feature of multi-unionism — wage drift, 'leap-frogging' and not merely the completion but the distortions of bargaining at plant level. Wage drift is the proportion by which actual earnings exceed formally negotiated rates over a period. It is particularly difficult to prevent where there are many different sets of piecework earnings among members of different unions. There were 180 different rates in Harland and Wolff's before the Boilermakers' amalgamation with the Blacksmiths and Shipwrights, and it was not until after the amalgamation that the structure could be rationalised. However, anomalies almost as gross are possible in single-union enterprises as well, and inter-union competition is sometimes blamed for faults which it did not create; although it does make correction more of a problem.

Printing and Building
We have seen already how some great industrial unions have

been dragged into a decline because their choice of industry was too narrow for long-term expansion: coal (and not energy); railways (and not transport). In others there has been a rapid concentration where union membership rather than the labour force has been contracting, as in building. In printing, on the other hand, union membership has increased with concentration while the labour force has been getting smaller. Printing has also witnessed the biggest failure of a union merger of recent years – the split in SOGAT – and successfully avoided competition among its workers by any of the conglomerate unions. But with sharp divisions surviving not only among but within member unions, printing is still a long way from harmony and such attempts as there have been at an agency arrangement for engineers, electricians and other maintenance workers have been heartily snubbed. Still, development in 'the print' has been particularly active, as these figures from TUC reports show:

1951: 14 TUC printing unions with 273,785 members.
1961: 13 TUC printing unions with 339,105 members.
1971: 7 TUC printing unions with 403,199 members.
(The figures include paperworkers and printers of packaging and similar products whose occupation has expanded while general printing has declined.)
1954: Printing Machine Managers (5,000 members) merged with the London Society of Compositors (13,500) as the London Typographical Society.
1962: Monotype Casters (900) merged with the Printing, Bookbinding and Paper Workers (160,000).
1963: LTS and Typographical Association (58,000) merged as NGA.
1964: Association of Correctors of the Press (1,500) and Press Telegraphists (1,500) transferred engagements to the NGA.
1965: National Society of Operative Printers and Assistants (48,000) and NUPBPW merged as SOGAT.
1967: Electro and Stereotypers (5,000) merged with the NGA.
1968: Lithographic Printers (10,000) merged with the NGA.
1971: SOGAT unmerged.

The seven unions, with their present membership and 1951 membership compared, are:
NUPBPW (SOGAT Div. A) 192,920 (123,716)

NGA	107,360	(81,631)*
NATSOPA	50,981	(35,278)
NUJ	24,503	(11,684)
SLADE	16,519	(10,823)
STA	6,906	(7,271)
Wall Paper Workers	4,010	(2,500)

These unions are diverse: NGA is a union of craft workers with some white-collar membership; the NUPBPW is predominantly a process workers' union with some craft and a few white-collar members; NATSOPA is a mixture of process workers, ancillary workers and white-collar staff. SLADE is a craft union, and the NUJ a general occupational union including publicists as well as journalists. The STA is the Scottish equivalent of the old London Society which has survived a number of flirtations. In some other countries, notably the United States, journalists are members of a general industrial union; in no country is the density of membership as high as in Britain at about 90 per cent. Both the NUJ and SLADE are somewhat apart from the other unions – the NUJ because of journalists' 'professional' aspirations, SLADE partly as a result of a single-handed strike a few years ago in which no other union supported it. The ultimate shape of trade unionism in paper and print is consequently uncertain; but it seems likely at least to escape conglomeration.

Construction, equally active in merger during the period, is comparatively a disaster. Building is a difficult industry in which to organise tight unions. Work is vagrant and discontinuous on large sites for large contractors, or steady but in small units for average local employers. The link between national and site level has always been uncertain. Years of full employment made it more uncertain still. The benefits of being in a union became less obvious than they were in the hard times before the war. Readily available work and high taxation made labour-only sub-contracting (where a man takes a lump sum to complete a specific job instead of working by the hour) increasingly attractive and frequently abused. Even the norms of enlightened employment policies may prove inappropriate in building, where the pattern of high earnings while a worker is young and strong, and easing off later, is still well established. Wates Brothers, who had the highest proportion of 'staff' workers, on the permanent payroll, of any British contractors, discovered that they also

* 1951 total membership of constituent unions.

had by far the highest average age of any major contractor and that it was beginning to affect their competitiveness. Finally, the big general unions were already well entrenched among builders' labourers: notably the TGWU, which had also recruited the majority of steel benders and fixers and all the organised bricklayers into its building trade group, which is almost as big as the combined ASW/AUBTW. The equivalent figures for construction are:

1951: 19 TUC unions with 599,011 members
1961: 18 TUC unions with 535,868 members
1971: 6 TUC unions with 375,628 members

These six unions probably represent a minority of TUC affiliated trade unionists engaged in construction; occupations not represented or barely represented include constructional engineers (AUEW), plumbing and electrical workers (EETU/PTU), heating engineers (merged with the sheet metal workers), steel benders and fixers, bricklayers and plasterers (mostly TGWU), gas fitters (NUGMW), and many labourers (TGWU, NUGMW, NUPE in particular).

1952: Builders' Labourers (11,000) merged with AUBTW (81,000).
1962: Scottish Painters (12,000) merged with Painters and Decorators (64,000).
1964: Packing Case Makers (4,000) merged with ASW (190,000).
1966: Street Masons (1,300) transferred engagements to AUBTW HDV (20,000) merged with SMW (50,000).
1967: PTU (55,000) merged with ETU (320,000) as EETU/PTU. Plasterers (11,000) transferred engagements to TGWU.
1968: Slaters and Tilers (2,000) transferred engagements to AUBTW. French Polishers (1,400) transferred engagements to Furniture Trade Operatives (60,000).
1969: Painters and Decorators and Building Technicians (2,000) transferred engagements to ASW.
Midland Glass Bevellers (400) transferred engagements to FTO.
1970: Sailmakers (165) transferred engagements to ASW.
1971: FTO and Wood-cutting Machinists (23,500) merged as FTAT. ASW and AUBTW merged as UCATT.

The six industrial unions, with 1971 and 1951 reported memberships, are:

UCATT	281,992 (388,987)*
FTAT	83,854 (106,881)*
Sign and Display	3,919 (2,528)
Asphalt Workers	2,924 (2,500)
Coopers	1,866 (3,623)
Basket Cane and Wicker	48 (510)

The different fortunes of the specialised unions in these industries are partly, of course, the result of the different character of the industries as well as the different institutions which their workers have set up. There are some other industries which arrived too late in the development of British unionism to have any serious prospect of developing industrial unions as such. Here the contrast between the American and British experience of the motor industry is instructive. When mass production of motor cars and components began in the United States, trade unionism for process workers was still a fledgling, bitterly resisted to the point of violence by employers. (It is still a regular feature of industrial life in the United States for large and respectable employers to use organised strike breakers in particularly rancorous disputes, and I remember being surprised to hear of Union Carbide some four years ago using helicopters to bring in gangs of 'blacklegs' at a plant in New York State; I was even more surprised to discover that a neighbour of mine who was a manager in the same division of the same company did not know about the incident.) The founders of the United Auto Workers were used to employing lawyers in suits and countersuits for assault, trespass and intimidation before the Wagner Act in 1935 made it possible at last to develop massive recognition across the board. The Second World War, with various emergency measures to keep production going, served to strengthen the hold of the union just as two world wars assisted British unions to recognition in different contexts.†

* 1951 total membership of constituent unions.

† Most managers expected to revert to pre-war 'normality' once the exigencies of battle were past. The story goes that the President of Ford summoned a senior UAW official to 'see what was happening' in the Dearborn plant, as part of a union election campaign. He pointed to three men, one with a bucket, one with a roll of posters, the third with a brush, sticking up the posters in the plant during production time. Wasn't this a scandalous example to set when the industry was shaking itself out of war conditions? The UAW man said that he could see that there was something badly wrong. He went up to the men and said: 'See here, how can you expect management to put up with this kind of thing? For God's sake stick these posters on straight.'

The CIO and later AFL/CIO agreements buttressed exclusive recognition, and by the end of the 1940s the UAW was effectively labour contractor for the whole American motor industry.

An Interest in Motors
In Britain, by contrast, general unionism was well established when motor manufacture was still virtually a cottage industry. On the car production lines the NUVB, the old coachworkers' union, the AEU and the TGWU competed with roughly equal success for assembly workers. Craft workers were included among the Engineers, the Foundry workers, the Sheet Metal Workers and the still independent Birmingham and Midland Sheet Metal Workers, the Electricians, the Patternmakers and several others. Some components factories were largely organised below skilled level by the NUGMW. As a result the large surviving car companies – one British-owned, British Leyland, and the three American-owned each has more than a dozen unions to negotiate with. For British Leyland in particular the problem is complicated by the rapid and anxious merger of companies, mostly in critical circumstances, with different traditions of management, conflicting payments systems and the inevitable disturbance of expectations which a major merger brings. This has been particularly exasperating for managers with experience of single-union operations in the United States and in Germany (the Metalworkers). In fact the motor industry is merely the most acute case of the mature but complicated trade unionism of all engineering. The motor industry is also highly organised in its production systems, highly paid, and unusually responsive to boom and slump. We have just seen again how a Government decision to ease credit restrictions has more immediate effect on the demand for new cars than on the demand for almost anything else: the demand for houses is less sensitive to marginal changes, since borrowing to buy a house is usually over a long term; the demand for other consumer durables like domestic equipment is less discouraged by credit restrictions because the amounts to be borrowed are so much smaller.

At the level of statesmanship, the problems of the engineering industry have been the hinge for merger proposals of the largest possible scale. The NUGMW has proposed a qualified form of merger of itself, the AUEW and the TGWU. No one rules even this out, but the three institutions are so different in structure that at least two and probably all of them would have to make great changes. The TGWU, proud of its industrial groups, considers that the necessary change would be in the other unions towards its pattern. The NUGMW is still organised as a general workers' union, making no membership distinctions and organised on a geographical basis, although it offered a special chemical section in its abortive negotiations with the CWU and has a cutlery branch based on the National Cutlery Union which it absorbed 15 years ago. The regular failure of more ambitious merger projects has started the union on a review of its structure with the objective of making it more attractive and flexible. Apart from picking up tiddlers from time to time, the AEU's Jeffersonian structure based on the district and very thinly officered – each official has an average of 6,000 members in his charge – has also prevented organic merger. The institutional life of the AEU sets its mark on a man, and it would be difficult to muster a majority of its officials in favour of reform, let alone a majority of its active members; and as we have seen already 14 per cent is a 'high poll' in a vote for General President in which political passions run strongly. But the AEU has been able to turn itself into the AUEW in successive mergers with the Foundryworkers, Constructional Engineers and DATA which made them into autonomous divisions with their own systems preserved up to national level.

Since the leadership of both the TGWU and the AUEW is at the moment left wing and the leadership of the NUGMW remains right of centre, a grand marriage is a remote possibility, and a union between the TGWU and the AUEW by themselves is only a little less unlikely. On the other hand, the TGWU has recently come into the merger business in a rush. Its biggest coup is merger with the NUVB after a decade of uncertainty. The NUVB merged with the automotive group of the TGWU and NUVB officers took over the leadership of existing TGWU members: a more attractive proposition in the end than the AUEW could offer. Instead of being split into three roughly equal union groups, assembly workers in the motor industry are now in two groups with the TGWU having about twice the membership of the AUEW. There is no certainty that this will make any particular improvement to industrial relations in the industry. The difference between one and two unions is much the same as the difference between one and three, and if two big fellows fall out they will make a more stubborn disagreement of it. The TGWU has also picked up the CWU, as we have seen – chemicals being another industry much younger than trade unionism and with USDAW active there as well as the two big general unions.

In its own special field of transport the TGWU has also won back the Scottish TGWU and merged with the Scottish Commercial Motormen and the Lightermen and Tugmen. It had also been making confident approaches to the National Union of Seamen, still recovering from the 1966 strike, still ideologically divided in its counsels, and dependent on tightly controlled closed shops to organise its members at all. The NUS for this reason defied the TUC ban on registering under the Industrial Relations Act and was duly suspended for applying for the 'approved closed shop' which the Act allows. Now it faces the possibility that more militant members might work up enough opposition to break or disrupt the closed shops, which are subject to challenge by ballot if enough members call for one. This has already happened to the Wall Paper Workers, a very small union which decided to remain registered and concluded agency shop agreements (requiring those who did not join the union in a designated employment to pay contributions instead). One member left the WPWU and joined the TGWU, and within a few months had put together the signatures of the 20 per cent of workers required to challenge the agency shop.

Laws about Union Mergers
Since the 1876 Act which made it necessary for a union merger to have the support of two-thirds of the members of each, there have been two Acts to make it easier. The first, in 1917, set off the great mergers of the 1920s, which were then followed by a long lull broken significantly only by the formation of the National Union of Dyers, Bleachers and Textile Workers, with 56,000 members still the largest clothmakers' union, in 1933; USDAW in 1947; and the conversion of the Miners' Federation into the notionally unitary but still largely federal NUM in 1944. In a sense the history of the NUM in the quarter of a century since has been the gradual consolidation of unity on a national level in a sequence of boom and decline in the coal industry, the reduction of membership by more than half, and the establishment of nationally uniform payments structures and ways of doing things. The national miners' strike at the beginning of 1972 which we shall look at later, was a very different matter from the national miners' strike of 1926, which began with a

lock-out and required the marshalling of several autonomous county federations in support of one of them; the 1972 confrontation although made possible by a conjunction of different regional motives was genuinely unitary in demanding better pay. The 1917 Act still required a two-thirds majority of those voting, and in spite of a TUC General Council policy favouring amalgamation, progress was slow until the second Trade Union (Amalgamations) Act in 1964. But just as the merger policy of Tom Mann and the notable merger which formed the NUR before the First World War were harbingers of the new wave of mergers which the 1917 Act made possible, so a significant number of important mergers arrived just before the 1964 Act.

Among them were the Boilermakers' amalgamation, the establishment of the NGA and the merger of the Scottish Painters with the major partner in London. Under the 1964 Act a simple majority of those voting in a small union is enough for transfer of engagements to (that is, incorporation in) a larger union; for a merger a simple majority of those voting in the merging unions is required. The vote is probably the simplest part of the proceedings. Marrying the rules of two separate institutions, making room for officials, taking account of special interests, merging property and even deciding on a title may require protracted negotiation. A change in the leadership of a union may either put paid to a promising negotiation or turn an outside chance into a moderately likely runner. The death at the end of 1970 of Sir Leslie Cannon dislodged some of the more obvious negatives about future mergers by the Electricians, for example: approaches by ASTMS, the AUEW and other unions with left-wing leadership ceased to be improbable. A common difficulty may eventually wear away the kind of intimate mistrust that is all too common among organisations of workers with different status in the same industry. It is a melancholy fact that it has taken either insecurity of employment or disquieting interest by a large general union to bring the little fellows in an industry together. The Dyers and Bleachers' amalgamation with the Textile Workers was the result of a virtual collapse of negotiations in the Yorkshire woollen industry after the hundred-odd little unions had lost control of their affairs and had no one to give them a lead in the miserable early years of the depression.

Splinter Unions

In the clothing industry, union membership is now almost wholly concentrated in three middle-sized unions – the Tailors and Garment Workers (117,573), Footwear, Leather and Allied Trades (78,630) and National Union of Hosiery and Knitwear Workers (64,407). There are other occupations where one or two stubborn splinter unions of significant size hold out against the major organisation – ASLEF has been holding out against the NUR for more than 60 years, although many engine drivers are members of the NUR already. The NAS (57,000 members) has been competing with the NUT (310,000) for a generation, although more schoolmasters are members of the NUT, because members of the NAS believe that the NUT is subject to the monstrous regiment of young women and consequently cannot negotiate properly for the career structure which will keep good family men happily in teaching. Teachers in technical institutions have their own union, which is affiliated to the TUC, and university teachers have theirs, which is not. COHSE, with some 90,000 members, has repeatedly turned down overtures from NUPE, more than four times the size; and their division is now deepened by the fact that COHSE is registered and suspended, while NUPE is not. NUBE, another registered and suspended union which is likely to have more to do with ASTMS as ASTMS starts organising in the City of London, turned down an ASTMS merger proposal with something like outrage. The Post Office Corporation has dealings at various levels with half a dozen unions – not counting the TSA.

As we have seen, the nature of work in an industry has an important effect on the form its trade unions take, and so has its ownership and control. But all trade unions have something in common, if only the quality observed by Professor Hugh Clegg of being an Opposition which can never be a Government. The notion of a grand, all-embracing national union has been in the back of many workers' minds since long before the short-lived experiment under Robert Owen in the second quarter of the nineteenth century. Separate unions also come under a cloud at times of stress because they seem to enshrine (and in a real sense do enshrine) particular interests rather than the general good. However, the reasons put forward for this criticism are variable and often conflicting. The purest absurdity is the assertion that trade union power prevents the operation of a free market in the public interest, and that trade unions, being accountable to no one but their members, become vehicles for pandering to their members' greed and desire to do ever less work for greater reward. A moment's examination will show that these objectives are not evil in themselves, being precisely parallel to those of managers. Managers' function is, or ought to be, bringing together resources for valuable purposes which will earn their enterprises a suitable reward, and as good an index of managerial efficiency as any is putting together these resources – materials, money and workers' talents – as effectively as possible, which means generating the greatest additional value for the least possible effort. Between the two interests of managers and those they manage has developed collective bargaining. Like American politics, collective bargaining is an expensive and time-consuming process. For the great mass of people who think in terms of two, it polarises matters which might be better left diffuse. It is under strong challenge.

The worst effect of collective bargaining is that it allows people to concentrate on things which are essentially divisive. It has not in fact significantly increased the workers' share in the profits of industry and commerce. Most of the major changes in the distribution of national wealth have come through political initiatives. There seems to be a tacit range of apportioning wealth between workers and proprietors, at least above a certain size of organisation, which collective bargaining does not change. Even the 'pecking order' of pay among industries is remarkably stable and changes only with technological revolution; it is resented even then. And the same holds good within unions. We have seen some examples of resentments and 'pecking orders' within large unions. We also find that the general unions have achieved very little by way of raising the comparative level of low-paid workers, although they talk about the objective more than any other unions. There is simply not the solidarity in a conglomerate to produce the necessary overall policy for collective bargaining. Like all busy men in charge of large organisations, trade union conglomerate leaders must take problems singly, winning a bargain here and losing one there. The density and willingness to fight of their membership varies from one area and industry to another. For every tightly organised plant there is one which is slack and probably more than one which is not organised at all.

What Does 'Collective Bargaining' Achieve? – The Miners' Strike

We therefore have the odd paradox in Britain that although collective bargaining affects about three-quarters of all wages and salaries, it is often impossible to determine precisely how. There are wage agreements which consist of an individual bargain first, and a retrospective calculation of how it is related to a collective bargain (this sort of thing is particularly common for small companies, or companies faced with a passing scarcity of qualified workers, which operate within broad national agreements like construction and engineering). In this context the power of large organisations is unequally applied, and in extreme situations like construction dribbles away without much application at all. With the severing of dealings between the Engineering Employers' Federation and the Confederation of Shipbuilding and Engineering Unions at the beginning of 1972, this process began to show itself. The unions set their sights on large, 'pace-making' settlements with large employers, and coherent local employers' associations tried to respond with a united front: it took a lock-out policy to establish national collective bargaining on a businesslike basis in the first place. There is no evidence that profitable settlements with large employers do 'set the pace' for small ones as this union policy implies. At best, the union leaders expect to do it over time. The fact remains that they never have done it, and that the 'going rate' for a class of worker in a particular area is at best an accepted rough estimate and at worst a mere fiction. It is a fair guess that if Britain does achieve an accepted national minimum wage which gradually moves proportionately higher, it will be a statutory figure and the list of permitted exemptions and ingenious evasions will tend to grow, as they have done in the United States.

It is easy to overestimate the power and resources of a large trade union. The TGWU is the biggest, with well over £20m. in funds and a million and three-quarters' membership. A simple calculation shows that the resources are in fact quite trivial – a few pounds for each member. They would be enough to establish a large manufacturing plant – employing, say, 5,000 workers – but not enough to cover 'start-up costs' by way of wages and training for the normal period that is required for a new plant to turn a profit. Some people call conglomerate trade unions 'paper tigers', but they are not tigers at all. They are more like very large ruminants which may flatten a bit of herbage here and there merely by stepping on it. Perhaps the supreme illustration of this came in the 1972 miners' strike, which will probably prove in the long run to have done more for low-paid workers in general than any action by general unions.

The initiative was clearly within the coal industry itself. Union leaders, notably Will Paynter, the general secretary, had concluded a series of settlements with the National Coal Board which tended to narrow differentials and eventually eliminated piece rates at the coal face. They could do this partly because there is a common cycle in a mineworker's life which finds work for exhausted faceworkers elsewhere in the mine or on the surface. Not all surface workers are former colliers, but the cycle is common enough to produce a link between them. At the same time, surface rates in mining tend to have some connection with pay for general labouring jobs in the area. At the end of 1971, the basic rate for surface work in mining was £18 a week, compared with £16·20 in agriculture. At the end of the strike, the mines rate had moved to £23, and the farm workers had something higher to aim at.

The day wage settlement in mining meant that some faceworkers in the Midlands lost an appreciable amount of weekly earnings. In the less profitable areas like South Wales and Scotland they moved up. The process was accompanied by the final stages of a massive reduction in the number of pits and the number of miners. Ironically enough, miners in the Midlands with a lot of manufacturing in the area saw their wages overtaken by those of factory workers, sometimes even by those of their wives. In remoter communities of miners' rows and miserable amenities, the miners remained at the top, or near the top, of the local earnings league but had nothing much to spend their extra earnings on. The effect of the strike in areas like this was a few holidays foregone, an accumulation of debts to local shops (which could hardly refuse credit and hope to stay in business), and less money for basic pleasures like betting and beer. In the Midlands, where miners had long lived and worked in an affluent society, there was no majority for strike action; but hurt pride and a sense of detachment from the great, new impersonal machines put the men solidly behind the strike once it began. Miners have a history of long strikes. Before the First World War some local strikes lasted a year or more. When the national strike in 1926 collapsed quickly, the Yorkshire miners, locked out by their employers in the original dispute which precipitated the crisis, carried on for six months. Although under nationalisation the disease of local unofficial wrangles about pay systems had eventually been arrested, the distinctive solidarity of the miners asserted itself again. Nationally, the miners demanded pride of place again in a 'national earnings league' in which they had slipped. They got it, whatever the future effects on their numbers and the size of the industry.

Their first strong card was the genuine feeling of being an industrial union (demonstrated on settlement day by their insistence on complementary pay increases for clerical workers, although they had not joined the strike). Other TUC unions, whose leaders tended to feel that the miners' action in defying a Government policy of wage restraint was unwise and unlikely to succeed, especially since the miners had no strike fund, did no more than tell their members not to cross picket lines. That day, the first day of the strike, the NUM leaders were notably depressed. In the areas some prominent leaders (who threw their hats in the air later when the strike succeeded) were full of doubt and foreboding. After all, a national miners' strike was unprecedented in anyone's working life. It was only when the NUM executive considered the full implications of picketing that they hit on a novel policy – to behave as if they were not only an industrial union for coal, but an industrial union for fuel generally. The extent of their picketing, which had never been matched in Britain before, took the Government, the Coal Board, the electricity industry and almost everyone else by surprise. Whether or not it was legal in the strict sense – does 'furtherance of a trade dispute' in mining justify action to immobilise coal that the industry had already sold, let alone oil and ancillary supplies for power stations? – it was effective. There has never been successful power bargaining in Britain to match it. Perhaps there never will be again. It took 46 years to work the miners up to such a pitch. There may not be any other group of workers in Britain who could organise themselves so effectively, and there is probably no other group of workers who would be allowed so much public tolerance in doing it. The miners' pickets would not have been effective if other trade unionists had not co-operated, or if a large enough proportion of British people generally had been prepared to resist them.

Limits of Authoritarian Government

The strike clearly showed the limits of authoritarian Government policy on wages. Since the end of 1970 the Government had been trying to keep wage settlements down without statutory controls. They relied instead on private exhortation to employers, pressure on employers in public service or publicly owned, and calculation of a steadily declining 'going rate' of settlements which was put about in conversation, implied with qualifications in Parliamentary answers, and in general settled in the minds of union leaders asking for money and managers doling it out. The paradox of collective bargaining has seldom been more apparent.

There seems to be no question that an industrial union worked up to a real sense of grievance in an industry with a clear pattern of payments has a decisive advantage if it feels strongly enough. Yet the difficulty of defining an 'industry' remains; it is a matter of assumptions. Sir Stanley Brown, chairman of the Central Electricity Generating Board, complained bitterly that by picketing power stations the miners had broken the rules. The electricity industry and the coal industry are constantly at odds because they are equal partners under the same ownership, with different commercial preoccupations. When the strike began, the electricity industry took more than half total coal output, and this was three-quarters of the electricity industry's fuel supply. Yet in a real sense they shared the energy industry with gas (also publicly owned), oil (privately owned), and atomic energy (an equivocal and controversial hybrid).

Short of a grand merger of several of the biggest organisations in the labour movement, there is no prospect of an energy industry union. Transport, as we have seen, is equally fragmented. The prospect of all these different institutions – unions, managements, work groups, industries – overlapping, competing, and often spending as much time on political lobbying of one kind or another as on 'free collective bargaining' has produced two schools of thought in sharp disagreement. On the one hand is the 'pluralist society' approach typified by the Donovan Commission and the distinguished academics who did its research. The Industrial Relations Act attempts to apply to this concept a number of notions about 'holding the ring' and letting the contestants get on with the tussle according to its Queensberry Rules. On the other hand is the 'orderly arrangement' school (which also makes wistful, wraithlike appearance in the Act), attracted by the idea of co-determination typified in German works councils and worker directors, and other European approaches to 'joint accountability' as in the Netherlands, where workers have the right to propose and veto candidates for the supervisory boards of companies. There is ample evidence to show that no man and by extension no work group is governed solely by 'them and us' approaches, and that the resolution of conflict of objectives does not normally require overt strife; there may always be other ways of sharing the power of decision. No structure of relations among large numbers of people can remain immobile, because the people themselves are moving all the time. Some researchers claim to see detailed patterns governing these movements – related to time-span of authority, according to Professor Jaques of Brunel University, or to responsibility for decision, according to Professor Paterson of Strathclyde.

Differentials during Commercial Change
Differentials – how much pay one worker or class of worker receives compared with others – always provoke controversy in times of change. One's impression of what is 'fair' is normally a much less fluid concept than the reality in which one lives in an innovative society. There seems to be a natural tendency to look for stable relations among and within occupations, and for various historical reasons Britain did become a comparatively stable industrial society much earlier than others. No other economy has yet reached the point where nine out of ten 'economically active' persons are paid wages or salaries; Britain reached it twenty years ago. One of the things which accompanied and probably reflected this was the development of a stable 'pecking order' among occupations, in which printers, railwaymen, electricians, miners and so on achieved a ranking which altered surprisingly little over many years. So ingrained was it that the Guillebaud Committee on railwaymen's pay in 1960, with the famous phrase that the nation 'having willed the end must will the means' to an efficient railway system, recommended a restoration of railwaymen to a position in the order that they had lost under collective bargaining and the other normal processes of commerce. The Wilberforce recommendations for miners after the strike in 1972 had something of the same thinking in them, and in due course, later in the year, the Government underwrote the coal industry with a large, non-

commercial application of public funds (although one must remember that this was partly to keep upsides with Europe, where the Ruhr coal industry, for example, reached an even greater dependence on public funds by a different route). A table of the stability of differentials was an important part of the evidence of the Ministry of Labour to the Donovan Commission in 1965–8.

Organised labour naturally puts a price on innovation, just as individuals do, whether the workers are air line pilots flying a new jet, railwaymen handling an advanced passenger train, or engineering workers moving away from piece rate to measured day work, or from one kind of machine to another. Technological innovation tends to move at an increasing pace, and at a pace that differs from one occupation to another. This means two things: first, that the training, experience or skills on which large numbers of workers depend for not only their pay but their ranking may rapidly become less relevant to the work required of them; secondly, that what distinguishes them at the place of work from other workers perhaps less trained or less skilled becomes blurred and increasingly hard to justify in traditional terms. At the same time, whole industries may become commercially less viable, either absolutely or comparatively, than they used to be, but their employees will rely on the solidarity built up in times of prosperity to resist simply being sacked in face of commercial pressures. Finally, the situation is complicated by that other technological and social change, the improvement in communications and education which makes people aware of other people's circumstances in a new and contentious way. At the same time, the improvement has not been as complete as it ought to be, and partial information and the singling out of exceptional cases has sometimes inclined workers to look for comparability with the best off in other industries or areas. The work of the National Board for Prices and Incomes as it reached workers at one remove had a disturbing as well as an informing effect; the abrupt abolition of the NBPI at this early stage of development tended to leave the disturbance, perhaps even accentuate it, while cutting off the information.

By the time that this book is printed, no doubt we shall have two boards, one for prices and one for incomes, as the Americans have done since President Nixon adopted British-style policies of restraint in 1971. At about the same time, the

American system will probably begin to come apart under the strain of collective bargaining in its due season in about half a dozen major industries. Meanwhile, as phase one, two, three, and so to infinity of more refined attempts at external control of pay bargaining develop in most industrial countries, the debate continues about getting agreement, about finding an acceptable 'pecking order' that can survive change without disruption, by which workers may move confidently from one occupation to another without worrying about their own security of prejudicing the security of others. Professor Phelps Brown has suggested that there should be a representative of the public interest in every major negotiation, to bring home to managers and trade unionists that something better than rate-setting in an exclusive group is required in a society like ours. Lord Brown, who as chairman of Glacier Metals developed an entirely new form of participative management, goes farther. He believes that differentials have become the central problem of industrial bargaining, a problem with which existing institutions cannot deal. He has suggested, at least as a subject for debate, that there should be an entirely new representative institution, with a place for all categories of occupation but not for employers as such, to set the rates for occupations from year to year in relation to one another. The important thing, to his mind, is that there should be no question of a mere majority vote: there should be unanimity, or somewhere with 5 per cent or so of unanimity – a sort of explicit annual revision of the 'pecking order' by agreement.

In putting forward this idea, Lord Brown is relying on his own experience in one company, where matters between workers and management are settled without a vote. There is a great deal to be said for the principle, because in the ordinary way a great many collective decisions are made without careful assessment of majorities, either dispensing altogether with voting or voting purely formally. One might go further and say that there are countless representative institutions nominally subject to majority vote which could hardly function effectively at all if there were constant voting. Voting is most appropriate when it concerns the election of people to do certain jobs (although even here it is often a formality); mere votes are frequently predictable, and too much reliance on votes regularly leads to vote-catching argument rather than earnest and practical work to find the right basis for acceptable policy. We see this fault particularly in the more abstract kind of political discussion and sometimes in legislation: the Industrial Relations Act itself is an example of implementing a 'mandate to legislate' (that is, a general election result in which legislation was part of the party policy) without adequate care about whether the details of the law would be acceptable in practice; besides, within itself the Act depends rather more heavily on ballots than experience suggests is necessary or helpful. There are many examples of harmonious job evaluation of one kind or another, of participative management and successful co-operative enterprise. Perhaps their central common quality is the element of full discussion, whether there is a vote or not, and concern to make workers feel that they have a share in the decision-making, so far as they want it, or are represented satisfactorily.

Exclusivity and Pride

The late Ted Hill, the Boilermakers' leader who laid the foundations for the amalgamation of the shipyard 'black trades' achieved by his successor, Danny McGarvey, and his colleagues, used to say that the detailed subdivisions of work in the yards which led to the huge crop of demarcation disputes for twenty years after the war had all been the employers' idea in the first place. Perhaps it would be fairer to say that they developed, condoned by both sides, without any clear consideration of where the development would lead. People being what they are, various other prejudices became attached to the pecking order. Danny McGarvey himself, in his first job in the yard, had to settle for one of the less favoured trades because he was a Roman Catholic; the original Boilermakers tended to non-conformity, freemasonry and a number of other allied social patterns. The patterns varied in some occupations from one part of the country to another.* There are also many examples of unions, or groups within unions, knit together by varying degrees of common interest, resisting a threat to their corporate identity which goes far wider than the simple, material facts of the work they do. Indeed, if people engaged on unpleasant work in distinctive conditions, like miners and dockers, had not developed

---

* Perhaps the most explicit general tendency of this kind was in the United States in the heyday of 'ethnic' consciousness, when New York cops tended to be Irish whereas Chicago cops tended to be German; New York dustmen were Italian and schoolteachers predominantly Jewish, and so on.

a strong sense of identity their terms would have been unendurable.

One of the products is exclusivity. Another is pride. In a collective bargaining system of the kind which traditional western approaches has produced, especially in the United States and Britain, pride is put on the line in every negotiation. In 1972 the miners' leaders claimed, inaccurately, that they were striking for a living wage. They did this because the theory of the process is that bargaining begins from a clean slate, although this is obviously not true. In 1926 the Yorkshire mine-owners locked out their men to enforce a cut in wages, which they felt was necessary because of the return to the Gold Standard. In 1972 the miners went on strike to restore (at least for some of them) purchasing power lost through inflation. The sense of being downtrodden was the same, and produced the same attitude, although with a different result. But in fact there was no taking away the 'living wage' of miners; what was at issue, and what is usually at issue, was the sharing of surplus above mere subsistence. This is particularly difficult in nationalised industries, where price-setting has never been really commercial; indeed, except in times of utter depression neither rail charges nor coal prices have been free since 1914. If collective bargaining is to survive as a method of establishing pay, public policy must find some way of confining it to the marginal parts of pay which it really affects, and remove the sense of a worker's whole livelihood and an industry's entire commercial prospects being on the line. If this does not happen the energy, commitment and cohesion of industrial unions is liable to lead to explosive encounters every so often, and they usually do disproportionate damage.

In the other aspects of trade union work – the monitoring of day-to-day dealings between managers and workers – the industrial union has clear advantages. Its leaders are more likely to be responsive to the needs of its members generally rather than to abstract notions which naturally develop in large and diverse institutions. Its frontiers of interest can be readily defined, and its officers can therefore more easily make harmonious transfer arrangements with other unions. Differentials problems within the industry can be settled more easily. There are dangers on the other side as well, but they are perhaps more associated with pride of craft than with pride of industry. It is not uncommon to hear from an officer of a craft union, for example:

'I represent (say) the electrical function in a plant'. This is never precisely true, since there are managers who represent it too, in so far as people can 'represent' a function. We are still a long way from resolving the confusions of the first industrial revolution a mere 200 years on.

Chapter 7

Tough at the Top

'Senates and great councils are often troubled with redundant, ebullient and peccant humours; with many diseases of the head, and more of the heart; with strong convulsions, with grievous contractions of the nerves and sinews in both hands, but especially of the right ... besides many others needless to mention.'
Swift

An Official's Career
There are only about 3,000 professional trade union officers in Britain, and of these some 500 are national officers: that is, a national officer of a trade union is a slightly rarer bird than a member of Parliament. His tenure of office is generally more secure as well, although there are exceptions and circumstances in which trade unions as well as other organisations accept the resignation of a scapegoat; they are very rare indeed. Almost all officers have a good deal of experience before they become paid officials, and some of them have specific training, especially recently. The CIR report on industrial relations training at the end of 1972 suggested that the trade union movement were making proportionately more of it at the appropriate level than management: TUC-sponsored courses at technical colleges and other institutions were attended by about 7,000 shop stewards and other workers in 1971–2; but in more than half the establishments the CIR surveyed not a single employee had any industrial relations training in 1970 – including nearly one in nine of establishments with more than 2,500 employees and one in five of establishments with between 1,000 and 2,500.

Vic Feather's celebrated claim in the 1970 TUC: 'We are experts on industrial relations', can therefore be said to have some statistical argument in its favour. But there is no generally accepted criterion for a trade union officer, either by qualifications or even by performance. As we saw in Chapter 1, trade unions follow different criteria from union to union and from time to time. Besides, a trade union officer may find it difficult to understand the important change that comes over him when he moves from the payroll of an ordinary employer (with whom he may have dealt as a shop steward or other lay official) to the payroll of the union itself. In general, this involves stopping being a 'job' worker, who expects to go on doing the same thing in much the same way, and becoming a 'career' worker, whose future depends on more than carrying out a limited task in a satisfactory manner. Inevitably, a trade union officer becomes much more closely identified with the union than he could be as an amateur official, and he also becomes removed by one stage from his former colleagues. Although in the ordinary way he will have privileged access to their work group and its thinking, like that of any other work group in his area of responsibility, he will no longer share in the group's decisions. Groups are exclusive and make their own decisions, we must remember; outsiders may influence individuals or swing a meeting, but their influence on group discussion is always at one remove and may be differently interpreted by different individuals in the group.

For some trade union officers a career is quickly over, or does not get far. There is also a minority whose members' careers begin in the service of the union rather than in its ranks: Sir Sidney Ford, former president of the NUM, and Alan Fisher, general secretary of NUPE, are good recent examples. A great many other unions confine some or all offices to members of the union qualified by trade or occupation. The AUEW and the TGWU are leading examples of this attitude among the major unions: they emphasise the representative quality of the union. There are others, notably the NUGMW, which tend the other way and have no compunction about employing horses for courses even if they are not home-bred: they emphasise the service function of the union and in the nature of things may lose something thereby and put more weight on its controlling function as well. But whatever the particular bias of a union, the general cast of officialdom sets its mark on people. Trade union officers usually have active and various lives. They are usually paid much less and have fewer defensive groups about them than managers with responsibility for much smaller numbers of people. They dispose of very small resources not only for the number of people they serve and represent, but often for the number of direct employees of the union. True, some white-collar unions set the pay of their officers according to scales in occupations they represent – the civil service, or teaching, or local government. The odd officer with literary ability or eloquence makes a bit on the side by writing and lecturing. But dedication is presumed, and indeed presumed upon.

Compared with other 'career' occupations, trade unionism offers only modest material satisfactions at least by way of direct payment. But a trade unionist rising in the movement can certainly get about – certainly more than managers at anything like the equivalent salary level. There is no doubt that this can cloud individual judgment of situations just as opaquely as the duty of servility can do it for many managers. Representing the rank and file, the trade union officer has a natural title to self-righteousness. He may be a prey to a sort of romanticism about the people he represents which is common also among managers in considering the people they manage. When a trade union officer goes into negotiation at national level, or intervenes in a dispute, he may show the style of commissar or fixer, he may appear as either advocate for the workers in an adversary situation or keeper of the union's conscience as upholder of agreements; he can never, in this country at any rate, appear as a labour contractor protecting the union against law suits (although the Industrial Relations Act is apparently designed to cast him in this role). What he also cannot do is know the workers involved in the way that the managers know them. He may have met only a handful of them personally, and he will have met them on a different basis. Trade union officers become experienced with groups (although in certain jobs in certain unions they may get out of touch through long service in the national bureaucracy); most of them must go on the assumption that their members are never wholly wrong. Managers perceive individuals and without careful training and constant reminders may not realise the exclusiveness and power of group behaviour.

'Knowing Your Own People'
Both managers and trade union officers who have come up from the shop floor are tempted to look on all shop floor groups in the afterlight of their own experience. They may assume that they know the people working on a shop floor now as intimately as they did when they were part of such a group. Even managers

without experience on the shop floor will make such an assumption. They claim to 'know their own people', although in the nature of things they may only experience a very lop-sided relation with 'their own people'. When the relation goes wrong and employees make a stand in groups, such a person is naturally inclined to discern a conspiracy by evil men, even to the extent of looking for 'reds under the bed' while they are blatantly at work on the counterpane. You only have to look at the mathematics of relations among people to see how size runs away with cosy assumptions of dealings between person and person. The number of personal ties in a group of three is three – the beginning of a 'crowd'. Among 20 people the possible number is 190. Among 100,000 people it is nearly 5,000 million,* and we must assume that only a tiny proportion of these possible relations even goes as far as a meeting. Their interrelations are symbolic: abstract, capable of being tested but unlikely to be tested by personal contact. One of the factors in the symbolic relation is the 'image' of leaders they have in common, so that there is the same kind of difference between the general secretary and the shop steward as there is between the tycoon and the supervisor. However, it is not as easy as that.

The relation between them is entirely different. In any properly managed institution there will be representation from below and authority from above, but the trade union inevitably inclines heavily to representation. After all, trade unions would not have developed at all if the state of affairs in Britain at the time had not produced a great and growing pressure for representation against authority. The services and guidance which the union provides are ancillary to that purpose. Unions as such are not productive institutions, any more than democratic government is a productive institution. They are moderating institutions, and they are anomalous in the sense that there is no specific place for them in the common structure of authority. This makes for endless cross-purposes and perplexities in dealings between managers and trade union officials, and in the outsider's perception of what goes on between them. An industrial union, for example, may have a natural interest in the continued prosperity of the industry but very little in that of a particular firm in the industry; yet its members in that firm may have an agonised interest in its future. The trade union

* The formula is $\frac{n}{2}(n-1)$, so that the possible direct relations among pairs in a group of 100,000 is 50,000 × 99,999.

movement has a natural interest in the continued prosperity of the country but an equally natural mistrust of the conventional ways of measuring prosperity. Above all, trade union activists are bound to dislike the convention of capitalism and private ownership, however moderated by their own activities, but since they are knit into it and take their colouration from it, if only by reaction, they have no significant power to change it as trade unionists. But they can impede it and impose conditions for other change, especially at places of work.

Nationalisation and the Work Group

Political action puts constraints on managers and owners; as we commented earlier, this year's paternalism is next year's statutory duty. What nationalisation in the form it has taken in coal and rail transport does is another matter; it has made possible certain achievements of rationalisation and rescue, removed the excesses of enmity between owner and employee which had devastated these industries, and perhaps not much more. A Treasury remit does not seem a much better background for running a railway than abstract conventions of commerce, and British Rail has been run down more drastically than any of its European counterparts, where a much smaller proportionate tonnage of freight goes by road. In 1972, when mines and railways in turn have been the focus of great symbolic confrontations between unions and government, the irrationality and asymmetry is all too clear. The fact that a corporation is publicly owned does not of itself make life brighter for its employees – or does not do so for very long – but is assumed to demand certain extra constraints on them. The difference between the rank-and-file worker and his managers remains much the same. Within this prescribed context there are amiable and disagreeable managers, trained and untrained managers, slack and diligent workers, passive and militant groups. Yet very few workers expect the millennium from their trade union or political leaders. Many of them want change, but not as a rule the kind of change that their managers want; above all, they want to have a say in the sort of change that they must tolerate. This attitude is frequently incomprehensible to an innovative manager, who may readily convince himself that change which seriously disturbs the people who work under him is not only right, other things being equal, but is right in an overriding way: the one most important matter.

Trade unions develop to protect people who are comparatively defenceless by themselves. For most people in this country, the only way to improve or, in situations like the present, protect their standard of living is by a wage claim. There will always be a minority who can do it otherwise, by taking an extra job, or running the risks of enterprise, or 'going over to the other side', or winning a lottery. Household income may vary according to the fortunes or opportunities of wife and children. But most workers reach maximum earnings early, before their family responsibilities arrive or about the same time, and face the prospect of lower earnings in late middle age. Unless they have a protector, which may be a trade union or in certain circumstances an individual, they become peculiarly vulnerable to arbitrary lay-off as well when they become older – all in the interests of 'efficiency'. This vulnerability is made greater by a common misunderstanding about the relation of the individual to the work group which is typified by the award of an industrial tribunal in Liverpool in June 1972, who refused a remedy for unfair dismissal to an elderly engineering worker, although clearly uneasy about the case:

Mr Banner had reached the age of 58, when his chances of new employment in the present state of the employment market would not be particularly good. This unfortunately is a matter which affects many employees in the older age groups, and it is not in our view sufficient reason for finding that employers must not dismiss a man of advancing years, but must first dismiss younger men who might, in the normal course of events, be expected to work at a faster rate and have a higher performance record.

In fact, work groups set their own standard of performance and to improve it is a collective, not an individual process. There is no reason to suppose that the standards of Mr Banner's work group were so high that he could not maintain them simply because of his age, and even if they were, research suggests that his colleagues would help him to keep up. There is no reason to suppose that his misfortune would make the rest work harder. It would be just as likely to make them leave, or determined to see that there was a stronger defensive organisation when they reached his age. True, as employers, trade unions stick as rigidly to age limits as most, but as representative institutions they are naturally bound to favour the principle of 'last in, first out', which the tribunal in Mr Banner's case explicitly rejected.

In the long run, it is the behaviour and decisions of managers which decide how much production and added value there is to be, to share among all workers. Research suggests that once a routine has been accepted, it is most effectively followed by an authoritarian system of command, but it becomes correspondingly difficult to change. (It took a long time to change the authoritarian system developed in the TGWU by Bevin and Deakin.) If everyone knows his place, and follows orders to the letter, collective decisions are efficiently followed. A more participative system with more wayward and natural communications makes more mistakes but is easier to correct. Consequently it meets change without disruption, being used to trial and error; whereas an authoritarian system upsets people when it changes course under outside pressure, social or economic, with the sense of 'disloyalty' on one side and 'exploitation' on the other.

Permanent Opposition or Giant's Strength?

Against this background the small company of trade union officers work. All sorts of epigrams have been coined to describe their peculiar position. Professor Clegg calls them the opposition that can never be a government. Conservative lawyers in the germinal days of industrial relations legislation perceived that they had 'a giant's strength'. They are asked to be agents, joint overseers, walking consciences, brothers together or dedicated and selfless reformers in the national interest, a large phrase which one interprets according to one's point of view. The strength is illusory, but the capacity for obstruction is considerable, although a good deal less considerable than many people imagine. There are trade unions in the world which command really large resources and go into business as principals: the German DGB (equivalent of the TUC) controls 78 per cent of the third largest merchant bank in West Germany, owns the largest property development company and runs the fastest-growing insurance enterprise. United States unions are often huge property owners. But some British unions have increased dues by as little as half since 1938, and they have fallen well below the pre-war convention – still common in some other countries – of giving the union an hour's pay a week. And, of course, the proportion of the national product going into wages and salaries remained roughly constant for nearly half a century until the distortion of the tax threshold by inflation pushed the proportion up a bit from 1968 onwards. This has the advantage that British unions have escaped the illusion that aggregations of wealth in their names give them countervailing power beyond the industrial dissent of their members. Their leaders have not escaped other illusions, and many of them are endlessly frustrated as a result.

Probably the greatest common illusion is that there is a natural solidarity of the working class which overrides everything else (like some managers' concept of efficient production) and provides a systematic frame on which to build an analysis of the present and a view of the future. Where trade unionists do this, they normally make the analysis first and find a doctrine afterwards to fit it – which is why university Marxists and shop-floor militants spend so much time at cross purposes. It is true that there is an objective fact of solidarity in certain circumstances, just as there is an objective fact of comparatively effortless production and even solely personal achievement (although this last is so rare and usually so private a matter as to be irrelevant to any discussion of industrial relations; group activity naturally inclines to moderate or control individual behaviour for collective ends, and where managers and work groups can accommodate their collective purposes you have industrial harmony because they tolerate one another). But solidarity is not an invariable fact or a fixed quantity. When it is there, it is much more important than any physical resources. For example, during the 1972 miners' strike the driver of an oil tanker pulled back into the depot within minutes of leaving it. The depot manager asked him why, and he said that he could not cross miners' picket lines. The manager did not believe that there could be pickets on the main railway link directly outside the depot, and there were none on railway property. The driver took him out on a shunter and let him see, draped over a bridge, a poster saying: 'Miners' picket line. Do not cross.'

Other things being equal, trade union leaders will get solidarity from their followers. That is why the 'cooling-off periods' and compulsory ballots designed to discover whether trade union members support their leaders in certain types of strike are unlikely ever to show a dissenting majority – especially if, as happened in the first use of these devices in the railway strike of 1972, the employer makes no use of the cooling-off period to seek a compromise. However, solidarity varies greatly from one union or occupational group to another, and is usually unqualified only at a time of conflict when the group of workers requiring it is clearly at odds with an employer. Trade union growth and merger would be very much easier if there were a continuing common interest overriding personal and institutional differences as something on which to build. Quirks of character among people and among unions tend on the whole to push them apart. The common ideals of the trade union movement are obvious enough. The impulse to get together is always there, and once union has been achieved it is remarkably difficult to break, even when there is a huge and bitter difference between members. One thing that never seemed likely during the ETU scandal was the disintegration of the union. One thing that has never seemed likely during the long and anxious argument about whether trade unions should register or not under the Industrial Relations Act has been the disintegration of the TUC, although some unions may be temporarily or permanently expelled. This is not to say that either unions or the TUC may not become less effective (or more ineffective than usual) under the strain of controversy, but that is a different thing.

The relations among the three railway unions illustrate the case very well. Ever since the Amalgamated Society of Railway Servants metamorphosed into the NUR, an industrial union covering all grades of railway employee but none of them exclusively, there has been no logical reason against a single railway union. Yet there have always been separate unions – ASLEF, organising the aristocrats who drive the trains, and TSSA (formerly the Railway Clerks), organising the white-collar workers, both in competition with the NUR. The separateness of the institutions has survived both nationalisation and the colossal decline in railway employment, and the experience of railway trade unionism as it has been and as it is shapes the personalities of the men who come to the top. The institutions are clearly quite different in their attitudes, and TSSA now organises, as we have seen, outside the rail industry as well as inside it. The NUR organises maintenance men and dockers because they are employed by the railways. ASLEF confines itself solely to drivers and their mates: the narrowest kind of trade unionism, covering one occupation in one industry with one employer. When George Woodcock was general secretary of the TUC, he used to exhort the leaders of the three unions to look to their common interest, and come together. When Vic Feather succeeded Mr Woodcock, he tried to bring the leaders together so that their institutional and personal differences would become less important. Perhaps the experience of 1972, in which the three unions kept a common line in resistance to Government pressure through the British Railways Board, has helped to clarify the union leaders' minds still further. If, for example, ASLEF had taken action alone it would have made the barriers higher.

Blackball Psychology
Consequently, one may say as a general rule that although good relations among the leaders of unions will not necessarily bring them together, bad feelings between the leaders will certainly keep the unions apart. In this respect unions are much more like clubs than like companies, at least when the companies have ceased to be identified with one person or one family. True, only a few individuals in a union have effective powers of blackballing by themselves, and these powers depend, of course, on their standing in their own union and their view of the other one. Clearly Jack Jones and Jack Cooper each has a much greater identity with his union as an institution than the thousands of general workers in the TGWU and the NUGMW where turnover of membership among the unskilled sometimes runs at more than a third a year. They share this closer identity with long-established managers of any institutions. They also have to take their members with them, and although now mergers need only a simple majority of members voting to carry the day, this is a much greater matter than the kind of barter required to merge companies; as we have recently seen in the takeover of Watneys by Grand Metropolitan Hotels, a corporate marriage is possible even if the views of those actively engaged in the conduct of one enterprise are overwhelmingly against it. Even absolute loathing of one another by the respective managers would have made a difference of at best a point or two in the acceptances. But moderate dislike among trade union leaders is enough in itself to put off a merger which in principle no one would care to resist.

Take the Patternmakers, a prosperous little union with 14,000 members of high skill strategically placed just after the design stage in all branches of engineering. Twenty years ago they would logically have merged with the Engineers. In the United States they are in the Machinists' Union, in Germany in the

Metalworkers'. But the drift of life in the AUEW has been repulsive to the Patternmakers as a group. Gerry Eastwood, the Patternmakers' leader, is a consistent opponent of Hugh Scanlon, the AUEW leader, in the Confederation of Engineering and Shipbuilding Unions. Nor is there much prospect of a merger with any of the other very large unions: the TGWU could not create an industrial group for 14,000 new recruits. The Boilermakers' Amalgamation is too specialised; the Sheet Metal Workers operate at a different stage of production and a different level of skill, and in any event have not been able to recruit the Birmingham and Midland local union which again is prosperous enough and self-conscious enough to take a great deal of persuading that any alliance is necessary apart from membership of the 'Confed' itself. Finance is, of course, an important consideration in a merger. Very small unions may ultimately run for cover because they can no longer provide even modest services to their members. Much larger ones may stagger after an expensive strike, or become worn down by a long process of shaky management and inadequate contributions by members. The prospect of being wound up for insolvency under the Companies Act must have been a marginal disincentive for some trade unions to go on the new register.

Trade unions and trade union leaders may never be absolute as some companies and some employers have seemed to be from time to time. True, where an employer is very remote from his workers, the union will fill a disproportionate part of the role which the system requires from union and employer together – the South Wales Miners Federation described by Will Paynter in his memoirs is a good example. But simply because they are not the employers, not the controllers of resources, but at best a brake on the controllers, trade union leaders cannot be the 'barons' and 'power brokers' that dramatic reporting sometimes makes them. Yet trade union leaders are extraordinarily well placed to observe if an enterprise of any size is well or badly run, especially in its industrial relations. Not long after becoming a shop steward, sometimes, and not long after becoming a paid officer, almost inevitably, a union leader is likely to come across a manager in charge of negotiations or involved in a dispute who is less variously experienced and, as likely as not, less shrewd than himself. Managers at that level are habitually also hamstrung by inadequate authority in conducting the negotiations and a tendency to underestimate the collective understanding of his or the company's predicament which the union members have. Skilled workers with no access to balance sheets will notice and draw their own conclusions from sudden and inexplicable economies – especially if they deal with either the men or the machines they use.

Symptoms of Good Ordering
We have become so accustomed to breaking up our view of an enterprise into specialities that it is easy to overlook the truism that symptoms of industrial good health tend to go together, and concentration on only one of them is pernicious. As it happened, three different authorities all made the point in the same week in the autumn of 1972. Ken Corfield of ITT commented to a seminar run by the Foundation for Business Responsibilities that not only were profit and loss accounts at an arbitrary moment in the production cycle (which the law requires) bound to be an educated guess, but that high profits when the paintwork was peeling were an indication of bad management in the long run. Bryan Harvey, chief inspector of factories, observed in presenting his annual report that an experienced inspector could be pretty sure when he went into an establishment that safety measures, technical efficiency and probably industrial relations and profit were good or bad together. The CIR, reporting on the duty of employers to give workers information, said that their study indicated that good industrial relations and satisfactory disclosure of information seemed to go together. This is a point, of course, which intelligent workers and union officers know perfectly well, even if they would not necessarily make it a neat generalisation. The CIR added that their finding did not necessarily mean that a rapid disclosure of information would necessarily mend bad industrial relations. Experience suggests that this is certainly true, depending on what is disclosed; a sudden rush of information after a long term of close-mouthed inefficiency may inspire not confidence but contempt, and a management may find it difficult to recover from the consequences.

Besides, the normal tolerant behaviour of an open society accepts that the less influence and authority society bestows on a person the greater freedom he ought to have to let off steam. It would be a poor thing if we were to tolerate for long complaints by millionaires about their straitened circumstances or by chief executives of large enterprises that they could get nothing done. However, the first complaints do occur, and the second are fairly common, usually with the rider that this ineffectiveness is an unnatural condition imposed upon them by trade unions. A good example was the passage from the presidential address to the Institute of Personnel Management in 1972 by T. P. Lyons, who said: 'Even in private industry the employer is little more than the medium through which the union forces the community to pay for higher wages for its members, because the increase is paid for in higher prices.' Perhaps the fact that so many experienced managers believe this to be true is a good enough reason for taking it seriously,* since they will presumably act as if it were true; it is the diagnosis on which Lord Brown based his ideas on a 'differentials Parliament' discussed in Chapter 6.

Unions as Scapegoats

The unions certainly have a part in the process – certainly some leaders of unions do – because in their representative capacity they over-emphasise the miseries of their members, talk a great deal in abstract terms of 'injustice', and as a result may actually impede the movement towards better things.† First of all, there is a limit to what they can obtain for their members simply because their members are many and the rentiers are few. Secondly, if they do not frighten managers (which normally happens only when the managers are low in the hierarchy, or given inadequate authority to meet their responsibility, or unusually ill qualified), they give them a stick to hit back with. To some extent the unions' role as a scapegoat for so many imperfections in British economic performance is the result of the unions' pressing too hard the melancholy lot of their members. Besides, self-righteousness itself becomes competitive, and where unions start falling out about which one has the more deserving mem-

* At the 1970 TUC a number of experienced union officers were talking about the unprecedented spinelessness of employers in the previous spring. The Conservatives at that time accused the Labour Government of leading a 'wage explosion' to win re-election. Yet this interpretation would lead to the unlikely conclusion that a large mass of employers wanted the Labour Government re-elected, since it was they who actually conceded the wage increases. There is some subtlety of collective psychology here which awaits an explanation.

† I have tried to avoid the word 'blame' in passages like these; we are always too ready to impute moral fault to one side or the other, and once we do so it makes it more difficult to determine what is happening.

bers, their critics prosper. The critics do not need to be subtle, either; when a rich man talks about 'the unions' greed' he must be very confident about his hearers' reactions. After all, the unions' members earn sums in a week that would not pay the rent of a bachelor flat in Belgravia, and give the union what would barely buy ten cigarettes.

The fact that they are not 'barons' and their members are not 'greedy' in any terms that make sense is apparent to all trade union leaders. That managers have a task of stewardship which is often badly executed is equally obvious. But there are many trade union officers in Britain with great organising gifts who do not recognise that there are limits to what they can do as trade unionists. Managers negotiating with trade union officials may from time to time say daft things, just as the trade union officials do; they never offer to change jobs with them. They seldom ask what the trade union officials would do if they were in the managers' position. Perhaps they should. The characteristic position of a trade union officer in a dispute is this: managers make a collective decision to apply some change in the workers' position (in this context a refusal to pay wage increases high enough to maintain the workers' standard of living implies change as surely as a proposed wage cut); the managers' decision is collective because many managers are normally involved in gathering the information on which it is based and several in the actual decision-making. The workers collectively make their decision on the managers' collective proposal, and reject it, with or without the guidance of their union officer. If they want to make a fight of it, his position is different from that of either workers or managers, and subtly different even from that of employers' association officials. The lines of formal authority which bind him are all abstract. He is not engaged in either productive or commercial activity, but in the settlement of connected matters of 'fair's fair' and so on, for which the only criterion is the satisfaction of his constituents.

It is perfectly possible for some constituents simply to want to be left alone for long periods. They may be rubbing along well enough with their employers, they may have to meet no major and unpleasant change, their pay may be running comfortably above national rates. Perhaps they have an employer who deliberately sets out to be more generous and solicitous than the average to keep the unions quiet, or out of the plant altogether. Perhaps they have an employer who is more generous and solicitous than most without any particular ulterior motives, or is seen to be so. Perhaps they have an employer who is so prosperous that his workers have become used to being significantly better off than their neighbours in the same kind of work. For most union officers quiescent groups of members like this are welcome, because most union officers are too busy to look for problems. The catch comes when there is change in one or other of these happy circumstances. As we have seen, no manager may expect simply to inherit the status of his predecessor, although he is sure to inherit his problems and pay for at least some of his mistakes. An employer can keep ahead of the game only so long as everything goes acceptably well, so far as his workers are concerned. For example, an employer is legally obliged merely to pay wages, but he is expected to pay real wages and if the value of money goes down faster than the wages he pays go up, he is in trouble. For the union officer who comes in to deal with the problem, it presents itself in simple terms: no union can accept a decline in the real earnings of its members.

At the same time, no union can prevent employers' being unable, either by bad luck or bad guidance, to maintain the real earnings of members. When the TUC committees meet to review large matters like the future of the economy and the interplay among unions, employers and government, they are faced by this bleak fact of economic organisation. It is a reality about the function of a trade union, and it is just as much a reality for trade union officers in totalitarian countries as in pluralistic ones – even if in a theoretical way revolutionary trade union members in Britain may feel that after the revolution they would have a chance to manage and make a better fist of it. There is, of course, nothing to prevent a trade union officer having managerial flair, and even to keep going a smallish organisation with smallish funds needs some flair although the objectives of the organisation are not productive. Ernest Bevin had the imagination and drive, as well as several of the blind spots, of a natural entrepreneur, and so the TGWU owns the splendidly placed property of Transport House without any of the risks of commerce hanging over it. In West Germany the DGB is a large commercial organisation without straightforward commercial motives. In Britain the Co-operative movement is in much the same situation, except that politics rather than running the show has confused and complicated its fortunes, and successive reorganisations for the sake of 'efficiency' have made the style and objectives of Co-op managers not conspicuously different from those of other managers. Like nationalised industry, the Co-op has outlived its special sense of identification with its workers' interests and dropped into terms of 'us' and 'them', blurred but not dissipated by the absence of private shareholders. Unions may reach such a pass as well.

'Us' and 'Them' Inside Unions
A worker need not necessarily have much more idea of his trade union – or the trade union in his place of work – than he has about the organisation of his employers. Normally he has a vague idea that the union is at least a working-class organisation and will be on his side if there is trouble. But as we saw in an earlier chapter this sense of identity may be damaged even without the intervention of another union; this happened in the Pilkington dispute. Pilkingtons and the local NUGMW organisation had stood still while change was occurring all about them; yet in terms of productive innovation and good relations between union and management they could not be faulted. Another 'us' and 'them' problem of a different kind was illustrated in the dissension-ridden history of the Alcan smelter site at Lynemouth in Northumberland, the subject of a CIR report in June 1972. For want of clear agreement on pay that covered the whole site in some kind of order, the work was disrupted by a series of stoppages playing off one employer against the others. One employer, bound by national agreement, stood out – the electrical contractor whose rates of wages were governed by the unique Joint Industrial Board for the electrical contracting industry which operates on the joint authority of the EETU and the employers. After a couple of years of skirmishing even unskilled workers on the site were earning more than the JIB rate for electricians, and in the end Alcan had to intervene to oblige the contractor to pay the electricians more than the JIB rate. A different aspect of the same dilemma has hit the TGWU in the battle between its docks and commercial section about containers.

These problems usually occur when there is some sharp departure in union behaviour from either its context or its function. The context of a large construction site does not necessarily follow a standard pattern, and the JIB agreement does. St Helens, which Pilkingtons dominated for so long, changed over the years from a one-company town at a time of restricted movement by most workers into a mere constituent of a much larger work area for a labour force accustomed to travelling farther. Containerisation in the docks has been a new and revolutionary change which the traditional TGWU approach to bargaining, using one section if possible as a lever to bring up another in the wage scale, could not meet. After all, in 1966 the docks were supposed to be settling down to a stable future with roughly the same labour force after decasualisation and the introduction of mechanical handling. It was just at that time that the shipping industry decided to go in for containers. The union expected that this would give more work inland but did not allow for the gross and rapid reduction in the need for men on the waterside. If union leaders had done, they might have pressed for a resettlement operation on the level of a small refugee migration, since more than 40,000 dockers seem likely to have left the industry in the ten years from 1966 to 1976, leaving a total of 20,000 at the most still at work. In the face of this massive dislocation the handful of jobs involved in places like Chobham Farm depot (just over sixty) is a fleabite and the action of dockers in 'blacking' such places a marginal distraction from the great central problem. It is, however, just the sort of distraction from great central problems which occupies disproportionate attention from journalists and lawyers.

Corporate Personalities and Real Responsibility

If the law cannot find a person it feels obliged to create one. In law BP or ICI or General Motors is each a person, like you and me. This sometimes leads to curious situations in minor courts. Counsel for a national catering company, one of whose managers had failed to observe its strict instructions about avoiding contamination of food by broken glass, pleaded guilty to the offence of selling jam with glass in it and admitted its record of more than a hundred other offences in the previous three years. For an ordinary person this would be a frightful situation; for a corporate person it may be almost unavoidable, depending on its corporate size. Lawyers have frequently tried to turn trade unions into persons in this way, and of course if unions register under the Industrial Relations Act there is no doubt about it. They become corporate bodies with perpetual succession. Since the distinction between an individual and his surroundings is always difficult to define absolutely, perhaps this is as good a way of going about it as the law can offer. But it is a good deal easier for a large company to discourage its managers from selling jam with broken glass in it than for a union to prevent symbolic outbursts of frustration from members who see their occupation slipping either in terms of numbers or in terms of pay. Most middle-class managers detest 'blacking', the instrument used by dockers against Chobham Farm and other container depots. They find it unsporting, 'sneaky' as compared with straight industrial action, because the men who are 'blacking' disrupt other people's business without losing pay. By contrast, a strike is a 'fair fight' if it follows the rules and everyone gets properly hurt.

Journalists also like their cult of personality. This is legitimate enough, since all life expresses itself in the behaviour and interplay of individuals. The trouble is that dwelling on the interplay of particular individuals – 'at 7 p.m. on 29 March 1972, Podger was in the Station Hotel at York after a meeting of the Saggarmakers, and met Pipkin on the way to London from his conference in Scarborough' – makes things appear accidental rather than the fruit of probabilities and determining causes. Most leaders who have had a narrow squeak think like the Duke of Wellington after Waterloo – 'By God, I do not think it would have done if I had not been there' – yet we have only to go behind the battle and ask ourselves whether, if Wellington had actually lost, Napoleon would have won the next one. There was no next battle for Wellington either. Industrial relations are not a series of battles, but of adjustments to change. There is always the possibility that Britain, a 'steady state' society since Culloden but with an inordinate amount of movement in it, may have a revolution, but it will not be through the activities of industrial relations; it would be because the 'steady state' structure of British society was not in the end adaptable and assimilative enough to meet the strains on it. Inflation, for example, is a disruptive change if it gets out of hand, is an indication that society somehow does not put the stability of money high enough to ensure that change occurs elsewhere. Victorian England was remarkably successful in maintaining the value of sterling, and the history of working class migration indicates one of the ways that Victorian England managed it. Trade unions exist to prevent excesses in putting the weight of adjustment to change on the people they represent, and being human institutions they may commit excesses of their own in the process.

Steady Jobs for Seasoned Men

In tune with this purpose, national union officers with few exceptions and local officers in the ordinary way may expect office until they retire, whether subject to constant re-election or not. (Occasionally they die in harness; although, so far as I know, no figures are available of the expectation of life of professional trade unionists, I suspect that it is above average.) We have seen that only the re-election clause in the ETU constitution made it possible for a court to unseat Frank Haxell from the post of general secretary; if he had been appointed until retirement, there would have been no election in which to be fraudulent and he would not have required the frauds in any event if he had been a more amiable man, as many Communist trade unionists are, or appear to be. The normal course of a career in a mature trade union is a staid business in which the membership may deny advancement but seldom take it away, and then only when something has gone blatantly wrong; there is some doubt about whether, when something goes wrong, the role of scapegoat falls to the right person, but this is even more true of the harsher world of management and politics. The labour movement is remarkably tolerant of its leaders. The contrast between the Labour and Conservative parties in this respect has often been noticed. In the union movement it means that as a rule change in alignment of its leadership is slow.

This may make union affairs a trifle flat for observers with a taste for the dramatic. A labour leader in controversial circumstances may acquire a reputation for successful infighting when all that he has to do is remain cool and keep his balance. But indeed, in this attitude workers as union members are not significantly different from workers as employees. In most industrial disputes workers want managers to change their minds or their behaviour, but seldom demand that they should dismiss one another, glad though many workers might be to see certain managers (or leaders) go. It is more common for workers to demand the dismissal of one of themselves who has behaved in an unacceptably deviant way – working too hard, or not joining the union, or making a fool of the union as an 'in and outer', or otherwise threatening their security as they see it. At some stage in the development of organisations, the personal contact which makes possible real individual malice seems to become diffused; the actions of individuals become significant as the actions of 'management' or 'union', although at a further, political stage where personal contact is irrelevant the institution may be personalised back again as 'Mr Jones's TGWU' or 'Mr Scanlon's AUEW' or 'Lord Stokes's British Leyland'. However, neither security in office nor the development of a synthetic public personality means that leaders can do as they please; although their position is buttressed by sentiment, they have to be as tough and realistic about what their members want as about what they can get for them.

Chapter 8

Quirks of Character

> *Long-horned and short, of many a different breed –*
> *Tall, tawny brutes from famous Lincoln levels*
>   *Or Durham feed*
> *With some of these unquiet, black-dwarf devils*
>   *From nether side of Tweed*
> *Or Firth of Forth –*
> *Looking half-wild with joy to leave the North.*
> Hood: 'The Stampede on Hounslow Heath'

Does Lancashire Count?
The late Charles Curran MP, once wrote an article suggesting that the rising militancy of British trade unionism in the middle 1950s was the result of waves of Welsh immigration into industrial centres of England. Professor Hoggart in his trendy and important book on *The Uses of Literacy* produced an array of working-class indicators which he had observed in his part of Yorkshire. For the average cartoonist, the trade unionist is as much a creature of thick head and hobnailed boots as the civil servant is a drowser among the teacups (a pair of concepts which fused in a watery and rather depressing way in the jokes about the civil servants' protests against the pay standstill at the beginning of 1973). There is almost no limit to the possibilities of symbolic association. I forget why Curran wrote what he did and what his evidence was; it must have been scanty if only because there are so few Welshmen, a variant on the standard conspiracy theory. Professor Hoggart's statements have been criticised by Yorkshiremen who claim that the idiosyncrasies were properly *Yorkshire* not *working-class*, and that Professor Hoggart did not see this because he moved from a Yorkshire working-class background into an academic middle

class in which regional differences were blurred and emulsified, so to speak, to a smooth consistency.

These critics may be wrong. Still, it is interesting that the controversy should exist at all, especially now that where there is a credible 'nationalist' politics, as in Wales and Scotland, nationalists pop up at moments of extreme exasperation with headquarters politics in London and occasionally win seats in Parliament. Britain is commercially one of the most centralised – possibly the most centralised – major country in the world. By modern standards it is 'no distance' (physically) from one end of Britain to the other; psychologically, for people who live confined lives in their early days, the distance may be immense, and psychology counts for a great deal. If we look at the reminiscences of Will Paynter, for example, a boy from the Welsh Valleys whose first taste of international travel was as a courier for the Comintern in the 1930s, we can see the candid and comical tensions of being, so to speak, an unauthorised diplomat. Paynter became a member of the Communist Party as a result of his experiences as a young miner, who was self-educated in the local libraries in the Valleys, taught himself shorthand once when his political activities and the state of the coal industry left him at a loose end, served his way to the general secretaryship of the union and before he retired co-operated with the Coal Board to bring off the incredible achievement of winning acceptance for a national powerloading agreement which not only levelled up the earnings of lower-paid areas but cost miners in some of the richer ones as much as five pounds a week. Paynter was the archetype of the red Welshman in his younger days, which is odd because his grandfather came from Gloucestershire.

In fact, one of the most disconcerting things about modern Britain, with its great cultural variety from one part of the country to the other, is the immense jumble of origins. Coal mines, factories, railway building and the growing demands of the civil service, the educational system and other innovations which have continued to pick up speed over the last four or five generations all involved huge migrations of people. Britain had more or less totally destroyed peasant agriculture by the beginning of the Second World War, long before any other country. Yet a number of concepts from an earlier day survived – of 'reservoirs of labour' and 'labour mobility' and regional consciousness of a rigid and immobilising kind. Perhaps one could do worse to illustrate the point than look at the 'domination of the trade union movement' by Lancashire, on the evidence at the beginning of 1973.

The first four unions in size in Britain have chief officers from Lancashire: Jack Jones, general secretary of the TGWU; Hugh Scanlon, general president of the AUEW; David Basnett, general secretary of the NUGMW, and Walter Anderson, general secretary of NALGO. David Basnett had also just succeeded another Lancastrian, Lord Cooper of Stockton Heath. A bit further down the scale in size, but bulking very large in the affairs of 1972, were the miners, and their general president, Joe Gormley, also comes from Lancashire. There may be some general geographical conclusions to be drawn from this impressive proportion, but I do not know what they are.

Jack Jones and Hugh Scanlon
The differences among these dignitaries are remarkable. Mr Jones is normally called a 'left-winger' along with Mr Scanlon; Mr Basnett a 'right-winger' along with Mr Anderson and Mr Gormley. But although Mr Jones has views and procedures which make his predecessors appear very far to the right, he is an institution man through and through. He started in the docks and engineering on Merseyside, with a Welsh surname and the formidable Irish given names of 'James Larkin' – a testimonial by his parents to the Irish socialist revolutionary who was shaking up Merseyside before the First World War. Jack Jones was a Liverpool councillor at 23 and was in Spain during the Civil War. His tough radicalism and desire to involve his members in decisions affecting them is beyond question. He is a big, broad-shouldered, emphatic man who writes logical and literate but never frivolous articles and speeches. Indeed, one unkind observer once said that 'Jack's cloth cap' (which he normally wears when visiting large groups of members but not otherwise) 'is like a preacher's vestments'. He became a full-time official in 1939, when he was only 26, made his name as an adept turner of the screw in West Midlands local bargaining, and had been thirty years in the professional service of the union before he became general secretary. He was, in effect, Frank Cousins's choice as successor. For most of his adult life the union – his union – has been the major institution in his field of concern.

This is true of Hugh Scanlon as well, but in a subtly different way. He was born in Australia but raised in Lancashire and trained as an instrument maker. He is a small, lively, expansive man, remarkably fit and alert and one of the sharpest negotiators in the union movement. Like Mr Paynter, he was an enthusiast (and still is) for self-education, and eager to make his mark in the world. He was a successful convenor of shop stewards at the big Trafford Park plant in Manchester when he was thirty. Afterwards, for sixteen years, he was divisional organiser for the North-west of England until he won a place on the national executive in 1963. The AUEW is very different in structure from the TGWU (or any of the others), with checks and balances based on the American constitution which allow a man to maintain an independent local view. Officials are re-elected every three years. Even after Mr Scanlon left the Communist Party in the 1950s (joining the Labour Party, he said, to change it from within), his practical union work and his simplistic approach to politics did not conflict. By 1963 his hard-line 'political morality' was well set; he had survived and indeed prospered as a leader of 'militant' opposition in the union to the magisterial leadership of Lord Carron. In 1967, when Lord Carron retired, Mr Scanlon stood for General President and won.

This was an electoral coup indeed. No one expected it, least of all John Boyd, the executive member for Scotland who had Lord Carron's support for the succession: an amiable but earnest big man, a Protestant evangelical with Salvation Army loyalties and a good example of the 'responsible' trade unionist. Perhaps unluckily for him, Mr Boyd was also chairman of the Labour Party that year, and the campaign against him made skilful use of the impatience of union members with wage restraint if they were activist at all. Mr Scanlon won on a 14 per cent poll, which was unusually high. At this point he may have fallen victim to the Guevara self-deception we noticed in Chapter 4. There was no doubt about his success in the union. It served to confirm all the views that he held, whether they were views of negotiation based on experience or views of wider political matters based on dogma. It is not that Mr Scanlon's general political outlook means that he is predictable; one of the things that his critics find most exasperating about him is the fact that he commands attention because he so often has something fresh to say. His friends find this a natural development of his long experience of 'free collective bargaining', looking for solutions that might possibly resolve a conflict to which both sides had come with a wide range of negotiable matters. As one of the six TUC representatives in the inflation talks with the Government and the CBI in 1972, Mr Scanlon was conspicuous for this quality; but of course the Government was not negotiating in any respect that an industrial negotiator would recognise, and probably cannot. Mr Scanlon also followed a policy of local bargaining in the engineering industry in 1972 which turned out to be unsuccessful, and the AUEW was the only big union which refused to defend itself in the National Industrial Relations Court when the court set about browsing on its funds by way of a remedy for contempt.

David Basnett, Jack Cooper and Walter Anderson
David Basnett is much younger than Mr Jones and Mr Scanlon. His father was an official of the NUGMW, and Mr Basnett was a bank clerk for a while before becoming a pilot during the Second World War. He became a full-time NUGMW official at 24, and by the time he succeeded Lord Cooper at the beginning of 1973 he had been a professional for 24 years, a member of the TUC General Council for six and a veteran of several official committees and commissions. Although he preferred a career with the union to a place at a university, one of Mr Basnett's jobs was as NUGMW education officer, when he not only pushed ahead with a large programme of membership education but had a leading share in giving the NUGMW the best funded and most professional research department in the movement. Mr Basnett is very tall, with a sardonic sense of humour but not much given to oratory. Although being a second-generation servant has a traditional pull in the NUGMW, to succeed Lord Cooper he had to beat a rival who was both President and an area secretary as Lord Cooper had been when he won. Lord Cooper (who was related by marriage to his predecessor, Sir Tom Williamson), is only five or six years older than Mr Jones and Mr Scanlon, but is a man so totally different in perceptions and style that upbringing in the same county fades into insignificance: an advocate of joining the European Common Market, a careful husbander of union funds, a strong believer in union discipline and a man of strong affections and long and intimate connections in the labour movement, the sort of public servant for whom the most wounding thing about the registration proposals under the Industrial Relations Act, with their offer of 'establishment', was

the implication that the unions, or at least the NUGMW, had not achieved respectability already.

Walter Anderson is a lawyer who left local government for the NALGO legal department in 1938 and worked his way to the chief executive job in that smoothest of all union bureaucracies. NALGO did not join the TUC until 1964, and before that occasionally flirted with the initiatives of the bank staff associations and similar bodies to establish some 'respectable' form of common organisation to set against the 'political' and 'irresponsible' qualities which they observed in the TUC. Mr Anderson retains the lawyer's and public servant's attitude to confidential proceedings, which is quite different from the attitude in the union movement at large. The TUC is political in the sense that, like Westminster and the parties in the country its members are given to the inspired or spontaneous 'leak' of information. Indeed, caution about giving information to the press or other agencies is something of a right-wing indicator in the union movement. Frank Foulkes, when he was general president of the ETU, had the reputation of providing a mass of accurate information, and I can recall the highly professional comment of one labour correspondent when it was clear beyond all doubt that the election scandal would mean the end of the Foulkes reign: 'It's a pity in a way; old Frank's the best leak we've ever had on the Confed.' (the Confederation of Shipbuilding and Engineering Unions). At the same time, Mr Anderson like other NALGO officials has found TUC membership a great broadener of horizons, as we saw earlier on, not only for NALGO but for other unions' views of NALGO. One of his surprises was to discover delegates from well-paid crafts who thought that NALGO had no low-paid members.

One of the effects of the reticence of the alleged 'right' is that the 'left' have much more of the running by way of publicity. When this is allied to the reality that the leaders of the biggest unions are the most powerful men in the movement, it means that there is far more public attention to 'left-wing' leaders of big unions. One particular personal quality of Mr Jones's accentuates the tendency even more. Mr Jones is a natural chairman. When he attends meetings of the TUC General Council, or other similar bodies, there is often a point where he makes a sort of compositing suggestion which may very well go on record afterwards as 'Jack Jones' or 'TGWU' policy accepted by the Council. A good example of that was when the

TUC was considering having talks on inflation with the Government and the CBI. It was in fact Walter Anderson who suggested that the natural place to hold them was the National Economic Development Council, on which the TUC had six representatives: Mr Jones, Mr Scanlon, Lord Cooper, Vic Feather (general secretary), Alf Allen, general secretary of the Shopworkers, and Sir Sidney Greene, general secretary of the NUR and chairman of the TUC economic committee. The discussion ebbed and flowed. A few members were against any talks at all. Some of the more refined leftists, like Dick Briginshaw of NATSOPA, thought that reference to the NEDC had the real advantage that anything would sink without trace there. But in the end it was Jack Jones who suggested that they should accept the idea of using the NEDC, while taking account of other opinions which would be represented through the TUC representatives; and word went out that the whole idea had come from Mr Jones.

Les Cannon and Frank Chapple
Trade union discussions can be extremely rancorous, and it is commonly said that the 'moderates' in the TUC General Council lack a leader at the beginning of 1973. The late Les Cannon of the EETU was not a leader of the moderates, because he was so impatient of what he considered the dithering and circular talk of his colleagues that he became, as one colleague put it, 'semi-detached'. Under Frank Chapple, who quickly established himself as Cannon's successor and was elected general president while remaining general secretary, the EETU leadership has become more astringent still. The EETU took a completely distinctive line in the debate at the 1972 Congress on suspending registered unions, and Mr Chapple's implied mockery of the proceedings so incensed George Smith of UCATT, the president, that Mr Smith did not 'notice' Mr Chapple's desire to speak. The result was a publicity coup for Mr Chapple: the speech that he would have given was printed in part or even in full in most newspapers. Mr Chapple, small, dark and Cockney, keeps pigeons, has an encyclopedic memory for members (a quality in which, it must be said, some union leaders are deficient), and is so seasoned by the wild work that we saw in Chapter 4 that there is probably no political operator in the union movement to touch him. He has a fund of down-to-earth epigrams: 'You've got to let the members blast you when they want; it's part of the job' being one that many union leaders would not accept.

Yet in spite of the divisions which are as open as the other outlines of this uniquely public pressure group, its members rub along together well enough for most of the time. If the common interest binding the TUC together had been brittle, it would have broken long ago under some of the pressures exercised on it; but since the common interest is elastic, the effects of the stretching are sometimes absurd in strict logical terms. When the TUC passed a disciplinary resolution on registration in 1971 and at the same time accepted a passage of the General Council's report which apparently contradicted the resolution, it was easy to mock until one considered what the alternative would be: a division of the TUC into mutually squabbling fragments. Only a romantic would suppose that a large, well-established institution like the TUC would readily behave like that, and only a considerable cynic would consider it desirable that it should.

During the tripartite talks on inflation, the TUC was greatly annoyed by reports that its six representatives had been divided among themselves in face of consistent postures by the Government and the CBI. The Prime Minister made a strong personal appeal to the TUC representatives to co-operate with the policy which the Government and its advisers had developed as the best possible in the circumstances. The TUC representatives heard this fairly glumly and replied in sequence as criticisms occurred to them; in particular, they wanted to talk about matters like rents which a Government statement later explained were excluded from the range of the talks. TUC representatives said different things, but the TUC resented the suggestion that they disagreed among themselves.

I suspect that there lies behind the common interpretation that the TUC is divided (on this occasion and on others) in a general and dangerous way an assumption that it is a system of unnatural alliances. Most active trade unionists do not agonise too much about matters of this kind; the alliance based on common interest has developed, and once it has developed there is a strong inclination to maintain it. There is nothing totalitarian about the union movement – it lacks the material resources which totalitarianism must have – and the further one moves from the rank and file the fewer the absolutes, as we noticed at the end of the last chapter.

In the TUC delegation to NEDC were two of the most senior and most overlooked union leaders of 1972 – Sir Sidney Greene and Alf Allen. Both have led their unions for several years, both are solid facts and figures men, and both lead unions with special problems. Sir Sidney's NUR membership has been running down rapidly, as we have seen; his own inclination to make the best bargain that he can across the board, conceding nothing of the traditional structure of railway employment unless the arguments for it are overwhelming, has unnerved more than one unprepared railway manager; it has also been clouded over by the enthusiastic noises of Ray Buckton, the new general secretary of ASLEF, who received far more publicity during the railway troubles. Sir Sidney, although on all occasions punctilious about the need to 'make recommendations to my executive' had his union well in hand; Mr Buckton is still proving himself.

Alf Allen was appointed to the original CIR, like Will Paynter, before the Industrial Relations Act made it unacceptable. Then USDAW had difficulties of its own with the Act. The bulk of USDAW membership is in the Co-operative movement. The Co-op officials' union registered, and USDAW was at first inclined to stay on the register to enjoy the advantage of concluding agency shops with the Co-op; only when the great bulk of the movement had clearly opted for de-registration and was prepared to discipline back-sliders did USDAW fall in line. Besides, neither Sir Sidney Greene nor Alf Allen are orators in any sense, and their speeches more often than not cover the less exhilarating parts of TUC work.

The Odd Men Out
Before going on to draw a few conclusions from this sketchy inspection of some important people, we should look at a particular class of union leader: the one who is thrown off, or kept off, the General Council. Being thrown off is very rare: it happened to Jack Peel of the Bleachers and Dyers in 1972 because of his style of controversy with left-wing leaders. If he had just been on the right, he would probably not have lost his seat; but he had a knack not only of making shrewd debating points but of challenging the pretensions of leaders of large unions. The Bleachers and Dyers is the biggest textiles union and has had a place on the General Council since it was formed nearly forty years ago, but the whole Congress votes on candidacies.

As we have seen, when Arthur Horner was general secretary of the NUM, the union regularly put him up for the General

Council and he always lost; at one stage the seat was held for several years by the representative of the North Wales Quarrymen (a union of some hundreds of members now absorbed in the TGWU). The TUC remains an anti-Communist organisation, although in 1972 it finally lifted the ban on Communists in trades councils; the late Bert Papworth was a member of the General Council while in the Communist Party and so was Will Paynter, but both for short terms more or less by accident. The method of kicking out Jack Peel was probably unprecedented. Like Frank Chapple at the same Congress, Mr Peel had a few extra television interviews and space in the papers, but both he and the TUC were losers.

There is another class of excluded leaders, very often lively and catching attention. Bryn Roberts, the autocratic general secretary of NUPE endlessly accused of 'poaching' by the TGWU and NUGMW, was a classic case before and after the war. Ray Buckton is one now: when railway employment was at its peak each of the three unions had a member on the General Council, but ASLEF has now lost its place. Mr Buckton is a big, enthusiastic Yorkshireman convinced that engine drivers are the salt of the earth and convinced (probably justly) that they and public employees generally are in a permanently false position. Lacking responsible TUC office, he was able to denounce the notion of any talks with the Government at all, a luxury at the time denied to General Council members.

At least there was no necessary personal element in the exclusion of Mr Buckton. ASLEF is, after all, the little railway union. There is nothing but personal considerations in the exclusion of Clive Jenkins of ASTMS. The leader of a union with 250,000 members in his middle forties can hardly still be called the awful child of the movement, but from his entrepreneurial style to his immoderately advanced opinions in international affairs and his extremes of humour (like the time that he told the TUC, which still has a very large number of practising Christians and many other members who are prim about certain things, that entry into Europe would be 'the biggest non-event since the immaculate conception') he gets on other trade unionists' nerves. He is suspected of leading a union that poaches members and rides the backs of other unions, and produces inflated membership figures by charging varying scales of contribution. However, although Mr Jenkins did not enjoy being excluded from the General Council when he stood for it, he exploits his position as a widely heard voice with all the more gusto for being among the groundlings. He started his career in Port Talbot (where Sir Geoffrey Howe, the legal artificer of the Industrial Relations Act, was a boy), and joined the obscure little engineering supervisors' union, ASSET, just after the war. He was lucky enough to work for it at London Airport, which made him prominent and experienced enough to become general secretary. The merger with the Scientific Workers and the huge growth in membership since make him the only leader of a large union who can claim in some sense to be its principal founder, the Bevin of the white collar.

Clive Jenkins's brother Tom is deputy general secretary of TSSA and seemed set to succeed Percy Coldrick when he retired. Mr Coldrick had the second railway seat on the General Council, and TSSA is nearly three times the size of ASLEF. But Tom Jenkins, dreaded in transport sector bargaining for the dogged precision with which he fastens on weaknesses in management arguments, lost the election for general secretary in the spring of 1973.

Provincial and Unqualified?
This survey has left out some of the most colourful and successful trade union leaders, but it could not be a who's who and it may help us to draw a few conclusions. First, there is no doubt of the impression that a disproportionate number of senior union officials come from outside the London area. This would not be surprising, since both heavy industry and hard times are more provincial than metropolitan experiences; it does not necessarily imply any direction or leadership behaviour. There are moderates and militants in every area: Lancashire is a militant area in engineering and a moderate one in mining. It may also be deceptive, since people in the middle and especially the upper class in Britain are culturally more uniform, and besides are expected to be more uniform. A career in management or government, on the whole, inclines the individual to take on the colouration of the colleagues among whom he moves. If there is any similar pressure on the trade unionist it is the other way: too smooth a diction might be an actual disadvantage, whatever the substance of the actual speech.

For some observers this accentuates the feeling that trade union leaders are unqualified, as indeed in formal terms they usually are.* Of all the persons we have mentioned in this chapter only Walter Anderson has a professional qualification as the phrase is formally understood. There is a point here which applies equally strongly to a certain kind of uneducated business entrepreneur (with the difference that such an entrepreneur is unlikely to get to the top of the CBI): the education system is supposed, at least to some extent, to prepare people to take responsibility for the government of others. The knowledge of the public good with which a student of parts finishes further education may be inexact, theoretical and unscientific, but it is traditional within a common pattern. Anyone formally taught about government is likely to have some formal ideas about government. For trade union leaders this is not necessarily so, and there is some reason to believe that even if the story of Citrine's theory of a separate TUC representation is myth, the union movement has developed some slightly divergent theory. Certainly, as we shall see, the union movement has developed in practice well away from the social theory behind common law. Besides, the difference between man-management, which treats of individuals, and industrial relations, which regulates dealings between collectives, is disregarded in the conduct and conversation of innumerable managers, officials and politicians every day. There are pleasant and unpleasant, clever and blockish, subtle and blunt, vain and modest men in trade union office as in any other office. I am not persuaded by twenty years' experience of reporting in Britain and other countries that managers are conspicuously more perceptive and intelligent as a class than trade union leaders.

Revising predictions to meet the unexpected is on the whole an easier process for trade union leaders than for managers. There are so few trade union leaders, they represent so many workers and they come up against such an enormous variety of situations, often novel, that in the course of a successful career which takes them to the top they must have operated frequently with almost no supervision in meeting a challenge where no established rule applies. It is true that their objectives are as often as not merely defensive and that on the rare occasions when a union hierarchy, let alone its membership, exercises

* An innocent example of this feeling from a moderately friendly source is in Peter Jenkins's *The Battle of Downing Street* where he gives a sardonic list of workers whom union leaders represented as if these experienced union servants were still at the lathe or the loom.

discipline over a union officer it may be harsh, but the continuing constraints on a manager on the make are much greater as a rule. There are still very few managers who are given adequate authority to reach a settlement at the level at which they negotiate. And a manager who takes an unauthorised risk in negotiation may see a superior take the credit if it comes off but leave him to take the blame if it does not. Most union leaders expect to take blame, like Frank Chapple, as part of their job. There will always be a number of critics of a negotiator who puts in a wage claim for, say £6 and settles for £4. The results are sometimes unpleasant.

Meeting Angry Members
Television viewers were able to see Frank Chapple himself being jostled by pickets from his own union as he went into the talks that led to the 1972 settlement. Jack Jones, general secretary of the TGWU, had angry dissidents invade Transport House and throw their weight about after the 1972 docks settlement. Lawrence Daly, the militant general secretary of the miners, was booed and jeered by union members who agreed with him in 1970 because he insisted on following the prescribed procedures before industrial action. This is not a new phenomenon. It is almost implicit in the nature of industrial life that where there is conflict, and a knot of angry men are mobbing another like sparrows after a cuckoo, he is more likely to be a union leader than a manager and (as we saw in the last chapter) more likely still to be another worker. To receive such treatment a manager would have to be provocative on a grand scale. I first saw this happen to a leader in 1958 after Frank Cousins, Jack Jones's predecessor, had unsuccessfully addressed a mass meeting of Covent Garden market porters on unofficial strike. As he left the building, with angry members crowding about him, the police offered to give him an escort. He turned back, saying: 'I don't need protection against my own men, even when they disagree with me.'

Not everyone has Mr Cousins's advantage of physical size and, on that occasion at least, the impression of majestic rage on tight leash. The effect was certainly dramatic and striking. But the simple fact is that the trade union officer, whatever his size, dignity or other capacity for persuasion, can never run away from his members and keep the place he needs in their estimation. By way of compensation, he can afford to be more open in his dealings than a manager normally can. It is always much easier to get a colourable account of conflict from the trade union side than from the management, at least while the conflict continues. Some trade union officers are all too ready to talk about their troubles without taking enough account of what effect it will have on the other side. Almost all managers are too cautious about what they say to either journalists or their own workers. Perhaps they are guided by a financial analogy and believe that one can hoard information like money; but information even more than money is valueless without use and the great neglected art in industrial relations is that of imparting information, anticipating questions, and learning in return. The trade union leader 'gets' messages from which the manager is normally insulated.

What he makes of them is another matter. We can take for granted that every senior trade union leader is more than ordinarily durable and worldly wise, a veteran of innumerable bargains, compromises and difficult meetings. But at some point in his career his prejudices will have hardened, and they will normally reflect a state of affairs which has long passed. In times of accelerating change induced by all sorts of factors in which unions have no part, this undoubtedly leads to difficulties. Trade unions do not, on the whole, accommodate 'whizz kids', partly because union members have abundant bruising experience of them in other positions of authority. On the other hand, it is quite common for youngsters to take the lead in unofficial action, or in difficult situations at plant level, and it is sometimes very difficult for the union machine to control them. Professionalism in trade union service has been a strong tradition in certain unions, and it may be growing a little. But a great mass of trade union leaders started their careers with some informal experience in 'extending the field of collective bargaining' – that is, asking for something that no one had asked for before and getting it.

Beyond Practical Experience
This common fact may lead to an odd political outlook. Where it matters most is in areas outside individual practical experience, paradoxical though it sounds. We have seen, in an earlier chapter, that trade unionists' concern with public policy depends to some extent on its direct practical relevance to their work as trade unionists. Going into Europe, or nuclear bombs, or even

German rearmament may be of first importance to individual and influential trade unionists, but they are not of central importance to all of them as trade unionists. This is true also of various other matters of public policy and political attitudes: they may even be important to the labour movement as a whole, but are not in the practical area of concern of a given individual. This is what Professor A. J. M. Sykes of Strathclyde calls the 'millenarian' area of trade unionism. He believes that perhaps a majority of trade union leaders are formally committed to a socialist millennium, but behave as if it will not and perhaps cannot ever come. For example, incomes policy of some kind seems a natural objective of socialism and more and more political economists who are neither dogmatically socialist nor dogmatically capitalist consider something of the kind inevitable. Yet 'left wing' trade unionists and 'right wing' Conservatives sometimes seem to be united in opposing it.

It is also possible, indeed common, for a shop steward or district officer of a union to do an extremely practical year's work in his particular area, but have a millenarian view of larger matters. The usual remedy for this is a process of steady commitment to the union as an institution at a continuously higher level. We must remember that in the 40 per cent turnover situation common in general unskilled work, the union itself is often the most comprehensive stabilising element in a whole field of employment, especially if there are many small employers whose level of management qualifications, as distinct from practical enterprise, may be no higher and is sometimes much lower than the practical industrial relations ability that union officials may simply have learnt on the job. The standard of solidity and expertise of employers' associations is very variable, from the considerable sophistication of a very big one like the Engineering Employers' Federation to little ones which may be either purely local, with a part-time official who is usually a lawyer, predominantly trade associations with an occasional appeal function, or very loose federations which intervene in industrial relations almost by accident.

Context of Individual Responsibility
From this emerges one final paradox: the union official is usually more left to his own devices than the manager, not less. He is responsible for far too many members to be totalitarian, but to a manager of limited experience and authority

and much more formal and continuous responsibility he may seem daunting or (in his influence on the employees) malicious. This brings us into the difficult field of individual responsibility in industrial relations. Try as we may to make this formal by some orderly rigmarole, we are forced back to the common requirement that, experience suggests, groups in general demand. They give their respect to leaders who give up something in return for leadership. They are sardonic about the characteristic Disraeliesque politician who shares the ambition mocked by Plato, 'first to achieve a competence and then to practise virtue' naively expressed by the poet Phokylides. Trade union leaders are individuals charged by groups with responsibility to prevent other individuals or smaller groups from exploiting them. Of course, no individual trade union leader is ever given a specific mandate in terms like that. But that is what he is there for.

Into this delicate relation comes the common lawyer, to whom the world is made up of persons, big and little. An institution is always a big person. Trade unions have always given the lawyers some difficulty, and for most of them this difficulty continues because they have refused to register and thus become a familiar class of legal persons, bodies corporate with perpetual succession and a common seal. The first requirement of the law in dealing with disputes between persons is to apportion blame, and where there is a straightforward adversary situation the lawyers will decently begin with the feeling that the onus is on the big person. In industrial relations this may prove to be an inadequate approach, because of the difficulty of apportioning blame where there is no malice, or even negligence, in any sense that counts, to any individual. Industrial relations is much more like traffic control than like matters of individual dealings where morality is an obvious and personal thing. Our record in industrial relations, happily, is a good deal better than our record in road travel; it is very rarely in either that it does not require a mistake by at least two parties to cause a serious accident.

In road traffic legislation we have at least learnt to discourage people from reckless zig-zagging in and out of the line of traffic. There is some standard of competence required from people taking the special responsibility of driving different classes of vehicle. In industrial relations the new Act actually gives licence to the reckless zig-zagger, if he is a worker who dislikes unions, and imposes only a general duty to have some idea of what one is doing, according to standards which are mostly undefined and sometimes defined in a way which runs contrary to industrial relations experience.

It is well known that in industrial strife people may be hurt through no fault of their own. Everyone has heard the story of the mental defective or the poor foolish widow who reported for work during a strike and had to be sacked when it ended because feeling was so bitter. But in fact it is only tolerance that prevents such incidents, and tolerance is not increased by giving a remedy against the union. The 'angry silence' is unpleasant for everyone, but it must be a very strange undertaking where workers' intolerance of this kind develops without examples the other way. Senior managers sometimes find it hard to appreciate the intolerable consequences for their humblest subordinates of small mistakes high in the scale. There are proportionately far fewer managers at the highest level who believe that they have ever given orders requiring a subordinate to do something immoral and callous, than there are junior managers who believe that they have been given orders which require them to do precisely that. So far as I know, there has been no similar study of trade union officials; the result would no doubt be the same (indeed, it might show interesting variations on what a trade union official may feel obliged *by his members* to do that he would rather not do).

Dangers of Collective Moralising

The case of Mr James Goad, whose case against the AUEW had cost the union £55,000 in fines by the end of 1972, illustrates the point. Mr Goad was a deviant in union terms. He was kept out of the union but not out of his job. He went for a legal remedy under the new legislation. He was suspended from his job as the stock of tolerance in the plant where he worked diminished. He became a celebrity, and like many celebrities suffered from making an off-the-cuff answer to a big question, saying that he would take an inordinate amount of money to give up his job altogether. The remedy had not been much use to him.

Meanwhile, the different cast of mind from the TGWU and other union leaders showed itself at the head of the AUEW, where the executive was dominated four-three by the 'left'. Unlike the TGWU, which had virtually compelled the TUC to endorse the principle that a member union might protect itself before the court by demanding that otherwise the TUC in general should pay the fines, the AUEW persisted in ignoring the court altogether. I suspect that something of the experience of the opposition within the opposition lay behind this decision. Mr Scanlon was not afraid to remind people that a great deal of the founding activities of trade unions was 'unlawful'. There were plenty of intelligent people who understood at best cloudily the NIRC's comment that the union's action was 'unlawful but not criminal' – a comment by way of reproof to a country solicitor who compared the union's behaviour with the bombing activities of the 'Angry Brigade'.

The thinking behind a remedy for Mr Goad is that if he has suffered someone must be to blame and owe him a remedy (although the court, in view of the union's boycott, had not by the end of 1972 decided what he had suffered, if anything). Much the same reasoning has come into the advocacy of incomes policy. Inflation, as we have seen, develops when there is not enough flexibility in other parts of the economic machine to maintain the value of the currency; in a country as dependent on economic activity in other parts of the world as Britain is, there has to be greater flexibility than in countries like the United States or France with comparatively greater resources. We measure productivity by averages – output per worker – but we do not achieve it by average individual performance but by collective performance. This involves collective regulation, and the individual worker may labour till exhaustion and make no difference if the work is wrongly ordered; to this extent the comment by Professor Galbraith at the end of Chapter 1 is valid. But it is not only foolish but dangerous to conclude that the flexibility must come predominantly from the earnings of organised labour merely because salaries and wages are the principal costs of commerce. There may be many other relations which are distorted and could be corrected. Above all, it is dangerous to make it a matter of collective morality. First, an accusation which appears unfair – and accusation of greed, even by association, from a rich man to a poor man is bound to appear unfair – stiffens rather than persuades. Yet after that a repetition that inflation implies collective immorality, instead of merely marginal although dangerous miscalculation or faulty ordering, may finally induce collective self-contempt and despair. This is hardly a moral objective, and the strongest characters the trade unions could produce would hardly rally their followers from its consequences.

Chapter 9

Day after Tomorrow

The ecologist must mistrust the questionnaire so beloved of the sociologist, because it fails to take sufficient notice of the ethos of a people. The questionnaire will not really give you scientific data.
F. Fraser Darling

Tactics and Attitudes of Unions
Trade unions have come a long way from their budding days as work groups presenting a united front to a single employer, or local cells trying to organise a particular craft, or whatever other determining step may have been taken. The status and tactics of most unions in 1972 are very different from the desperate and experimental tactics of, say, 1850. They have always been slightly mystifying institutions, even to the people who run them. Although they apply most of their energies now to collective bargaining and the power calculations that accompany it,* the share of wages (perhaps as distinct from salaries) in the gross national product has barely increased in half a century; social security has been a more effective instrument of redistribution of wealth by taking a higher proportion of income by way of national insurance and tax contributions. Unions, especially British unions, tend to be unimaginative in their variation of tactics.

This is partly because innovation in union tactics is greeted with dismay or with condescension by the 'moulders of opinion'. Dismay is particularly marked if the innovation is both tough

* Although they do pay more in provident benefit than strike benefit. In 1968 they paid nearly ten times as much; the proportion spent on strike benefit has been rising steadily since. Of course, not all strikers get strike benefit and their families qualify for supplementary benefit; the present Government has made this qualification less generous, but I doubt if it made much difference. Strikes are not 'level-headed business decisions'.

and successful, like the miners' picketing in 1972, or if it involves real or apparent licence to troublemakers. Authoritarian leadership in the docks, for example, broke down irreparably more than twenty years ago. The TGWU's difficulties with the NASD 'poaching' and the endless succession of unofficial strikes and unofficial leaders made some opening to a representative style inevitable. Yet Frank Cousins and Jack Jones successively were criticised for 'surrendering' to militants. 'Respectable' observers were uneasy when the Devlin Committee in 1966 said that there should be a proper shop steward system in the docks, and pointed out later how many of the 'unofficial liaison' leaders had become shop stewards. The real point was that recognition changed their behaviour; strife in the docks diminished. Yet even then port employers were still complaining that the union's dock groups (representative area councils within the union for scrutinising and passing judgment on negotiations) had no standing in the TGWU rule book or in national agreements.

We have seen that the experience of many trade union officials includes 'extending the area of collective bargaining' almost by accident. In many respects the fortunes of a union and its officials are full of unexpected turns which neither unions nor employers can predict. Most people are ready to say what a union's 'job' is or ought to be – usually with a good deal more confidence than is justified by their knowledge of what it actually does. There is also, I believe, a strong underlying feeling that it would be pleasanter if trade unions were able to achieve their purposes without so much strife, and this is not mere sentimentality either. But it is perfectly possible for someone to believe this and remain a solid union member.

Someone who feels obliged to take sides in a conflict may dislike it, and dislike other men's even more. He may nevertheless see the blame as the employer's, at least in his case. As we saw in the introduction, the trade union movement is a very public pressure group, although not necessarily outstandingly effective. As a result, pollsters are likely to ask the public simple questions about trade unions and compile equivocal or meaningless answers. Even if it were logically inconsistent to tell a pollster one day that there were too many strikes and take part in one the next day (which it is not), it would still be understandable. Another favourite question is whether 'the unions' power should be curbed'. What unions? Power towards whom?

The proposition disintegrates as soon as one tries to put flesh on it. If opinion polls took the trouble to be specific, and asked people to comment on what they knew about or had experienced, I suspect that there would be a considerable change of emphasis in the material they put together.

Occupations Set Their Mark

You need to be bold nowadays to make large predictions. We know, for example, that there is not enough zinc, or copper, or other non-ferrous metals so far discovered to allow the population of the world at large to use as much per head as the Americans do. We do not know how these metals will be used a generation ahead in advanced economies or what new materials may have been developed. By extension, we do not know what people will be doing for a living and in what respects it will have changed from what their parents are doing now. All the indications are that the change will continue to be rapid. We know that all occupations set their mark on a person. Sometimes it is crudely physical. Without corrective measures, dentists and dockers are liable to have bad backs, the first from posture and the second from strain; miners and blast-furnacemen develop distinctive scars; sewage workers and some food processors and chemical operatives lose their sense of smell. Pop musicians, road repair gangs, sheet metal workers and production line workers in engineering tend to become hard of hearing because of the amplification equipment, pneumatic hammers and general clangour respectively. These and many others like them are obvious enough examples of cause and effect.

Much more subtle are the effects on attitudes not only of what a man does, but where and on what terms he does it, where he was born, what language he speaks, what values and expectations he acquired while growing up. Besides, of this list or any list of occupations we can no more be sure that they will all survive than we can be sure about the future of materials. But we do know that there are certain tendencies and tensions in human behaviour that are likely to be with us as far ahead as we can see. We must hope that the variety and complication and interdependence will continue to increase, without becoming destructive. All our social arrangements are on a narrow path between specialised docility that kills them off as institutions like in-bred Pharaohs, and revolting individualism that makes conflict unbearable.

Odd things happen constantly in the ordinary way. It goes without saying that among a hundred million people a million-to-one chance comes up a hundred times in any given period. The impossible, of course, never happens, but the far-fetched is a commonplace. Given the speed of communications nowadays, conspicuous oddities among hundreds of millions of people become common knowledge. To bring home the results of innovation, advertisers in particular talk the language of exaggeration, keeping expectations slightly ahead of the ability to provide.

If anything, in recent years much trade union activity has widened the gap a little more. The double talk required of managers, reassuring owners or shareholders on the one hand about future prosperity and warning workers on the other of the imminent disaster implicit in a wage claim, does not help much either. Facing these conflicting signals, people in general remain remarkably sane. We cannot define sanity, just as the World Health Organisation has struggled unsuccessfully to define good health. We know that we have lost something when we become emotionally disturbed or physically ill. The trouble about institutions is that the bigger they get, the more difficult it is to detect whether they are making life in general more or less humane, or indeed whether or not they are already in a state of fatal decline. Harmless weaknesses or eccentricities which are tolerable in a village or small town where everyone knows the individual concerned assume a different aspect in the anonymity of large communities; sometimes instead of the occasional deviant understood and supported by a small community one finds pockets of many of them in a large one. (I knew an eccentric Irishman in New York who called it 'a great town for village eejits'.) A sick company with a turnover of a billion dollars or an outdated industry with half a million workers can do immense damage in its death throes, probably killing a few bright little enterprises in the process. When we look at the behaviour and prospects of trade unions, we must ask what they ought to be to meet the expectations for which they were founded.

The Theory of Countervailing Power

As institutions, unions are bound to grow, consolidate and merge in response to the development of society in general and employers' organisations in particular. This is the theory of 'countervailing power': as employing organisations extend and buttress their power and autonomy, employees' organisations should do the same. But although unions may have to be big to play their part in setting the context for industrial relations, the measure of their success must be how well they deal with individual situations, whether they involve a few members or many. On the one hand, we have the beginnings of international organisation to bargain with international companies, although they are not much more yet than gleams in the eyes of very large unions like the Auto Workers in the United States, the TGWU in Britain and the Metalworkers in West Germany, or of extremely sanguine and venturesome organisations like ASTMS. Some union internationals are more active than others. The Chemical Workers (ICF) have set up an organisation to negotiate with Dunlop-Pirelli, the English-Italian merger, and are developing permanent world councils of local and national affiliated bodies, including representatives from plants, to explore new bases for bargaining with about two dozen of the largest multinational enterprises within the next few years. The TGWU proposals for transnational bargaining in the motor industry in Europe will probably come under the wing of the Metalworkers' International (IMF). In both chemicals and the motor industry there have been contacts at unofficial level among shop stewards and workers' leaders for some time.

In the European Economic Community the trade unions have formal representation on the economic and social committee and the standing committee on employment. This is a new and complicated operating ground for the British labour movement (although it has been active in international trade unionism as long as anyone). Politically, a minority of trade union leaders in Britain care for the prospect before them in Europe, but no one, least of all their European colleagues, expects them not to be a major influence. British organised labour is big, flexible and self-confident (perhaps even self-righteous); in spite of the clumsy postures required by the Industrial Relations Act, the confidence survives.

However, in operating internationally the TUC and its members have problems which employers do not have. Since they deploy resources for production, employers may operate internationally without worrying unduly about the variations of national law or, within limits, national commercial practice. In dealing with other businesses, they deal on equal terms so far as the law is concerned. Trade unions organise people for their collective protection against undue liberties by employers. National law varies a great deal in the context that it sets for this process. The balance between collective bargaining and state regulation varies and is subject to regular revision. At one extreme is the United States, where collective bargaining is the main concern of a highly commercial trade union movement – bargaining which sets out in controlling detail relations between union and employer from national to factory level. At the other extreme is West Germany, where an elaborate code for joint regulation at company level does not require the participation of unions at all, although they are more likely to win majorities of works councils than not. In organised plants in the United States the individual contract of employment has hardly any significance. In Western Europe it remains the basic agreement on which the superstructure of management and organisation is built. Finally, national trade union movements are pulled into international activity not so much by broad aspirations (although international solidarity has always been an ideal, like 'one big union') but by the development of the organisations they have to deal with.

The Only Jobs in Town
All trade unions must take some account of the people at Kiltartan Cross* (or whatever other place their members may be) or in the end they may turn against the union as well as other apparently interlinked and equally remote parts of a power structure. Of course, a small community may simply accept an economic death sentence. If the only factory in the town is taken over by a big group and closed there is not much that the local employees can do about it. In a similar factory where there are alternative jobs, they may not bother much. Only rarely do we get a spontaneous revolt from the local workers without official union blessing, like the famous 'work-in' at Upper Clyde Shipbuilders which we discuss later in this chapter. It is true that the principal leaders of this revolt were both members of the Communist Party. It is also true that in

* 'My country is Kiltartan Cross,
My countrymen Kiltartan's poor;
No likely end could bring them loss
Or leave them happier than before.'
Yeats

Germany as a result of the 1972 works council legislation, an employer may not close a plant without first consulting the works council, providing them with the information they need, and receiving their social plan for the resettlement of the workers. Indeed, the employer is obliged to accept the social plan unless he can make a case before arbitration for rejecting or varying it. Anyone who is satisfied with the state of British democracy or inclined to see any unofficial workers' action as subversive should consider that it is easier or less expensive or both to close a works and strip its assets for the benefit of shareholders who need never have heard of it in Britain than almost anywhere else in Western Europe.

Lackeys and Libertarians

It is much easier to trace the history of trade unions as institutions, with their national and local and industrial variations, than it is to assess their real contribution to the satisfaction of their members' requirements. It is as difficult to assess this contribution as it is to trace the real centre of decision-making and innovation in a very large company. We have seen in the Clayton Dewandre case that the NUGMW and TGWU sections met different needs of different workers, depending on their age and taste for a quiet life. I have known companies where the collective leadership of trade union groups was appreciably more stable than the collective leadership of their management. This can produce considerable distress and much greater strain on managers than on workers' leaders. There is a class of managerial behaviour which is rather like the quality attributed by the ancient Romans to household slaves, who were intimately linked to their masters by the personal value of their services, and their subordination. By leave of the master, they were indulged in a certain impertinence and forwardness to others, but paid the price in the necessary obsequiousness to the master himself. The Romans described this behaviour as 'vernile', to distinguish it from the sullen and alienated 'servile' behaviour required of other slaves. It might be a tonic to revive the word in English, because we do not seem to have another which so perfectly describes the pathological lackey, the person who may derive high status and high pay from doing trivial things for important people.

People who are too obviously vernile inevitably pay for it in the attitudes of other people towards them. Like all such subtleties, this can be carried to extremes, as any reporter knows when someone, some time, calls him a capitalist lackey. John Barbour's poem about Robert Bruce some 600 years ago was the first known use of the word 'freedom' in its modern sense in Western European literature:

> 'Freedom all solace to man gives:
> He lives at ease who freely lives.'

Scotsmen, with the requirement to make do with very little set on them by the spareness of their soil and climate, have always been prominent in putting their pride before their bread, if their temperament inclined them that way, or keeping the Sabbath and everything else that they could lay their hands on if their personality and circumstances were different. But all too often the 'solace' that freedom gives is the freedom to persecute or to dominate. The same spirit of liberty that we read into Barbour has been cited to support many excesses, yet his definition of the *symptoms* of freedom keeps its freshness in all the countless multitude of words that assault us on the subject year in and year out. Trade unions are very definitely concerned with freedom in this sense, about the struggle within a man as well as among men; the struggle between the need to work together and the need to be noticed, between 'let's get organised' and 'get off my back'.

As we have seen, specialisation to get a task done, however valuable it may be, is by its nature unpleasant except for the organiser. If a group organises the specialisation by mutual discussion – Joe do this, Jack do that, and so on – it is more acceptable but uninstitutional. As organisation becomes more complex, the humbler and less remarkable individuals have less and less perceived choice of what they are to do compared with the choice that they might have and the choice that is available to people with greater talents or pushfulness, or a better start in life. The situation becomes even more unendurable as change accelerates and specialisation in the more unsatisfying economic tasks becomes more exacting. It is highly efficient when everyone is used to it and while its routines remain adequate and match external needs, but it is not well suited to meeting change. Its very efficiency in handling routines reduces the healthy experience of learning from mistakes, and may even come to convince people that they do not make mistakes, a statement which is obviously absurd. Generalisation, bringing as many people as possible into the discussion of policies and possibilities, may never reach the peak of authoritarian efficiency* but it makes participants used to correcting error.

Twilight of 'Scientific Management'
All systems have their day, and perhaps one of the systems which is near the end of its day is 'scientific management' in the sense in which it is normally used, which is the application of mechanical measures to the behaviour of people at work. Flesh and blood can stand it, but humanity will not stand it indefinitely. Unfortunately, a trade union may become as mechanically set in its ways as any other institution. For example, British Railways pay engine drivers (or motormen, as the word is now) bonuses which depend on the distance their train travels. This has made a sort of aristocracy out of long-distance drivers, and now a favoured aristocracy because their job is proportionately easier than it used to be and absolutely less wearing than the job of stop-and-start drivers of trains on densely used, short-distance services like London suburban lines. Besides, the London drivers live in a high-wage area with little unemployment. But it is the unions, or at least their leaders, who resist change in this situation. Unions may make miscalculations about the needs of different classes of membership, as the TGWU did in the docks container affair. If a national structure works too smoothly, it may not be responsive enough; young American and German workers are increasingly dissatisfied with a representative system which facilitates production but diminishes spontaneity. Spontaneity certainly has a place in industrial relations, so long as it is not merely wilful and heedless of other interests. But the necessary candour and tranquillity to make it possible is a rare combination.

European Influences: Councils and Directorships
We have seen that in Britain the way from a work group to a national trade union is a long and winding road, and that left to unregulated development a labour movement becomes a loose coalition of very various institutions. British employers' organisations have something of the same quality, of course; to see the opposite one has to look at Sweden, where the effectiveness of the lock-out makes commentators describe both sides of

* However, it also avoids the temptations, of which the greatest is the refusal to admit that anything has gone wrong.

industry as having 'the nuclear bomb' and they are so highly organised that national collective agreements covering all workers are honoured more securely than statute law in many less disciplined cultures. Although international merger may seem a natural step forward, it will be a much more difficult step than amalgamation in one country. At the moment the EEC Commission has begun the process of harmonising company law. There is one directive already in force about the presentation of statistics, and four or five others are under consideration. There is also a draft statute for Europeon companies: that is, companies which will be registered as European and not of any particular member country, although they will have all the privileges of national companies. The natural inclination of the Commission is to provide for workers' participation according to the most advanced practice, which they believe to be the German and Dutch.

Dutch and German companies have two boards. One is representative and 'supervisory': its members appoint those of the other board, which consists of the most senior managers. They may not be on the supervisory board as well. Under German law, the shareholders and workers elect equal numbers of members of the supervisory board in the coal and steel industry, and the shareholders elect two to the workers' one in other public companies over a certain size. Dutch law provides for workers and shareholders each to have the power of nomination and veto over candidates for the supervisory board, but the existing members decide which of the unvetoed, nominated candidates are acceptable. All western European countries outside Scandinavia and Italy require representative works councils by law; Scandinavia and Italy provide for them by collective agreement. However, they are various institutions; honouring of either law or agreement is variable from country to country. In Germany works councils have a large veto power over management decisions that affect employment. The powers of Dutch works councils are less formidable on paper, but the Netherlands have in addition collective agreements which take practice there quite as far. Every western European country also has statutory compensation for redundancy. The EEC Commission has now put up proposals for a European company with a structure, supervisory board and works council on the German model; for a harmonisation of national company law requiring workers' representatives (or the Dutch system) for the supervisory board; and one for harmonisation on 'collective dismissal' which would make it impossible to lay off more than a few workers for redundancy without scrutiny by a public authority and a 'social plan' to guarantee the workers' future over and above mere severance pay.

These are still only proposals, and they have to go through an elaborate screening process before the Council of Ministers makes the final decisions. They will all be novel in Britain, where the union movement is suspicious of any attempt to inhibit them by depending on statutory remedies and formal representation. But whatever the outcome European company law – either for a supranational or a domestic undertaking – will be a simple problem compared with the eventual controversy about the standing of the European trade union, let alone the international trade union. It seems on the face of it impossible to run an international trade union from a haven from any involved country's industrial relations laws as companies use tax havens, or to force municipal law to become less restrictive of any institution. Tactically, international operation will call for policies less and less like the 'monitoring and veto' to which we have become accustomed in Britain.

What Form for Supranational Bargaining?

At the beginning of Chapter 1 we said that a trade union is successful when it is convincing. At international level, the most promising course for trade unions will probably bear little resemblance to traditional tactics of domestic strife. After all, it took all the years of organising in the coalfields until 1972 to produce a genuine national coal strike (the 1926 'General Strike' began as a lock-out); how long would it take to produce a European strike? A European lock-out is probably slightly more likely, and commentators from European countries where lock-outs are still a regular part of the employers' armament have no doubt about its effectiveness compared with a strike. Besides, such a clash would appear Titanic and remote to far too many workers. We are more likely to see international co-operation in riding the backs of employers, extracting information, calling them to account by 'consumer information campaigns' and other propaganda devices, and by measures of consolidation like bargaining at the same time for employees of the same company in different countries. This last tactic has two advantages. There is bound to be some convenience in it for the common employer, if he plays his cards properly, since even monitoring let alone exploiting disparate arrangements in neighbouring countries is an expensive and, not infrequently, inaccurate process; for the union or unions it gives a basis of convenience and legitimacy for industrial action, either selectively or across the board. Industrial action itself in disparate systems might not achieve much (although 'blacking' across national frontiers has a considerable history, especially in transport), but its potentialities and legitimacy might concentrate the minds of employers considerably in negotiating terms.

Conditions for a 'Work-in'
We have seen repeatedly that trade unions if they are to grow must be open institutions, instruments and beneficiaries of social change as well as monitors. At one time or another, much of their most significant development has depended on respectably unlawful behaviour. Probably the most striking recent example of this in Britain has been the 'work-in' on the Clyde when Upper Clyde Shipbuilders went into liquidation. This response captured the sympathy of millions of people who are not in any sense revolutionary. At root the work-in was an appeal to a 'legitimacy' more profound than the formal rules of company ownership and management, a denial that workers' interests count for no more than their formal contracts allow them when an enterprise goes down with no employment to succeed it. The denial, like other labour innovations, has to be convincing. There was a great deal against success in the Upper Clyde yards. The standard of management on the Clyde had certainly been low, or at least failed to keep pace with circumstances, but the workers in general had more than matched the excesses of management and many conscientious and talented executives had failed to find the response that they would have deserved in a less harsh context. The Government had put a great deal of money into the insolvent company and was being asked for more. If UCS had gone down quietly, as dozens of smaller concerns did during the same period, its demise would have left Govan and Clydebank bitter and desperate, but most of the country would have shown the traditional stoicism in face of others' misfortune.

On the other hand, the decision to go on working was unexpected and impressive. There was an element of self-rehabilitation in it, since the 'work-in' leaders required higher standards of behaviour on the job than many workers had been prepared to give to the unsuccessful management. There had to be an impression of callousness and injustice strong enough to persuade outsiders that not all had been done that could be done to protect thousands of jobs in a distressed area. There had to be a level of workers' organisation in the yards strong enough to maintain discipline and administer hundreds of thousands of pounds. And there had to be a response. The final settlement actually required far more money from the Government than the subsidy refused UCS; but the reaction to the work-in produced from Govan Shipbuilders and Marathon Manufacturing at least the promise of enterprises which would eventually be viable.

There is no question that the work-in was in strict terms unlawful; its justification lay in showing that the workers could be made to produce better results if there were something to rouse their enthusiasm, and that a serious application of enterprise in everyone's interests could produce a possible solution for even a desperate case. Of course, this was an application of power; but it was a much more convincing application than a last despairing strike would have been, and dozens of smaller work-ins since the one on the Clyde began have established a new constraint of accountability on fugitive managements. But for every dozen there are a hundred who get away.

For years British trade unionists have been accustomed to behave with impunity in ways that other countries' laws forbid. Perhaps this has been more of a safety valve than a positive advantage to union members as a whole. Yet the behaviour of trade unions is intimately linked to the ordinary social behaviour and assumptions of a people. Everybody wants freedom and prosperity, and comparatively speaking, making the comparison with a hundred years ago or with an underdeveloped country, people of the industrial world assume that they have got them, but not as much as they would like. The messages are conflicting. How much freedom of choice, how much life-enhancing variety, do people really have? How much should they have? In the nature of things, trade union answers to questions like these are quite different from the commercial answers to the international questions that companies ask. Commercial partnerships involve comparatively few people deploying large resources in proportion to their numbers for limited objectives. The size of the resources, the growth of production or exchange, and the growth of profit are all simply measured; although in the context of eternity they may not mean very much, in the context of today they are the justification of enterprise. For these limited purposes, a commercial enterprise normally has ample access to information and in many countries a great deal of power to control information, by advertising, public relations and the general fact of 'respectable' assumptions shared among substantial people in a given society.

Trade unions do not have these ready measures of success. They organise large numbers of people in a monitoring and advisory and sometimes resisting sense, but call on very little of their personal resources, let alone the resources required for their work. Attempts to co-ordinate trade union activities in different countries, let alone merge them, are vulnerable to national prejudices and lack of sympathy among the controllers of public information. They are also vulnerable to wild political views, for roughly the same reasons that make commercial enterprise easier internationally as well. A Communist or Trotskyist international venture requires only a few people, but in the appropriate circumstances it can cause a lot of trouble. We may therefore expect that the organised response in depth of the trade union movement to the international company, or even the European company, will be slow and uneven and possibly depend in the end as much on indirect political action and local initiative as on formal trade union co-ordination. The big American unions have been trying for about a generation to keep some sort of inhibition on American companies which go international; they see this as the 'export of American jobs'. They have tried, sporadically, to develop interest in other countries in joint resistance, but even assuming their diagnosis to be right, it is hard to persuade a labour movement to resist the 'import of jobs' even if there is full employment. After all, the imported jobs might be 'better' jobs.

Anarchy of International Commerce
Governments of considerable countries are anxious about the power and anarchy of international commerce. Standard Oil of New Jersey disposes every year of resources equivalent to about 15 per cent of the gross national product of Britain. Although this is only a money calculation and even in the twilight of Britain's tradition of cheap food and cheap raw materials there is a surviving margin compared with Western Europe, the dis-

posal is in some respects more absolute and more private than any GNP except the odd absolute sheikhdom. International companies also have a tremendous influence on the flow of funds; they may not initiate speculation, but since they require large and expert international exchange departments to protect themselves, they give great weight to international speculative movements by responding to them in the predictable expert way. International companies are not subject to international discipline, and a great many of them are now so big or so ingenious that they contrive to avoid any national discipline that is a serious inconvenience. Trade unions, on the other hand, are subject to the national discipline both of their members and, in various degrees, of their national systems of law.

Even if alliance between movements as different as the trade unions of the different EEC countries is tenuous to start with, it will have to come or the unions will be kicked out of the way by some other movement of workers looking for the reliefs and satisfactions that the existing institutions do not give them. Probably there has never been a labour explosion in Britain to match the French strikes of 1968 which took all authority, including the unions, by surprise and, after they had settled, brought about significant legislative changes not only in France but in other EEC countries, and made 'participation' a slogan for change in management approaches not only in the EEC but in Scandinavia. The law of the allegedly highly capitalist EEC countries includes provisions for workers' participation which most British managers know only as proposals from the left-wing Institute of Workers' Control: another example of the road from outrageousness to respectability that we saw in the BOAC stewards' policies in Chapter 4. But the proof of the pudding is in the eating. A formal legal system may sound splendid but be limited in application. Fewer than half of French companies which should have works councils by law actually do have them. For years the presence of workers' representatives on the supervisory boards of German companies gave German unions an immense amount of commercial information, but since there was no statutory protection for union representatives at the workplace the unions were restricted in getting the social information they needed to further their members' interests until a series of collective agreements in 1968 – sixteen years after the passing of the Works Councils Act – and finally an amendment to the law in 1971.

How Strong Should Union Structure Be?

Where European union movements are divided and weak, they are deeply divided. Where they are united and structurally strong, the very strength of the structure causes misgivings among some British unions. If the trade union movement becomes too strongly organised or too commercial in its attitudes, it may eventually find itself doing managers' jobs for them. It may find itself having no distinctive job of its own at all. When the British Government was pushing the Industrial Relations Act through Parliament, Mr Robert Carr, then Secretary of State for Employment, liked to say that employers would be prepared to pay a little more – perhaps a lot more – in a wage agreement in return for a legally enforceable contract with the union and a guarantee against strikes. Yet there is reason to doubt that unions exist to push up wages; if they did exist for that purpose, surely they would be better at it. Certainly they do not exist to help employers to exercise discipline, but to see that whatever employers do, does not work against the perceived interests of their members. To be sure, their members may not perceive their interests very well, or they may not see them as constant growth.

Survey after survey has shown that perception of the union as a wage-increasing mechanism varies according to three criteria at least – age, organisation of the industry, and one's position in it. In a society where working men on the whole begin to lose their earning power in middle life, people above the age of 40 or so do not look to unions to get them more, but to maintain what they have; and they cease to be much excited by the prospect of a rapidly rising standard of living. Younger workers are more easily prodded, and in inflationary times they are forced on by the rising cost of setting up a house, whether they buy the house or only the furniture (and if they buy only the furniture they are likely to be pushed on by higher rents); besides, they have had an easier upbringing and in an increasing number of industries face growing difficulty in earning extra at special times like the arrival and increase of a family. There are also, of course, more youngsters of all classes nowadays who 'drop out' deliberately rather than by pressure of circumstances, avoiding the 'rat race' and incidentally escaping the long and weary business of persuading the rulers of a highly artificial society to behave naturally. But I suspect that the 'drop-out' problem can be exaggerated and demands a less drastic change in middle-aged values than some alarmists think to be moderated.

Quick Pickings or Security?
Where an industry is organised in a highly commercial way, with private ownership and rapid response to market changes (either because of tax and credit changes or because it is naturally unstable), workers are likely to look to the union, or their particular section of it, for quick pickings. The motor industry is a case in point. It is also an example of another impetus to commercial unionism. Rapid merger and amalgamation in an industry which is not actually declining seems to set off wage demands as a compensation for falling security. Where the industry is declining as well – that is, actually has less money to pay workers – they may be prepared, if they are led by officers who regard security highly, to fall behind the average increase in wages for a time. In the end, this cannot last because members see it as a reduction in wages (which indeed in equity it is) and will eventually rebel. Overmanning is often a form of self-indulgence by managers or proprietors, because there is a kind of personality which derives satisfaction from knowledge of the numbers of men subordinate to him. This is a cruel and damaging form of self-indulgence when it is carried, as it often is, beyond the point where such a manager can find the resources or contacts to place his extra underlings in alternative jobs. Managers ought to take account of the full use of all resources, including people's talents, and so long as our society is organised much as it is today, they owe a duty of stewardship to their employees as well as their shareholders, or whoever else happens to have the final say: the Treasury, the borough council or (if the employer is a trade union) the national executive.

As for position, we find that managers and supervisors incline to look on the trade unions primarily as engines for increasing wages. So do union officers and shop stewards to a lesser extent. It is rare to find a majority of shop floor workers who regard increasing pay as the prime purpose of the union, although it is certainly unfashionable to find many who do not consider it one of the purposes. But the difference in emphasis is so marked between professional managers and bargainers and their constituents that there must surely be a lesson here. Somehow, in the machine, in the structure of institutions that has developed, basic impulses and allocations of responsibility have been lost.

Trade unions do not deal in resources but in attitudes and collective behaviour. Their stock-in-trade and their principal objectives are security and self-respect; if society does not give them to their members collectively, they will take them as best they can, and no doubt the resultant substitutes are sometimes unsatisfactory. Managers, tycoons, principal civil servants and colleagues according to their degree do dispose of resources. It is only because, left alone, they are so reckless and capricious about human resources that we have trade unions at all. It is because managers tend to parsimony and control, as a class, that unions have developed the habit of asking for money rather than deciding whether the money offered is adequate. It is because information about money is hard to come by that so many groups of workers merely think of a number which will keep them ahead of the game, add a proportion for bargaining, and begin to haggle.

The best works councils in West Germany, and the best productivity agreements in Britain, have illustrated how, with the required amount of shared information, managers and workers can reach agreement in the interests of both. Their experience emphasises the real virtue of clear written agreements in industrial relations, which is subtly different from the advantage of clear written agreements between equals. The advantage is the process of getting it, which both helps the negotiators to understand each other, and clarifies their minds. Things ought to be easier afterwards, although not automatically, because it depends on how well the negotiators of both sides explain the agreement to members and other managers respectively. Besides, it must leave room for movement. Anyone in human society who thinks that he does not live on a moving platform is deceiving himself. We have heard a great deal recently of where the present trend of events is taking us, but since there are so many trends in one field and another it is easy to be deceived. What we ought to see over the next few years are moves towards greater autonomy of workers in their jobs; further limitations on the notion of private property as conferring control over large organisations with the duty only to pay wages and, if necessary, redundancy money; and increasing legislative action to preserve scarce resources because market pressure does not seem to be adequate.

Restoring Human Satisfactions: Job Design and Structuring
Moves towards the first are beginning with job design and job structuring. Job design puts together a group of things to do to suit the talents of an individual worker. Job structuring means putting together several parts of a process that has been 'scientifically' reduced to the most elementary components, particularly on a production line. Structuring began in the manufacturing of electrical equipment, but Volvo in Sweden have now applied it even to car assembly: a group of so many workers are left to put together so many cars a week, deciding for themselves how they allocate the work and even how many days they come into the plant, so long as they reach the norm.* In the United States a computer 'software' company is experimenting with programmes to supply to individual workers the precise wage and benefits combinations that suit them. These experiments and others like them are increasingly necessary now to moderate the effects of more and more sophisticated mechanisation which has so far been used to feed on itself rather than furnish the specifically human needs of the people who look after the machines. Very large machines, which one by one are economically more important than the individual labours of many men, intensify the unpleasantness of subordination to a common task. They also increase the gratification of routine management, and widen the gulf between the machine minder and the manager. In human terms the objective ought to be to restore by all available methods the human satisfactions bruised by brute mechanical efficiency.

If it becomes necessary to challenge property rights to achieve this end, they will be challenged even further. Probably, given the existence of compound interest and exponential growth, high taxation is the alternative to revolution. Without one or the other, the only way to prevent property owners becoming endlessly richer would be to encourage them to destroy themselves by riotous and degenerate living, and in spite of the livelier assumptions of fiction the majority of property owners do not do so with enough zeal. Even prosperous gangsters eventually try to put the substance of their gains into 'legitimate'

* One of the large American companies has more striking plans still in this field; the problem is to build into very great capital investment physical changes of plant to combine the economies of scale with the most acceptable and efficient operations for twentieth-century workers who resent their reduction to moron activity by 'scientific management'.

business. But high taxation and other transfers of ownership to the state have their disadvantages. Bureaucrats may not always be sure what to do with the money, once they have got it, beyond controlling it with scrupulous care. Nationalised industry has not proved a conspicuous psychological success, and the combination of Treasury remits and Conservative resistance to letting these publicly-owned institutions behave like privately-owned ones and grow judiciously has caused further uneasiness. And nationalisation has not prevented the worker being separated from his tools. Yet the argument for another look at ownership is that the concept of private property as applied to large industrial enterprises is becoming increasingly ludicrous. It is not so much that it is 'immoral', which is what the Socialists and Communists call it, but it is irrational and misleading.

Challenge of Arrogant Autonomy: Will Unions Meet It?
It is normally so difficult to estimate who owns a large enterprise that if it applies for liquidation a large team of highly qualified accountants spend weeks dissecting the corpse. How much more difficult it is to assess the ownership of a going concern at some arbitrary point in its year's work, when plans are being made, work begun or completed, bargains struck which together may change the formal pattern of ownership of work in progress, and obligation for it, quite appreciably in a few months. Besides, the owners of capital become more and more impersonal. The danger therefore increases that enterprises become institutions under the autonomous control of managers who technically own practically nothing but effectively regard shareholders as just another group to be paid off once or twice a year. Autonomous management therefore becomes based on a notion of ownership which is no longer a reality, and consequently no longer carries accountability. It is not surprising that trade unions show a tendency to develop a similar arrogant autonomy in reaction. Neither helps the workers much in their search for the more substantial satisfactions of life. The Danish trade union movement have now drawn up a scheme for capital-sharing which would give workers an increasingly large stake in the equity of their enterprises. Some private companies in Britain have carried the process to the stage where the majority shareholder is the employees' trust. In such circumstances managers retain control; they may even find it easier, since to

many workers it appears more legitimate. We are likely to hear much more of such approaches.

As for resources, the market criterion of scarcity is too mechanical and short-sighted to meet the anxieties of the crowded modern world. In a perfect market, no doubt, all engines would switch to oil until all the oil was used up, and then return to coal while nuclear power generation gradually attained a more favourable commercial equation, either as coal's price rose with scarcity or nuclear power's dropped with improving technology. The use of land for building would eventually cause such a scarcity of land for agriculture that the prices would balance out again, and so on. A shortage of one kind of service or skill would eventually produce the high demand that would bring a crash course of training. Since there is no such thing as a perfect market, none of these things happens. That is the trouble about theory. By definition, we should all be as happy under perfect competition as under the final achievement of Communism, but all known practitioners stick well short of half way. In a system of unregulated competition, entrepreneurs who achieve power set about eliminating competition as soon as they can. In the first stage of the dictatorship of the proletariat, its agents set about consolidating it when theory predicts that it will wither away. But in the end corrective movements develop; it may be that machines in the hands of minorities have become so powerful that a further diminution of individual choice lies ahead; we must assume that humanity will not readily collapse and die through failure to understand itself.

If trade unions do not continue to meet human needs, something else will develop instead of them. One sometimes hears the hypothetical question, are trade unions necessary? Of course they are; that is why they exist. They would not have been necessary if the human demands they seek to meet had been met otherwise. There would not be a society for the prevention of cruelty to children if everyone were kind, and no doubt Nero would be ruler of the known world still if he had really been a god. As the range of surveillance spreads geographically, we may see the development of unprecedented 'internationals' with practical objectives as daunting to individual governments as Exxon's operations are now. We may find them remaining intercessory and lobbying bodies with international conventions giving more statutory standing to individual work groups at their places of work. We cannot tell; all we have to go on is the vast and sometimes conflicting message of what has happened before, and the continuing challenge of behaving naturally and candidly in a world of artificiality and cross-purposes.

Index

of persons named or quoted in the text

Airlie, Jimmy 95, 111
Aldington, Lord 57
Al-Ghazali 34
Allen, Alf 192 *seq*
Anderson, Walter 49, 114, 188 *seq*
Archer, Jeffrey 81

Bain, George S. 114
Banner, John 171
Basil, Douglas C. 53
Basnett, David 188 *seq*
Beeching, Lord 81
Behan, Brian 75, 108
Behrend, Hilde 132
Bell, Clive 90 *seq*
Bevan, Aneurin 86
Bevin, Ernest 42, 61, 68, 94, 172, 180
Birch, Reg 108
Black, Jimmy 75
Bleakley, David 112
Blairford, Bill 97
Boyd, John 189
Briginshaw, Richard 192
Brooke, Rupert 66
Brown, Lord (Wilfred) 162, 178
Brown, Sir Stanley 159
Bruce, Robert 211
Buckton, Ray 194 *seq*
Byrne, Jock 100 *seq*

Caesar, Julius 71
Cannon, Sir Leslie 50, 96, 99 *seq*, 153, 192
Carlyle, Thomas 68
Carr, Robert 219
Carron, Lord (Bill) 86, 189
Cassidy, Hugh 75, 106
Castro, Fidel and Raoul 104 *seq*
Caughey, Charles 46*n*
Chapple, Frank 99 *seq*, 192, 198
Churchill, Sir Winston 93
Citrine, Lord (Walter) 93 *seq*, 197
Clegg, Hugh 154, 172

Coates, Ken 108
Coldrick, Percy 196
Cole, G. D. H. 80, 102
Collier, John 88
Cooper, Lord (Jack) 175, 188 *seq*
Cousins, Frank 48, 68, 86, 188, 198, 205
Corfield, Kenneth G. 177
Cowper, William 87
Cromwell, Oliver 68
Curran, Charles 186

Darling, F. Fraser 204
Daly, Lawrence 103, 198
Davies, Dai 69
Deakin, Arthur 68, 172
Denning, Lord 121
Devlin, Lord 205
Donovan, Lord 60, 92, 159, 161
Donovan, Anthony F. 128*n*, 130
Drake, Sir Francis 66

Eastwood, Gerry 176
Ellis, I. G. 128*n*
Evans, Sir Lincoln 69

Feather, Vic 111, 166, 175
Fisher, Alan 167
Ford, Sidney 103, 167
Foulkes, Frank 96, 99 *seq*, 191
Friedenberg, Edgar Z. 133
Fryer, Peter 105, 108

Galbraith, J. Kenneth 37, 203
Garner, Robert 107
Garnett, John 70, 98
Goad, James 46*n*, 202 *seq*
Gormley, Joe 103, 188
Gould, Bill 143
Grantham, Roy 14
Greene, Sir Sidney 192 *seq*
Guevara, Ernesto ('Che') 104, 189
Guillebaud, C. W. 160

Halpin, Kevin 73, 97
Harvey, Bryan 177
Haxell, Frank 96, 100 seq, 184
Healy, Gerry 108
Hemingway, Ernest 76
Herzberg, Fred 133
Hill, J. W. 122
Hill, Ted 163
Hogarth, Bill 124
Hoggart, Richard 186
Hood, Thomas 186
Horner, Arthur 103, 194
Howe, Sir Geoffrey 195
Hughes, John 49 seq
Hyde, Douglas 104, 109

James I and VI 140
Jaques, Elliot 160
Jenkins, Clive 99, 124n, 195
Jenkins, Peter 197n
Jenkins, Tom 196
Jones, Jack 57, 108, 175, 185, 188, 198, 205
Joyce, James 104

Kerrigan, Peter 99, 108
Kingston, Dennis 100
Korzybski, Alfred 113

La Rochefoucauld, François, duc de 66
Lawther, Sir William 103
Lin Yutang 39
Lynch, Frank 124
Lynch, Matt 75, 106
Lyons, T. P. 178

McBride, Ralph 75
MacDonald, Ramsay 96
McGarvey, Danny 163
McHarg, Ian L. 83, 85
McLennan, Bob 96
McLoughlin, Johnny 75, 76
Maitland, Sid 75, 97 seq
Mann, Tom 153
Marsh, Arthur 44
Marx, Karl 31, 62, 80
Matthews, Jim 78, 97

Napoleon I 183
Neal, Len 35
Nicholas, Sir Harry 49

Nixon, Richard M. 161
Northcliffe, Lord 54
Norton, Harry 78

Orbell, Eric 121
Owen, Robert 154

Papworth, Bert 195
Paterson, Tom 160
Paul, Bill 88
Paynter, Will 103, 157, 187, 189, 194, 195
Peel, Jack 194
Phokylides 201
Pinner, Ernie 100
Plato 201

Reid, Jimmy 95, 111
Richard I 84
Roberts, Bryn 47, 195
Rolph, C. H. 99
Rylands, Sir William 57

Saleeby, Caleb 142
Scanlon, Hugh 108, 176, 185, 188 seq
Schutz, Bill 113
Seeger, Pete 19
Simpson, H. McK. 128n
Smith, Charles (Lord Delacourt-Smith) 56
Smyth, H. G. 128n
Stamp, Lord Justice 122
Steiner, Rudolf 85
Stokes, Lord (Donald) 185
Stuart, Ian 175
Swift, Jonathan 166
Sykes, A. J. M. 200

Taylor, A. J. P. 28
Tiffin, Arthur 68
Tyler, Wat 35

Vestey, Lord 31

Webb, Sidney and Beatrice (Lord and Lady Passfield) 80
Wellington, Duke of 183
Wilberforce, Lord 160
Williamson, Sir Tom 190
Winn, Mr Justice 107
Woodcock, George 80, 93, 174